OPERATION
TROJAN HORSE

Other Anomalist Books by John A. Keel

Jadoo
The Eighth Tower

OPERATION TROJAN HORSE:
The Classic Breakthrough Study of UFOs

John A. Keel

ANOMALIST BOOKS
*San Antonio * Charlottesville*

Contents

Foreword

Any appraisal of the "flying saucer mystery" must be all inclusive and must attempt a study of the apparent hoaxes, as well as an examination of the many events now generally accepted as being totally authentic. The data must be reviewed quantitatively, no matter how arduous the task becomes. There is a natural tendency to concentrate on only those facets which seem most interesting, or which seem to provide the best evidence. The phenomenon of unidentified flying objects is a gigantic iceberg, and the truly important aspects are hidden far beneath the surface. Nearly all of the UFO literature of the past twenty years has leaned toward the trivia, the random sightings which are actually irrelevant to the whole, and to the meaningless side issues of government policy, dissection of personalities, and the conflicts which have arisen within the various factions of the UFO cultists.

For the past four years I have worked full time, seven days a week, without a vacation, to investigate and research UFO events in total depth, hacking my way systematically through all of the myths and beliefs which surround this fascinating subject. This book is a summation of that effort. The original manuscript was more than 2,000 pages long. It has been boiled down and carefully edited to its present length. In the process, a good deal of documentation and many details have been deleted or heavily condensed. I had hoped to include full acknowledgment of my many sources and of the many people who helped me in this task. But that proved to be impossible.

More than 2,000 books were reviewed in the course of this study, in addition to uncounted thousands of magazines, newsletters, and newspapers. Since it is not feasible to list them all, I have included a selected bibliography, listing those works which proved to be the most valid and useful. Very few of these books deal with the subject of flying saucers directly. History, psychiatry, religion, and the occult have proven to be far more important to an understanding of the whole than the many books which simply recount the endless sightings of aerial anomalies.

I have tried to apply the standard rules of scholarship wherever possible, going directly to the original sources in most cases instead of relying upon the distilled and often distorted versions of these events which were later published in various media. This involved tracking down and interviewing, either by phone or in person, the people who had the experiences or, at least, conferring with the investigators who personally checked into some cases and were able to supply taped interviews with the witnesses and other documentation. In the earlier, historical cases I have tried to accumulate at least three independent published citations for each event. Many possibly important events were rejected simply because it proved impossible to uncover satisfactory documentation.

My files include thousands of letters, affidavits, and other materials encompassing many unpublished cases which correlated with and confirmed the events and conclusions discussed in this book. Numerous other researchers around the world have confirmed may findings through events in their own areas.

The real problems hidden behind the UFO phenomenon are staggering and so complex that they will seem almost incomprehensible at first. The popular beliefs and speculations are largely founded upon biased reporting, gross misinterpretations, and the inability to see beyond the limits of any one of many frames of reference. Cunning techniques of deception and psychological warfare have been employed by the UFO source to keep us confused and skeptical. Man's tendency to create a deep and inflexible belief on the basis of little or no evidence has been exploited. These beliefs have created tunnel vision and blinded many to the real nature of the phenomenon, making it necessary for me to examine and analyze many of these beliefs in this text.

Some readers will be offended and enraged by what I have to say and how I have chosen to say it. It is not my intention to attack any belief or frame of reference. Rather, I have tried to demonstrate how all of these things blend together into a larger whole.

John A. Keel
New York City
1969

1

The Secret War

On Wednesday, October 5, 1960, a formation of unidentified flying objects was picked up on the sophisticated computerized radar screens of an early-warning station at Thule, Greenland. Its exact course was quickly charted. It appeared to be heading toward North America from the direction of the Soviet Union. Within minutes the red telephones at Strategic Air Command headquarters in Omaha, Nebraska, were jangling, and the well-trained crews of SAC were galloping to their planes at airfields all over the world. Atomic-bomb-laden B-52s already in the air were circling tensely, their crews waiting for the final signal to head for predetermined targets deep within the Soviet Union.

SAC headquarters broadcast an anxious signal to Thule for further confirmation. There was no answer. Generals chewed on their cigars nervously. Had Thule already been hit?

Suddenly the mysterious blips on the radar screens changed course and disappeared. Later it was learned that "an iceberg had cut the submarine cable" connecting Thule to the United States. It was a very odd coincidence that the "iceberg" chose that precise time to strike. But the mystery of unidentified flying objects is filled with remarkable and seemingly unrelated coincidences.

World War III did not start that day. But it might have. Weeks later, when news of the enigmatic radar signals leaked out, three Labor members of the British House of Commons, Mr. Emrys-Hughes, Mrs. Hart, and Mr. Swingler, stood up and demanded an explanation. The U.S. Air Force replied that the radar signals had actually bounced off the moon and had been misinterpreted. The story appeared in the *Guardian,* a leading newspaper in Manchester, England, on November 30, and a week later it was buried on page 71 of the *New York Times.*

Could modern military radar really convert the moon into a formation of flying saucers? I have excellent reasons for doubting it. In May 1967, I toured a secret radar installation in New Jersey at the Air Force's own invitation, and I was extremely impressed by the complexity and efficiency of the equipment there. By pressing a few buttons, the radar operators can not only instantly detect every aircraft within range, but giant computers also provide complete and instant information on the speed, altitude, direction, and ETA (estimated time of arrival) of each plane. Even the aircraft's flight number appears on the radar screen! Unknown objects can be immediately picked out in the maze of air traffic, and a routine procedure is followed to identify them quickly. If these procedures fail, jet lighters are scrambled to take a look. It is improbable, if not impossible altogether, for the moon or any other distant celestial object to fool this elaborate system.

There have been frequent radar sightings of UFOs for the past twenty years, not only on military radar but on the sets of weather bureaus and airports. Often in these cases ground witnesses have also reported seeing the objects visually. When the Federal Aviation Agency tower at the Greensboro-High Point Airport in Greensboro, North Carolina, picked up an unidentified flying object early on the morning of July 27, 1966, several police officers in the High Point-Randolph County area also reported seeing unidentifiable objects buzzing the vicinity. They said the objects appeared to be at an altitude of 500 feet and described them as being round, brilliant red-green, and appeared to be emitting flashes of light.

The government's official position toward flying saucers has been totally negative since 1953, although a great deal of attention has been paid to the subject behind the scenes. Obviously any phenomenon that could possibly trigger World War Ill accidentally has to be taken seriously.

An extensive flying saucer "flap" (numerous sightings occurring simultaneously in many widely scattered areas) broke in March 1966, and the then-Secretary of Defense, Robert S. McNamara, had been well briefed by the Air Force before the subject was interjected into a hearing of the House Foreign Affairs Committee on March 30, 1966. Representative Cornelius E. Gallagher of New Jersey, a state where scores of UFO sightings had been reported that month, asked Secretary McNamara if he thought there was "anything at all" to the flying saucer mystery.

"I think not," McNamara replied. "I have talked to the Secretary of the Air Force and the Air Force Director of Research and Engineering, and neither of them places any credence in the reports we have received to date."

Ironically, at 8 A.M. that very day, C. Phillip Lambert and Donny Russell Rose, both stable men with good reputations, were driving to work outside of Charleston, South Carolina, when they reportedly noticed a strange circular object spinning in the clear sky above the Southern Trucking Company terminal on Meeting Street Road. They stopped their car and watched the object for about eight minutes.

"It looked like a sterling-silver disk," Lambert said. "It was about fourteen feet tall and twenty feet in diameter. We just happened to look up into the sky; it was such a pretty day. I know we saw it; we were both wide awake, and neither of us drinks."

A veteran of eight years in the airborne infantry, Lambert estimated that the object was 800 or 900 feet above the ground when they first saw it. It appeared to be spinning rapidly and was constantly shifting from one position to another.

This was what ufologists call a Type I sighting—a low-level object observed and reported by reliable witnesses. March 30, 1966, was a flap date, and local newspapers from coast to coast carried dozens of other Type I sightings that day. Many of them involved police officers, pilots, and other above-average witnesses. Weeks later, when all of the clippings and reports for that day had been collected by the author, we found that extensive sightings had also been reported in the following states: Michigan, New York (Long Island), Ohio, New Jersey, Wisconsin, Iowa, and other sections of South Carolina. This was a typical minor flap, and like most flaps, it received no national publicity, and none of the sightings was published outside of its place of origin.

While all of this was going on, Secretary McNamara was blithely repeating the long-established Air Force line behind the closed doors at the House hearing.

"People are beginning to attach significance to this matter," Representative Gallagher told the Secretary that day.

"There is no indication that they are anything other than illusions," McNamara responded blandly.

How do you suppose those two men in South Carolina responded when they read that statement? For years now thousands of witnesses have been reacting with anger and bewilderment to the official pronouncements and explanations. The governmental attitude has succeeded in maintaining skepticism among those who have never seen a UFO and has helped foster the general disinterest of the press in the subject. As a result, most of the reported UFO activity has gone unnoticed, and the alarming scope of the phenomenon is unknown except to the relatively small handful of organizations and individuals who have tried to keep tabs on the sightings.

When I first decided to look into these matters in March 1966, I subscribed to several newspaper clipping services, and I was stunned by the results. I often received as many as 150 clippings for a single day! My immediate reaction, of course, was one of disbelief. I thought that all of the newspapers in the country had thrown objectivity out the window and were participating in some kind of gigantic put-on. It seemed impossible that so many unidentifiable things were flying around our sacred skies without being seriously noticed by both the military and the scientific community.

Reliability of Reports

My first task, therefore, was to determine just how reliable all of these reports were. I began by placing frequent long-distance calls to the reporters and editors of some of the newspapers that seemed to be carrying UFO stories week after week. Not only did they sound like reasonable people, but they all assured me that they were only publishing the more interesting or best-validated stories that were being reported to them. Many were concentrating only on those sightings reported by police officers and local officials. It quickly became clear that literally thousands of sightings were being reported by ordinary citizens but were going completely unpublished. The published sightings represented only a fraction of the whole!

I also called many of the witnesses in the published accounts and learned, to my further dismay, that the newspaper stories had only outlined a part of their total experiences. Some of them claimed the objects had pursued their cars, had landed briefly beside the road near them, or *had even reappeared later over their homes.* Innumerable witnesses complained that their eyes had become red and swollen after their sighting and had remained that way for days afterward. Others said they had experienced peculiar tingling sensations or waves of heat as the objects passed over. I must admit that I experienced an emotional reaction to all of this at first, trying to convince myself that the phenomenon was more hysterical in nature than physical, but the more I heard the more I was forced to realize that all of these people were coming up with the same incredible details.

It became apparent that the only way to properly investigate this situation was to travel to the various flap areas personally and interview the witnesses in depth, applying the standard journalistic techniques that I had learned from being a reporter and writer for two long decades. So in the spring of 1966 I began a long series of treks that eventually took me through twenty states, where I interviewed thousands of people, hundreds of them in depth. Occasionally I encountered a publicity seeker or an outright liar, but such people were easy to spot. The majority of the people I met were ordinary, honest human beings. Many were reluctant to discuss their experiences with me at all until I had won their confidence and assured them that I was not going to ridicule or slander them. Some had had such unusual and unbelievable sightings that they were afraid to recount them until they were certain that I would give them a sincere hearing. In my typical reporter fashion I only extracted information and gave little or none in return. I seldom let the witnesses know that other people in other sections of the country had told me identical stories which seemed to corroborate their own experiences. The details of many of these stories were unpublished and unknown to even hardcore UFO buffs. By maintaining this secrecy, I was able to make unique correlations that might not otherwise have been possible.

As I traveled, I naturally visited local newspapers and spent time with the editors and reporters who had been handling the UFO reports in their areas. They were all competent newsmen, many with years of experience behind them, and when I met the witnesses whose stories they had written and published, I realized what a skillful and objective job they had done. So I developed a new respect for the clippings that were pouring into my mailbox. Most newspaper stories were reliable sources for basic information.

Likewise, I found that most of the material being published by the various civilian UFO organizations had been carefully sifted and investigated to the best of their ability, even though some of these organizations did tend to over interpret their material, over speculate, and add the coloring of their own beliefs. They also had an exasperating tendency to delete reported details that they felt *were* objectionable or detracted from their "cause."

Sadly, this is even more true today than it was in the 1960s. The few remaining UFO groups have become cults with strong religious overtones, far more concerned with their petty feuds and vendettas than with the UFOs themselves. However, the witnesses, I concluded, have been giving honest descriptions of what they have seen, and their local newspapers have been giving objective accounts of what they reported. The nature and the meaning of what they saw is another matter. And the answer could not be found in newspaper clippings. However, it was possible that those clippings could supply some broad data about the overall phenomenon. None of the UFO organizations had made any effort at all to extract such data. The U.S. Air Force had tried in the early 1950s but had apparently given up in despair. So my next job was to translate the seemingly random clippings and reports of investigated cases into some form of statistical information.

Patterns in the Phenomenon

More than 10,000 clippings and reports reached me in 1966 (in contrast with the 1,060 reports *allegedly* received by the Air Force during that same period). I had checked out many of these cases personally and had become convinced of their validity. Throughout 1967, I devoted my spare time to sorting this great mass of material, categorizing it, and boiling it down into valid statistical form. It was an enormous job, and I had to do it alone. I threw out most of the "lights in the sky" types of reports and concentrated on the Type I cases. I obtained astronomical data on meteors, etc., for the year, and from the National Aeronautics and Space Administration I obtained information on all of the year's rocket launches. By checking the UFO reports against this data, I was able to sift out the possible or probable misinterpretations that were bound to occur.

My first interest was to uncover whatever patterns or cycles that might exist in the flap dates. I ended up with two files: one containing the Type I sightings (730 in all, or 7.3 percent of the total); and the other, the best of the Type II sightings (high-altitude objects performing in a controlled manner and distinct from normal aircraft and natural phenomena). There were 2,600 reports in the second group. Thus I was working with 33.3 percent of the total. (Radio and TV surveys that rule the industry work on a far smaller sampling, claiming that a survey of 1,500 TV viewers represents the viewing habits of the whole country.)

As soon as I had organized the sightings by dates, the first significant pattern became apparent. This was that sightings tended to collect around specific days of the week. Wednesday had the greatest number of sightings, and these were usually reported between the hours of 8 to 11 P.M.

Day	Percentage of Total Reports
Wednesday	20.5
Thursday	17.5
Friday	15.5
Saturday	15.0
Monday	13.5
Sunday	11.0
Tuesday	7.0

Of the sampling used, .5 percent were not dated.

If the UFO phenomenon had a purely psychological basis, then there should be more sightings on Saturday night when more people are out of doors, traveling to and from entertainments, etc. Instead we find that the greatest number of sightings are reported on Wednesday, and then they slowly taper off through the rest of week. The lowest number occurs on Tuesday. This inexplicable "Wednesday phenomenon" proved very valid and was repeated throughout 1967 and 1968. It was later found to be valid, with minor variations, in other countries.

This does not mean that flying saucers are out in force every Wednesday night. But when there is a large flap, it nearly always takes place on Wednesday. The one notable exception is the flap of August 16, 1966, a Tuesday night, in which thousands of people in five states witnessed unusual aerial phenomena.

By carefully studying the geographical locations of the reported sightings during these flaps, we came upon another puzzling factor. The reports seemed to cluster within the boundaries of specific states. For example, during the flap of August 16 there were hundreds of sightings in Arkansas. These seemed to be concentrated into two belts which ran the length of the state from north to south. Yet we did not receive a single report from the neighboring states of Oklahoma, Mississippi, Tennessee, or

Louisiana that night. Minnesota and Wisconsin, both far to the north of Arkansas, participated in that same flap. But the majority of the sightings seemed to be concentrated in Minnesota, and the UFOs seemed to confine their activities within the political boundaries of that state, too. Random sightings were also reported in distant New Jersey that night, and a few sightings were reported in South Dakota, right on the border with Minnesota.

Certainly if the UFOs were meteors or other natural phenomena, they would also be reported in adjoining states. Cross-state sightings are not as common as the skeptics would like to believe. In addition, the objects often linger for hours in one area. At Fort Smith, Arkansas, newsman John Garner took his KFSA microphone into the streets and broadcast a description of the strange multicolored lights that cavorted over the city for hours as great crowds of people watched. Another newsman, Ken Bock of KDRS, Paragould, Arkansas, did the same that night.

In my studies of several other flaps I have discovered this same baffling geographical factor. If the UFOs are actually machines of some sort, their pilots seem to be familiar not only with our calendar but also with the political boundaries of our states. They not only concentrate their activities on Wednesday nights, they also carefully explore our states methodically from border to border.

Does this sound like the work of Martians or extraterrestrial strangers? Or does it sound like the work of someone who is using our maps and our calendars and may, therefore, know a great deal about us, even though we know little about "them"?

The skeptics try to explain away the published UFO stories by saying that a mass hysteria builds up in flap areas and that everyone starts seeing the things once a few reports have been published. This is patently untrue. Nearly all the published reports of flap dates appear on the same day. There is no time lag, no building up of reports. Random individuals in widely separated areas all apparently see unidentifiable objects on the same night and dutifully report their observations to their local police or newspapers, seldom realizing that anyone else has seen something that night. The next day the newspapers in several areas, or even several different states, carry the reports. The flap has come and gone in a single day. Even then, people reading the Arkansas *Gazette* never learn that other papers in other states have been filled with UFO accounts on that same day. Most UFO buffs, who depend upon one another and assorted friends for clippings, are never aware of the full extent of the flap. With the exception of the North American Newspaper Alliance, no news service assigns men to keep track of these things and tabulate them. So while an occasional sighting may be sent out by a wire service, data on the overall situation are simply not available.

Anatomy of a Flap

In March-April 1967, the published UFO sightings outstripped all previous years. I received more than 2,000 clippings and reports in March alone and was able to investigate many of them firsthand. Yet the major news media ignored this flap, perhaps because none of the editors realized it was happening. Instead of the mythical censorship so lovingly expounded in some cultist circles, we have a lack of communication and a complete lack of research. The indifference so long fostered by the official government position has resulted in a general indifference.

The biggest flap in March 1967 occurred on Wednesday, March 8. Let's review briefly some of the sightings reported on that day:

1 Minnesota: "A strange object in the sky hovering around above our homes here is giving some of us folks the shivers. It's becoming such a mysterious light or flying saucer that we can almost work our imaginations into seeing it land some green men from outer space into our backyard. The thing moves with a gliding motion with brilliant light and sometimes just hovering and sometimes moving with utmost speed. *It appears each night at 8 o'clock and stays for about one hour before it fades away.*" (Floodwood, Minnesota, *Rural Forum*, March 9, 1967.)

2. Michigan: "Police said they received eight reports that a UFO hovered over Liggett School about 8 P.M. Wednesday." The

Air Force and Grosse Pointe Woods police were investigating reports of a "burning orange oval" that had been photographed by two persons that week. "There was definitely something out there," said Major Raymond Nyls, Selfridge Air Force Base operations officer. "Too many people saw it." (Detroit, Michigan, *Free Press,* March 11, 1967.)

3. Oklahoma: At 8:45 P.M. on Wednesday night Mrs. Homer Smith stepped onto her back porch and "was astounded to see a twirling object with colored lights" going over Ninth Street headed south. She called her ten-year-old son, and he saw it, too. She said the UFO was traveling and twirling so fast that it was difficult to count the lights on it, but they were colored, and what she believed to be the rear of the ship had what looked like "spits of fire coming from it." (Henryetta, Oklahoma, *Daily Free Lance,* March 19, 1967.)

4. Arkansas: Mrs. Ned Warnock of Brinkley, Arkansas, viewed an object from her kitchen window that night. "It was a reddish orange," she said. "And it changed to a silver-white color just before it took off. It was round and pretty large. It was real low but gained height and speed as it took off. It was moving too fast for a star." She alerted her neighbors, Mr. and Mrs. J.H. Folkerts, and they also saw the object. (Clarendon, Arkansas, *The Monroe County Sun,* March 16, 1967.)

5. Maryland: Two residents and a police officer observed an object that appeared circular, with "a shiny gold bottom." When it hovered, the top glowed red. It flew an oval-shaped path, going back and forth from Fort Meade to Laurel three times before taking off. (Laurel, Maryland, *Prince George's County News,* March 16, 1967.)

6. Montana: Mr. Richard Haagland of Stevensville, Montana, reported to the Missoula County sheriff's office that he had seen a circular flying object which "dropped three balls of fire before disappearing at 8:20 P.M. Wednesday night." (Missoula, Montana, *Missoulian-Sentinel, March 9, 1967.*)

7. Montana: "Many people have seen unidentified flying

objects in the Ekalaka, Lame Jones, and Willard areas. The report is that they seem to hover about a mile from the ground, 'fly' up and down, or in any direction that seems to pleasure them. They are lit up with red and green lights and are apt to be seen in the early night.

"The report to the *Times* office by Mrs. Harry Hanson of Willard relates that Stanley Ketchum has seen them at what seems to be a closer range than most, and any attempt at trying to get close to them makes them literally disappear into thin air." (Baker, Montana, *Fallon County Times*, March 9, 1967.)

8. Missouri: Mr. J. Sloan Muir of Caledonia, Missouri, observed a flashing light from his kitchen window at 7:15 P.M. last Wednesday and called his wife. They said it was "a shiny, metal, oblong globe, shaped something like a watermelon. Around the perimeter were many beautiful multicolored lights-green and red mostly, but also white, blue, and yellow, running into orange." They estimated that it was about 35 feet long and said they watched it for fifteen or twenty minutes before it flew out of sight. (Bardstown, Kentucky, *Kentucky Standard*, March 16, 1967.)

9. Missouri: "In the past two-and-one-half weeks 75 to 100 persons have reported sightings in the Osage Beach and Linn Creek areas." (Versailles, Missouri, *Versailles Leader-Statesman*, March 16, 1967.)

10. Missouri: Mrs. Phyllis Rowles of Bunceton, Missouri, reported seeing a multicolored object at 8 P.M., Wednesday. She described it as having flashing blue, green and white lights. It hovered for two hours, moving in an up-and-down motion. Many others in the area had similar sightings, including Leo Case, a newsman for station KRMS. (Boonville, Missouri, *Daily News*, March 9, 1967.)

11. Illinois: Mr. and Mrs. Lonnie Davis were driving on Route 30 around noon when "they saw a beam of light come from a wide-open area south of them." They stopped and observed a strange object for three or four minutes. "It was very brilliant," Mrs. Davis said. "And cast a red and blue color. It was circle-shaped. It

seemed to come toward us but gained height until it went in back of a small cloud. We watched for about ten minutes more, but it never appeared again."

Ronald Kolberg of Aurora, Illinois, said he and other residents of his neighborhood "have noticed an unusual light in the sky west of their area every night for a few months." (Aurora, Illinois, *Beacon-News,* March 9, 1967.)

12. Illinois: Several witnesses in Pontiac, Illinois, reported sightings to the state police on Wednesday. They said a white light flashed occasionally with a less frequent red light and a periodic green light. The object appeared between 10 P.M. and midnight and moved up and down slowly. "More than a dozen people have seen the object this week." (Pontiac, Illinois, *Leader,* March 10, 1967.)

13. Illinois: Knox County Deputy Sheriff Frank Courson and twenty other persons watched a pulsating white and red circular object for several hours on Wednesday night. The object resembled an upside-down bowl and appeared to be about 2,000 feet off the ground. Deputy Courson added that "a similar object crossed over his car Monday as he drove along Interstate 74 near Galesburg, Illinois, but he was scared to tell anyone about it then."

There were also reports of UFO sightings Wednesday night in Warren and Henry counties, west of Galesburg. (Associated Press story, widely circulated, March 10, 1967.)

14. Illinois: State police and scores of others watched UFOs near Flanagan, Illinois, on Wednesday night. A state trooper named Kennedy said he had followed the object to U.S. 51 where he met two Woodford County deputies who had been watching it approach Minonk from the east. The object was a brilliant bluish-white and red. (Bloomington, Illinois, *Pantagraph,* March 10, 1967.)

15. Illinois: "Flying saucer reports, one of them from a veteran policeman and pilot, flooded the Knox County sheriff's office in Galesburg Thursday. Dozens of similar reports poured into police departments in Moline, Illinois." (Chicago, Illinois, *News,* March

9, 1967.)

16. Iowa: "On Wednesday, Thursday, and Friday nights of last week unidentified flying objects were reported by several persons... including Dr. and Mrs. W.G. Tietz, Connie Dagit and her younger brother, Jack Chadwick, and John Kiwala. The UFOs west of Eldora were all reported at approximately the same time nightly, at about 8:30 P.M. UFOs have also been reported in the Steamboat Rock area." (Eldora, Iowa, *Herald-Ledger*, March 14, 1967.)

17. Iowa: A "saucer-shaped blue light" was observed Wednesday night hovering above Dam 18 north of Burlington, Iowa. Deputy Sheriff Homer Dickson said he thought it might have been a "reflection of a spotlight on the ice." "Wednesday's sighting was the latest of several reported in the Burlington area the past two weeks." (Burlington, Iowa, newspaper. Name obliterated. March 9, 1967.)

18. Iowa: Mrs. L. E. Koppenhaver reported seeing "a big red ball" sailing over her house at 9:45 P.M., Wednesday. "You know how the setting sun gets a red glow on it?" she said. "Well, that was what this thing looked like. Only this object was very mobile, moving almost out of sight, the bright glow diminishing to a small light. I've seen satellites before, but this was nothing like them. It moved so fast and maneuvered so quickly." Her father, Walter Engstrom, said he also saw the same object. (Boone, Iowa, *News-Republican*, March 10, 1967.)

19. Kansas: Mr. Jake Jansonius of Prairie View, Kansas, was driving home about 10 P.M. Wednesday night "when the sky lit up and a bright blue object of some kind appeared." While he was watching it, it shot straight up in the air, and half of it turned fiery red as "three blazing tails reached toward the ground." It moved to the west and then dropped down, out of his line of vision. He drove a short distance when "the sky lit up poof in one big flash, and immediately ahead of me the saucer-shaped object began to spread apart-one half still blue, the other fiery red. As the distance widened between the two parts, a connecting band which appeared

to be about one and a half feet thick formed, and while I watched, the object broke up and disappeared in a flash." (Phillipsburg, Kansas, *Review,* March 16, 1967.)

20. Kansas: Several police officers in Marion, Kansas, watched an unidentified flying object Wednesday night between 8:00 and 8:30 P.M. Marion police dispatcher Sterling Frame and others viewed it through binoculars and stated it changed color: red, green and yellow. "They all agree they saw it. There's no question about that." (Marion, Kansas, *Marion County Record,* March 9, 1967.)

21. Kansas: "Around 9:00 Wednesday night, several Towanda youths were parked along the road northwest of town when they observed revolving red, white and blue lights flashing in the sky above the Wilson field in the vicinity of a city water well." The boys fetched City Marshal Virgil Osborne, and he went with them to the area and viewed the lights himself. Osborne said, "The trees along the river were lighted up from the reflection as the mysterious object moved over them." A line of cars led by Osborne followed the object as it continued its course without changing direction or altitude until it was out of sight. (Whitewater, Kansas, *Independent,* March 9, 1967.)

22. Kansas: Sheriff G. L. Sullivan and Police Chief Al Kisner watched a hovering object for more than an hour on Wednesday evening near Goodland, Kansas. They said the thing resembled a sphere from 12 to 14 feet long with an object attached to the bottom which appeared to be about 12 feet in diameter. There were three lights on it—red, green and amber.

A Goodland policeman, Ron Weehunt, reported seeing an oval-shaped, domed object about fifty feet long that same evening. He said it flew over the city at moderate speed and appeared at an altitude of 1,000 to 1,500 feet. (Norton, Kansas, *Telegram,* March 14, 1967.)

These twenty-two reports are a mere sampling, but they provide an idea of what happened on a single Wednesday night in March 1967. This was not an exceptional flap. It was, in fact, a rather ordinary one, and none of these incidents is of special interest. There were seventy-four flap dates in 1966, many of them much larger than that of March 8, 1967.

The flap of March 8 seemed to be largely concentrated in the states of Kansas and Illinois. In fact, much of the UFO activity in recent years has been focused on the Midwestern states. Until the fall of 1967, a simple pattern seems to have emerged: less densely populated areas had a higher ratio of sightings than heavily populated sections. The Air Force discovered this odd fact back in the late 1940s. If this were a purely psychological phenomenon, then there should be more reports in the more densely populated areas. Instead, the reverse has been true. The objects still apparently prefer remote sectors such as hill country, deserts, forested areas, swamplands, and *places where the risk of being observed is the least.* As you will note from the sample cases mentioned previously, the majority of the sightings were made between 7:30 and 9:30 P.M. But throughout rural America, most of the population is at home and planted in front of the TV sets at that hour, particularly on weekday nights. In other studies we have determined that the majority of the reported landings occur very late at night in very isolated locales, where the chances of being observed are very slight. In most farming areas, the people are early risers, and therefore most of the population is in bed before 10 P.M. It is after 10 P.M. that the unidentified flying objects cut loose. When they do happen to be observed on the ground, it is either by accident *or design.* And usually they take off the moment they have been discovered, or they inexplicably disappear into thin air!

Already we can arrive at one disturbing conclusion based upon these basic factors of behavior. If these lights are actually machines operated by intelligent entities, they obviously don't want to be caught. They come in the dead of night, operating in areas where the risks of being observed are slight. They pick the middle of the week for their peak activities, and they confine themselves rather methodically to the political boundaries of specific states at specific times. All of this smacks uneasily of a covert military operation, a secret build-up in remote areas.

Unfortunately, it is not all this simple. The first major UFO flap in the Midwest took place in 1897. There's something else going on here. If secrecy is "their" goal, then both our newspaper wire services and our government have happily been obliging them. What are the reasons? And, more important, what are the pitfalls? If strange unidentified flying machines are operating freely in our midst, I wonder if we can really accept what Secretary of Defense McNamara told the House Committee on Foreign Affairs on March 30, 1966: "I think that every report so far has been investigated," he said. "And in every instance we have found a more reasonable explanation than that it represents an object from outer space or a potential threat to our security."

The newspapers of March 9, 1967, quoted Dr. J. Allen Hynek as dismissing a number of the March 8 sightings as being the planet Venus. But I worry about the report of two Erie, Pennsylvania, policemen, William Rutledge and Donald Peck, who said they watched a strange light over Lake Erie for two hours on Wednesday, August 3, 1966. It appeared as a bright light when they first noticed it at 4:45 A.M. It moved east, they said, stopped, turned red, and disappeared. A moment later it reappeared and was now a bluish white. They watched it until 6:55 A.M. As the sun came up and dawn flooded the sky, the object ceased to be a mere light. It became a definite silvery object, possibly metallic, and finally it headed north toward Canada and disappeared.

Could all of these other strange lights in the sky also be silver metallic objects when viewed in daylight? If so, then we can forget about all of the theories of swamp gas, meteors, plasma, and natural phenomena that have been bandied about by the skeptics for so many years.

2
To Hell with the Answer!
What's the Question?

At 8 P.M. on Wednesday, October 4, 1967, I was driving a rented car along the Long Island Expressway about twenty miles outside of New York City when I noticed a large brilliant sphere of light bouncing through the sky on a course parallel to my own. It caught my eye because I had seen many such lights in many places for the preceding two years. There was something special and very familiar about the crystal-like purity of its whiteness, and it was brighter than any star in the sky. On top of it I could make out a second light, a smaller fiercely red glow that flickered slightly in contrast with the steadiness of the larger sphere beneath it. Although Kennedy Airport was nearby, I knew that this was not the bright strobe landing light of an airplane. I've seen many of those, too, in my travels.

When I reached Huntington, Long Island, that night, I found cars parked along the roads and scores of people, including several police officers, standing in the fields staring at the sky in wonder. The enigmatic light that had "followed" me was joining four others overhead. All were low, hovering silently, slowly bobbing and weaving like illuminated yo-yos tethered to invisible strings.

"What do you think they are?" one elderly gentleman asked me.

"I've never seen anything like it before," the man muttered, marveling that such things could be. "I always thought they were just so much nonsense."

I nodded and got back into my car. I had a long way to go that night and many problems on my mind. I seem to have had nothing but problems since I got into the flying saucer business.

A few miles south of Huntington, in the tiny hamlet of Melville, another man had problems. The night before, on October 3, 1967, Phillip Burkhardt, an aerospace computer systems engineer who holds a bachelor of science degree in mathematics and a masters in philosophy, was alerted by two teenagers, Shawn Kearns, thirteen, and Donald Burkhardt, fourteen, his son. They called him outside his home on Roundtree Drive to look at an odd machine hovering just above the trees a few yards away.

"It was disk-shaped," Burkhardt said later. "It was silvery or metallic white in color and seemed to be illuminated by lights—a set of rectangular-shaped lights that blinked on and off and seemed to be revolving across the lower portion of the object, from left to right. Another light emanated from the top but was not blinking. There was no noise such as an engine would make."

The object dropped down behind the crest of a ridge, and Burkhardt returned to his house to get a pair of binoculars. Then he and several others set out to find the thing again. They drove to a nearby road, spotted it, and watched it as it flew out of sight. Burkhardt tried to determine if the object was running the legally required red and green lights that even experimental craft must display. If it did, he couldn't see them.

After phoning the Suffolk Air Force Base in Westhampton Beach, Long Island, and answering questions for half an hour, the scientist and the two boys returned to the area of the sighting and examined the ground with flashlights.

"We detected a peculiar odor," Mr. Burkhardt noted. "It was comparable to burning chemicals or electrical wiring and confined to the immediate area… a sand and gravel-covered clearing."

Because this sighting was not made public until a month later, few people outside of the immediate vicinity knew of it. But within days after the incident, Mrs. Burkhardt told me, they began to receive a series of peculiar phone calls. The phone would ring, but there would be no one on the other end. Sometimes the phone would continue to ring even after the receiver was picked up. Also, the Burkhardt phone bill began to show a puzzling increase over the previous monthly average.

Melville, we might note, had frequent and inexplicable power failures throughout 1967, as did Huntington. For Phillip Burkhardt, unidentified flying objects are no longer a controversial subject or a matter of belief or disbelief. He knows they exist.

How Long Has This Been Going On?

History prefers fantasy to fact. Legend endures while truth coughs up blood, which dries and fades. We prefer to teach our children that Christopher Columbus was a hero and have buried his glaring faults. We choose to pass on the nonsense that the Great Chicago Fire of October 8, 1871, was ignited when Mrs. O'Leary's discontented cow kicked over a lantern, and we forget that that fire was actually caused by a gigantic, still-unexplained fireball that swept low across the skies of several states, destroying dozens of communities and creating a kind of death and havoc which would not be seen again until the great fire raids of World War ll.*

A thousand years from now Hitler may be remembered as a somewhat eccentric manufacturer of soap. And man's clumsy, stiff-legged attempt to leap into space may merely supplement the older tale of Icarus flying too close to the sun on wings of wax.

We are more enthralled with our interpretations of great events than with the events themselves, and we gingerly alter the facts generation after generation until history reads the way we think it should read.

If you want to believe the fancy-ridden scribes who have painstakingly recorded their versions of man's long history, you may be ready to accept the fact that unidentified flying objects have *always* been up there. Certainly the histories and legends of

---

* In Chapter Four of his book *Mysterious Fires and Lights,* researcher Vincent H. Gaddis documented the spectacular and disastrous fires that swept across Iowa, Minnesota, Indiana, Illinois, Wisconsin, and the Dakotas. Wisconsin suffered the greatest loss of life, with 1,500 deaths recorded in Green Bay alone on that horrible night. Four times as many people were killed in Peshtigo, Wisconsin, as in Chicago.

every country and every race, including the isolated Eskimos, are filled with stories of inexplicable aerial happenings.

How valid is our history, and where is the point that history and myth intermingle and become one?

Several great religions have been founded on the contents of the Holy Bible. Millions of people have accepted it as truth—as the Gospel—for the past 2,000 years. Yet the Bible gives us several different and contradictory versions of the same events, including the life and death of Christ, all purportedly written by eyewitnesses and all of them different in many significant details. Which is the true account? The devout accept them all. Few believers would reject the existence of Christ because of these differences.

Unlike most UFO researchers, I have read the Bible carefully several times. In view of what we now know—or suspect—about flying saucers, many of the Biblical accounts of things in the sky take on a new meaning and even corroborate some of the things happening today. They were given a religious interpretation in those ancient days when all natural phenomena and all catastrophes were blamed on a Superior Being.

Today we kneel before the altar of science, and our scientific ignorance receives the blame for what we do not know or cannot understand. The game's the same, only the rules have changed slightly.

We no longer run to the temple when we see a strange, unearthly object in the sky. We run to the Air Force or to the learned astronomers. In ancient times the priests would tell us that we had sinned, and therefore God was showing us signs in the sky. Today our learned leaders simply tell us that we are mistaken—or crazy—or both. The next time we see something in the sky, we keep it to ourselves.

But the damnable things keep coming back anyway. Maybe they never went away.

The first photograph of an unidentified flying object was taken back in 1883 by a Mexican astronomer named Jose Bonilla. He had been observing the sun from his observatory at Zacatecas on

August 12 of that year when he was taken aback by the sudden appearance of a long parade of circular objects that slowly flitted across the solar disk. Altogether he counted 143 of the things, and because his telescope was equipped with a newfangled gadget called a camera, he shot some pictures of them. When developed, the film showed a series of cigar- and spindle-shaped objects which were obviously solid and noncelestial. Professor Bonilla dutifully wrote up a scholarly report of the event filled with mathematical calculations (he estimated that the objects had actually passed over the earth at an altitude of about 200,000 miles), attached copies of his pictures and sent the whole thing off to the French journal *L'Astronomie.* His colleagues no doubt read it with chagrin, and because they could not explain what he had seen, they forgot about the whole business and turned to more fruitful pursuits—such as counting the rings of Saturn.

Five years before Professor Bonilla's embarrassing observation, a farmer in Texas reported seeing a large circular object pass overhead at high speed. His name was John Martin, and when he told a reporter from the Dennison, Texas, *Daily News* about it, he made history of sorts by describing it as a "saucer." The date of his sighting was Thursday, January 24, 1878. His neighbors probably called him Crazy John after that, never realizing that he was not the first, and certainly would not be the last, to see what had been up there all along.

In April 1897, thousands of people throughout the United States were seeing huge "airships" over their towns and farms. Scores of witnesses even claimed to have met and talked with the pilots. According to the New York *Herald,* Monday, April 12, 1897, a news dealer in Rogers Park, Illinois, took two photographs of a cigar-shaped craft. "I had read for some days about the airship," the news dealer, Walter McCann, was quoted as saying. "But I thought it must be a fake."

Because so many people were coming up with airship stories, and many of them were even signing affidavits swearing to the truth of what they had seen, newspapermen naturally turned to the greatest scientific authority of the time, Thomas Alva Edison.

"You can take it from me that it is a pure fake," Edison declared on April 22, 1897. "I have no doubt that airships will be successfully constructed in the near future but…it is absolutely impossible to imagine that a man could construct a successful airship and keep the matter a secret. When I was young, we used to construct big colored paper balloons, inflate them with gas, and they would float about for days. I guess someone has been up to that fine game out west.

"Whenever an airship is made, it will not be in the form of a balloon. It will be a mechanical contrivance, which will be raised by means of a powerful motor, which must be made of a very light weight. At present no one has discovered such a motor, but we never know what will happen. We may wake up tomorrow morning and hear of some invention which sets us all eagerly to work within a few hours, as was the case with the Roentgen rays. Then success may come. I am not, however, figuring on inventing an airship. I prefer to devote my time to objects which have some commercial value. At the best, airships would only be toys."

Forty-one years later, however, a young man named Orson Welles disagreed with Edison. The opening lines of his historic "War of the Worlds" broadcast on October 30, 1938, were almost prophetic: "We know now that in the early years of the twentieth century this world was being watched closely by intelligences greater than man's and yet as mortal as his own," Welles' sonorous voice declared. "We know now that as human beings busied themselves about their various concerns they were scrutinized and studied, perhaps almost as narrowly as a man with a microscope might scrutinize the transient creatures that swarm and multiply in a drop of water. With infinite complacence people went to and fro over the earth about their little affairs, serene in the assurance of their dominion over this small spinning fragment of solar driftwood, which by chance or design man has inherited out of the dark mystery of time and space. Yet across an immense ethereal gulf, minds that are to our minds as ours are to the beasts in the jungle, intellects vast, cool, and unsympathetic, regarded this earth with envious eyes and slowly and surely drew their plans against us."

Until the last few years no real effort was made to dig out and examine the many published accounts of those 1897 "airships." And even now the work is being done by a small, dedicated band of ufologists. There are great lessons to be learned from those early incidents, and many interesting clues scattered among the accounts. Ufology is just now beginning to come into being as an inexact science, and the field is a disorganized bedlam of egos and controversies and divergent opinions.

The most popular theory is that the flying saucers are born and bred on some other planet and that they visit us occasionally to drink our water and bask in our sun. But all of the available evidence and all of the patterns indicated in the now-massive sighting data tend to negate this charming theory.

The Lightning and the Thunder

When a bolt of lightning lashes across the sky, it exists for only a fraction of a second, but it is often followed by a deep rumble that can persist for several seconds. We know that the lightning produced the thunder, and we do not separate the two. However, during the nearly fifty years of the UFO controversy there has been a tendency to pay more attention to the thunder than to the sightings that precipitated the noise. In a way, the thunder has drowned out and obscured the cause. For years scientists and skeptics questioned the reliability of the witnesses, forcing the UFO researchers to expend inordinate effort trying to prove that the witnesses did, indeed, see *something* instead of trying to ascertain exactly what it was that was seen.

The problem was escalated by the fact that the witnesses to seemingly solid ("hard") objects rarely produced details which could be matched with other "hard" sightings. Thus the basic data—the descriptions of the objects seen—were filled with puzzling contradictions that weakened rather than supported the popular explanations and hypotheses. But there are actually definite hidden correlations within those contradictions, and we will be dealing with them at length in future chapters.

In Chapter 1 we outlined twenty-two typical reports. Most of these were of luminous objects that behaved in peculiar, unnatural ways. The great majority of *all* sightings throughout history have been of "soft" luminous objects, or objects that were transparent, translucent, changed size and shape, or appeared and disappeared suddenly. Sightings of seemingly solid metallic objects have always been quite rare. The "soft" sightings, being more numerous, comprise the real phenomenon and deserve the most study. The scope, frequency and distribution of the sightings make the popular extraterrestrial (interplanetary) hypothesis completely untenable. These important negative factors will also be explored in depth further on.

Apparently the U.S. Air Force intelligence teams realized early in the game (1947-49) that it would be logistically impossible for any foreign power, or even any extraterrestrial source, to maintain such a huge force of flying machines in the Western Hemisphere without suffering an accident that would expose the whole operation, or without producing patterns which would reveal their bases. There was never any real question about the reliability of the witnesses. Pilots, top military men, and whole crews of ships had seen unidentified flying objects during World War II and had submitted excellent technical reports to military intelligence.

The real problem remained: What *had* these people seen? The general behavior of the objects clearly indicated that they were paraphysical (*i.e.,* not composed of solid matter). They were clocked at incredible speeds within the atmosphere but did not produce sonic booms. They performed impossible maneuvers that defied the laws of inertia. They appeared and disappeared suddenly, like ghosts. Because there was no way in which their paraphysicality could be supported and explained scientifically, the Air Force specialists were obliged to settle upon an alternate hypothesis that could be accepted by the public and the scientific community. Dr. J. Allen Hynek, an astronomer and AF consultant, suggested the "natural phenomena" explanation after finding they could successfully fit most of the sighting descriptions into explanations of meteors, swamp gas, weather balloons and the like, to everyone's satisfaction—except the original witnesses. This left them with only a small residue of inexplicable "hard" sightings, which they shelved with a shrug.

Captain Edward Ruppelt, head of the Air Force's Project Blue Book in the early 1950s, wrote a book, *Report on Unidentified Flying Objects,* in which he freely discussed all of this. That book, published in 1956, still stands as the best standard reference on the subject.

The explosion of public interest in the UFO phenomenon in 1947 attracted many highly qualified professional scientists, researchers, and authors. Working independently, they quietly assessed the incoming evidence and slowly evolved complex theories that accounted for the paraphysicality of the objects. Unfortunately for them, the idea of extraterrestrial visitants had very strong emotional appeal, and the many amateur enthusiasts who were drawn to the subject quickly accepted the ET hypothesis on the strength of superficial, circumstantial evidence and pseudoscientific speculation. Their growing beliefs were augmented by the appearance of the "contactees"—people who professed that they had actually met the UFO pilots and had even flown to other planets aboard the objects.

Ironically, the UFO enthusiasts divided into factions over the contactee issue. Some accepted the contactees totally, while others rejected such stories and concentrated on trying to prove the reliability of witnesses and on the search for some kind of solid physical evidence that the UFOs were machines representing "a superior intelligence with an advanced technology." Friction between these factions increased over the years and added to the burgeoning controversy.

In the early years the Air Force was relatively free with UFO information, and Captain Ruppelt lent considerable support to

Donald E. Keyhoe, a retired Marine Corps major-turned-author, providing him with many official reports for his books and magazine articles. The Pentagon spokesman for Project Blue Book, Albert M. Chop, even went so far as to write the cover blurb for a Keyhoe book in 1953, stating:

"We in the Air Force recognize Major Keyhoe as a responsible, accurate reporter. His long association and cooperation with the Air Force, in our study of unidentified flying objects, qualifies him as a leading civilian authority on this investigation.

"All the sighting reports and other information he has listed have been cleared and made available to Major Keyhoe from Air Technical Intelligence records, at his request.

"The Air Force, and its investigating agency, Project Blue Book, is aware of Major Keyhoe's conclusion that the "flying saucers" are from another planet. The Air Force has never denied that this possibility exists. Some of the personnel believe that there may be some strange natural phenomena completely unknown to us, but that if the apparently controlled maneuvers reported by competent observers are correct, then the only remaining explanation is the interplanetary answer."

The Man Who Invented Flying Saucers

Ruppelt's book describes how the Air Force investigators made a strenuous effort to fit their evidence into an extraterrestrial framework. In January 1953, a panel of top scientists and CIA officials reviewed this evidence and rejected it. Instead of grandly announcing that flying saucers from another planet were visiting us, the panel suggested that the public be re-educated to believe that the sightings were inspired by natural phenomena, misinterpretations of known objects, and so on. The Air Force files were buttoned up, and an order was issued to forbid Air Force personnel from discussing UFO data. The move inspired the cry of "UFO censorship!" that persists to this day.

There was even division within the government on the true nature of the phenomenon!

On the West Coast, a brilliant man named Dr. Meade Layne had launched his own UFO study in 1947, and he was soon exploring the then little-known contactee aspects. By 1950, he was issuing privately published books explaining and defining the paraphysical nature of the objects and the parapsychological elements of the contactee syndrome. The ET believers rejected his theories and continued their fruitless search for physical evidence.

In England, the RAF had established a wartime UFO study project in 1943 under the direction of Lieutenant General Massey, but the results of that effort were never released. In 1944, a Chicago editor named Ray Palmer started to publish UFO-oriented fiction in his magazine *Amazing Stories,* and he was quickly inundated with thousands of letters from people who claimed to have seen the objects or had some kind of close experience with them. Palmer was later the cofounder of *Fate* magazine and devoted his life to the subject.

Other thoroughgoing researchers started to move toward the paraphysical concept in the early 1950s. The British science writer Gerald Heard published *Is Another World Watching?* in 1950, in which he examined the extraterrestrial theory pro and con and postulated his "bee" concept, suggesting that the objects might represent a mindless order organized by some larger intelligence. Another famous English science writer, Arthur C. Clarke, turned his attention to UFOs in 1953 and wrote articles pointing out that the general data suggested the objects were paraphysical and not too likely to be extraterrestrial.

If there was an actual turning point in ufology, it occurred in 1955. That year the "secret" was widely and repeatedly published by many superbly qualified investigators. Many UFO students reviewed this well documented material and quietly abandoned the subject, feeling that the mystery had been competently solved. A few held on until they were able to confirm the published evidence to their own satisfaction. Then they dropped out, leaving a vacuum in the field that was erratically filled by cultists and the emotionally disturbed types who were attracted more by the cloak-and-dagger aspects and the anarchistic possibilities of the allegations of official censorship.

A new UFO wave over England in 1950 inspired a new RAF investigation that was continued behind the scenes for five years. On April 24, 1955, an RAF spokesman told the press that the UFO study was completed but that the findings would be withheld from the public because they would only create more controversy and could not be adequately explained without revealing "certain top secrets." This enigmatic statement hardly satisfied anyone, but soon afterward RAF Air Marshal Lord Dowding, the man who had directed the Battle of Britain in 1940, gave a public lecture in which he openly discussed the paraphysical aspects of the phenomenon and declared the UFO occupants were immortal, could render themselves invisible to human eyes, and could even take on human form and walk and work among us unnoticed. This was very strong stuff in 1955, and the UFO enthusiasts didn't quite know what to make of it. The cultists still circulate his earlier pro-extraterrestrial statements made before he reached the paraphysical stage.

Still another excellent British researcher and reputable author, Harold T. Wilkins, stressed the paraphysical aspects in his 1955 book, *Flying Saucers Uncensored*. In the earlier stages of his research he had concluded that much of the evidence pointed to hostile intent, but later, as he developed a better understanding of the paraphysical factors, he modified this conclusion.

An astrophysicist, Morris K. Jessup, published a series of books from 1954 to 1957, filled with historical correlations and mind-bending theories about the paraphysical side of the phenomenon. R. De Witt Miller, a columnist for *Coronet* magazine, also spent years studying the subject and drawing upon the testimony submitted by thousands of his readers. He produced a well-documented summary of his paraphysical conclusions in a 1955 book called *You Do Take It with You*. An unfortunate title, perhaps, but the book is a fine examination of the implications of the main phenomenon.

The U.S. Air Force made its major contribution to the

subject in 1955 with the publication of *Project Blue Book Special Report No. 14*. This was undoubtedly the most important single contribution to the UFO problem. It was a statistical survey and computer study prepared for the Air Force by the Battelle Memorial Institute, containing 240 charts and graphs detailing the geographical distribution of sightings and other vital data. It was the only quantitative study ever produced by anyone. Many dismissed *Special Report No. 14* as "another whitewash," because the basic conclusion of the study was that there was no evidence of extraterrestrial origin and no suggestion that an advanced technology was involved. When I carried out my own statistical studies using thousands of reports from the 1960s, I was startled to discover that my findings merely verified the material in *Special Report No. 14*. It was embarrassing, at first, to realize that an objective examination of the evidence proved that the UFO enthusiasts were wrong and the Air Force was right.

Sensible research must be dictated by this basic precept: Any acceptable theory must offer an explanation for all the data. The paraphysical hypothesis meets this criterion. The extraterrestrial hypothesis does not. The UFO enthusiasts have solved this problem by selecting only those sightings and events that seem to fit the extraterrestrial thesis. They have rejected a major portion of the real evidence for this reason and, in many cases, have actually suppressed (by ignoring and not publishing) events that point to some other conclusion. Once this process of selection began, the problem became more confusing and the mystery more mysterious. The UFO publications were filled with selected sightings, and professional writers preparing books and magazine articles sifted out the best of those sightings, unaware that a major part of the real data was being deliberately ignored.

After the 1955 explosion of paraphysical information, ufology slipped into a Dark Age of confusion and bewildering misrepresentation. The Air Force paid only token attention to the phenomenon, explaining it away successfully for years as natural phenomena. The UFO enthusiasts became convinced of

"Air Force suppression of the truth," and a considerable part of the UFO literature published after 1955 was devoted to wild-eyed speculations about why the government was trying to keep UFOs a secret from the public. Because the professional writers and researchers had deserted the subject, the general quality of UFO literature hit a new low, most of it filled with pseudoscience and amateurish speculation. The factions within the UFO camp spent most of their efforts on feuding and fussing with the Air Force and with one another. There was very little actual research into UFO matters at all between 1955 and 1966.

As part of the hype for Ruppelt's 1956 book, the Intelligence Community in Washington, D.C. held a well-publicized symposium for four days in June 1956. Everybody attended: most of the top CIA officials, the German rocket scientists who would later achieve great fame with our NASA program, and leading aviation industrialists such as William Lear of Lear Jets. They decided to establish a civilian UFO organization to be called the National Investigation Committees on Aerial Phenomena (NI-CAP). A physicist named Townsend Brown was named to head it. Charter memberships cost $100, a great deal of money in 1956. It seemed as if something was finally going to be done.

There are other examples of sensible researchers who tried to penetrate the thunder of the UFO enthusiasts and reach the lightning. In 1954, Wilbert B. Smith, superintendent of Radio Regulations Engineering, Department of Transport, Ottawa, Canada, became the head of a semiofficial Canadian UFO study dubbed Project Magnet. Smith had fine credentials, and the UFO enthusiasts were thrilled with the announcement. But as the years passed, Smith began to realize that the quickest way to the source of the problem was through a study of the contactees. In some cases the UFO "entities" had actually passed on scientific information that Smith was able to check and confirm in his laboratory. Toward the end of his life (he died of cancer on December 27, 1962), he gave lectures and wrote papers about what he had learned.

"I began for the first time in my life to realize the basic

oneness of the universe-science, philosophy, and all that is in it," he remarked in 1958. "Substance and energy are all facets of the same jewel, and before any one facet can be appreciated, the form of the jewel itself must be perceived."

As usual, the extraterrestrial believers thought their scientist had gone crackers. They didn't want to hear about philosophy and energy. They wanted to discuss Venusians and the Air Force plot to hide the truth. It is unfortunate that a large part of Smith's papers and findings are still unpublished and undiscussed.

Another engineer, a graduate of Yale and the Massachusetts Institute of Technology, became interested in flying saucers in 1953. Upon his retirement in 1954, he and his wife toured the country interviewing UFO witnesses and, inevitably, contactee claimants. His name is Bryant Reeve. Like the rest of us, he began with the hope and expectation of finding evidence for the extraterrestrial hypothesis. He thought in the same physical terms of all engineers and scientists. But as he plunged deeper and deeper into this complex subject, he reached into philosophy and metaphysics just as Smith had. Finally, in 1965, he published a book called *The Advent of the Cosmic Viewpoint*. After long and careful investigation, he had concluded that the UFO sightings themselves were actually irrelevant and were merely part of the larger paraphysical phenomenon.

Kenneth Arnold, the private pilot whose sighting on June 24, 1947, set off the first modern flying saucer scare, quietly investigated UFOs in depth for years, and then in 1955 he, too, issued public statements expressing his belief that the objects were actually some form of living energy and were not necessarily marvelous spaceships.

In 1957, Ray Palmer started a new magazine called *Flying Saucers*. In the early issues he titillated his readers by hinting that he knew the secret. Then, in 1958, he published his conclusion that UFOs were not from some other planet, offering as an alternative a complex theory about secret civilizations with paraphysical or psychic ties to the human race. (As early as 1949, he had editorialized that saucers were extra-dimensional not extra-terrestrial.) He stubbornly stuck to his guns and published a number of small magazines devoted largely to the psychical aspects of the phenomenon. After a twelve-year struggle, his *Flying* Saucers had managed to build up a meager readership of only 4,000 paid subscribers and 6,000 newsstand sales despite nationwide distribution.

Palmer's anti-extraterrestrial stand isolated him from the ufological mainstream, and he was widely criticized and ostracized by the ET believers.

Dr. Leon Davidson, a physicist who worked on the atomic bomb project, became interested in UFOs in the early 1950s. Because of his status, the Air Force permitted him to view official UFO photos and movies. Eventually he turned to investigating the bewildering contactee cases, and his trained mind soon detected a hoax. Like other objective researchers, he conceded that the controversial contactees were telling the truth as they knew it. He recognized that these people were being tricked through some hypnotic process, but he was unable to accept any paraphysical explanation. Instead, he finally evolved a theory pointing the finger of guilt at the CIA. He speculated that the CIA was deliberately creating these events as a diversionary tactic in the Cold War. A very small proportion of the data did seem to fit this conclusion, but ultimately it proved to be insupportable.

For many years Al Chop, an Air Force information officer, lent his name to the board of governors of Major's Keyhoe's organization, the National Investigations Committee on Aerial Phenomena (NICAP). But in 1966, he withdrew his name, and in personal correspondence and in appearances on radio programs he declared that he no longer accepted the idea that flying saucers were real, physical machines. He explained the turn of mind with the wry statement, "I used to believe in Santa Claus, too."

Many other early UFO investigators, most of them far above average in education and intellectual capacity, arrived at similar negative conclusions after long and careful independent study. Some, such as Dr. Donald Menzel, a Harvard astronomer, recognized that people were seeing something and had tried to explain the phenomenon within the restrictions of their own scientific disciplines. Dr. Menzel argued convincingly for a mirage and air-inversion theory.

Two authorities well known to the UFO field, Ivan T. Sanderson, a noted biologist and anthropologist, and Dr. Jacques Vallee, a NASA astronomer and computer expert, studied the extraterrestrial theory for years and finally turned toward the paraphysical hypothesis.

What exactly is the paraphysical hypothesis? It is the central theme of this book. It can best be summarized by the remarks of RAF Air Marshal Sir Victor Goddard, KCB, CBE, MA, a very high-ranking member of the British government. On May 3, 1969, he gave a public lecture at Caxton Hall in London, in which he cited these main points:

"That while it may be that some operators of UFO are normally the paraphysical denizens of a planet other than Earth, there is no logical need for this to be so. For, if the materiality of UFO is paraphysical (and consequently normally invisible), UFO could more plausibly be creations of an invisible world coincident with the space of our physical Earth planet than creations in the paraphysical realms of any other physical planet in the solar system... Given that real UFO are paraphysical, capable of reflecting light like ghosts; and given also that (according to many observers) they remain visible as they change position at ultrahigh speeds from one point to another, it follows that those that remain visible in transition do not dematerialize for that swift transition, and therefore, their mass must be of a diaphanous (very diffuse) nature, and their substance relatively etheric... The observed validity of this supports the paraphysical assertion and makes the likelihood of UFO being Earth-created greater than the likelihood of their creation on another planet... The astral world of illusion, which (on psychical evidence) is greatly inhabited by illusion-prone spirits, is well known for its multifarious imaginative activities and exhortations. Seemingly some of its denizens are eager to exemplify principalities and powers. Others pronounce upon morality, spirituality, Deity, etc. All of these astral exponents who invoke human consciousness may be sincere, but many of their theses may be framed to propagate some special phantasm, perhaps of an earlier incarnation, or to indulge an inveterate and continuing technological urge toward materialistic progress, or simply to astonish and disturb the gullible for the devil of it."

Sir Victor's remarks are, admittedly, even harder to believe than the claims of the various UFO cults. If you are not familiar with the massive, well-documented occult and religious literature, his words may be incomprehensible to you. In essence, he means that the UFO phenomenon is actually a staggering cosmic put-on: a joke perpetrated by invisible entities who have always delighted in frightening, confusing and misleading the human race. The activities of these entities have been carefully recorded throughout history, and we will be leaning heavily on those historical records in this book.

Recently the U.S. Government Printing Office issued a publication compiled by the Library of Congress for the Air Force Office of Scientific Research: *UFOs and Related Subjects: An Annotated Bibliography.* In preparing this work, the senior bibliographer, Miss Lynn E. Catoe, actually read thousands of UFO articles, books and publications. In her preface to this 400-page book she states:

"A large part of the available UFO literature is closely linked with mysticism and the metaphysical. It deals with subjects like mental telepathy, automatic writing, and invisible entities, as well as phenomena like poltergeist manifestations and possession... Many of the UFO reports now being published in the popular press recount alleged incidents that are strikingly similar to demoniac possession and psychic phenomena which has long been known to theologians and parapsychologists."

Dr. Edward U. Condon, the physicist who headed Colorado University's Air Force-financed two-year UFO study, has been criticized because he devoted part of his time to examining the claims of the controversial contactees. He earned the undying wrath of the cultists when his final report was published in January 1969, and he stressed an anti-extraterrestrial conclusion. He asserted that his scientific teams had failed to find any evidence of extraterrestrial origin or of serious UFO censorship on the part of the government. But both of these myths have been implanted too deeply in the UFO literature to be killed off so easily. The Library of Congress' objective bibliography even had sections devoted to news management, censorship, and CIA plots. Was all of this just another government whitewash, as the cultists contend?

In April 1969, Dr. Condon delivered a speech before the American Philosophical Society in Philadelphia, in which he was gently derisive of the popular UFO beliefs: "Some UFOs *may* be such [extraterrestrial] visitors, it may be postulated," Dr. Condon said, "and some writers go so far as to say that they *actually are.* To discover clear, unambiguous evidence on this point would be a scientific discovery of the first magnitude, one which I would be quite happy to make. We found no such evidence, and so state in our report …We concluded that it is not worthwhile to carry on a continuing study of UFOs in the manner which has been done so far: that of going out into the field to interview persons who say they have seen something peculiar. The difficulty about using objective means of study lies in the rarity of the apparitions, their short duration, and the tendency of observers not to report their experience until long after it has ended …These difficulties led us to conclude that it is quite unproductive of results of scientific value to study UFOs in the traditional manner. But, contrary to popular belief, we do not rule out all future study.

"Perhaps we need a National Magic Agency (pronounced 'enema') to make a large and expensive study of all these matters, including the future scientific study of UFOs, if any," he concluded.

The real UFO story must encompass all of the many manifestations being observed. It is a story of ghosts and phantoms and strange mental aberrations; of an invisible world that surrounds us and occasionally engulfs us; of prophets and prophecies, and gods and demons. It is a world of illusion and hallucination where the unreal seems very real, and where reality itself is distorted by strange forces which can seemingly manipulate space, time, and physical matter—forces that are almost entirely beyond our powers of comprehension.

Nearly all of those who have finally come to an understanding of the true nature of the phenomenon have quietly abandoned the subject because they found it impossible to articulate their findings and make the incredible credible. They were not silenced by the Air Force or the CIA, as the cultists believe. They were rendered mute by the awesome and overwhelming realization that man is not alone; that the human race is merely a trifling part of something much bigger.

That something is at the core of all human beliefs, ranging from the ancient myths of Greece, India and China to the modern myths of the friendly Venusians.

Whatever "it" is, it is often inimical to the human race, and the manifestations range from childish mischief to acts of horrifying destruction. The phenomenon has driven many people mad; but it has also produced miraculous cures. A cosmic system of checks and balances seems to be an actual fact. There are now well-documented cases of people being seriously injured, even killed, by flying saucers. But there are equally well-documented events in which the mysterious objects and their enterprising occupants have interceded directly in human affairs and thwarted disaster.

Many flying saucers seem to be nothing more than a disguise for some hidden phenomenon. They are like Trojan horses descending into our forests and farm fields, promising salvation and offering us the splendor of some great supercivilization in the sky. But while the statuesque long-haired "Venusians" have been chatting benignly with isolated traveling salesmen and farm wives, a multitude of shimmering lights and metallic disks have been silently busying themselves in the forests of Canada, the Outback country of Australia, and the swamps of Michigan.

Before we can find any answers, we must first find the right questions to ask. We must understand the exact nature of these visitors, and of ourselves.

3
The World of Illusion

There have been hundreds of incidents in which electromagnetic effects, such as the stalling of automobile engines and power failures, have been noted and documented. Early ufologists were already aware of the fact that electromagnetism played a large role in many UFO events. The late Frank Scully, a reporter for *Variety,* wrote a contactee-oriented book in 1950, *Behind the Flying Saucers,* which contained a long chapter on electromagnetism.

Now we have enough data to properly interpret the overall meaning of this force in the phenomenon. We will try to simplify it here, going a step at a time, before we outline the material that verifies these conclusions.

Radio beams are waves of electromagnetic energy. They vibrate at various frequencies, and we separate them or tune them by adjusting the length of the waves with coils and condensers. Your local radio station is broadcasting a signal of electrical pulses, each pulse adjusted to a specific length. When you tune your radio to the station, you move a series of metal plates which sort out the various wavelengths and enable your radio to pick up and amplify only the signal coming in at a certain point—or frequency—of the electromagnetic spectrum.

Your eyes are also receivers tuned to very specific wavelengths of the spectrum, and they turn the signals from those wavelengths into pulses, which are fed to your brain. Your brain, in turn, is also a very sophisticated, little-understood receiver, and it is tuned to wavelengths far beyond the receiving capabilities of manufactured electronic instruments. Most people are running around with crude biological "crystal sets" in their heads and are not consciously receiving any of the sophisticated signals. However, about one-third of the world's population possesses a more finely tuned instrument.

These people experience telepathy, prophetic dreams, and other bizarre signals from some central source. If you are one of that 30 percent, you know precisely what I mean. If you belong to the larger, ungifted two-thirds, you probably regard all this as nonsense, and we may never be able to convince you otherwise.

Now let's try to define this whole process.

When moving electrons pass through a wire, a small magnetic field is created around the wire. If the current fluctuates, or vibrates, this fluctuation will also appear in the magnetic field. A voice speaking through a telephone mouthpiece (or microphone) causes the current flowing through the phone to fluctuate, or oscillate. Your voice thus causes a flow of electrons to vibrate. At the other end, a magnet in the receiver responds to this fluctuation, and the minute vibrations are magnified. A thin piece of metal in the earpiece is vibrated in turn by the magnet, and these vibrations oscillate the air in the form of sound waves, which can be sensed by your ears and auditory system.

Technicians are undoubtedly gnashing their teeth over my explanations here, but again, I am trying to oversimplify these things. It is necessary to understand elemental electronics before we can move on to our next point.

Your voice causes the electricity in your telephone to vibrate at a very specific frequency. When that metal plate (diaphragm) at the other end responds to the magnet, it vibrates at this same frequency and duplicates your voice almost exactly. A part of you— your individual voice—has been transformed into electrical waves, transferred to a distant point, and then reassembled into sound waves that duplicate exactly every inflection and nuance in your voice. This is a very primitive form of teleportation.

The wire carrying your voice is surrounded by a magnetic field that is also vibrating at your own personal frequency. If there are, say, twenty telephone wires on a pole, all conducting signals, we now have the technology to tune in a device to your personal frequency and intercept your telephone conversation instantly without cutting into any wires or tapping any lines. In other words, a panel truck carrying the necessary equipment need only park near a telephone pole bearing a wire hooked up to your phone. The operator can then tune in to your line (your personal frequency) in the same way that you tune into your favorite radio program by adjusting a condenser which cuts out all other frequencies.

This method for tapping telephones is absolutely undetectable. It does not produce any clicks or noises on the phone at either end. However, the process can be reversed, and an operator can tune into the frequency of your telephone line and talk to you by radio waves vibrating at the very low frequency of the telephone current. Or, if he so desires, he can insert static, strange sounds, etc., onto your line. He can even place phone calls through the telephone system using your line (and you will be billed for them).

The equipment needed for this kind of tampering is most complicated and expensive. It is highly unlikely that any ordinary practical joker would be able to obtain and operate such equipment. But my studies, investigations, and nationwide polls prove that somebody is using such equipment or is exploiting these principles.

The telephone companies themselves now utilize high frequency radio for long-distance telephone calls. Microwave relay towers now dot the countryside. Telephone signals are stepped up to high-frequency radio waves and projected from tower to tower across the country. In the past few years there have been thousands of reports of low-level UFOs hovering directly above these microwave relay towers. Some researchers, such as Ivan T. Sanderson, have perused similar reports and suggested that perhaps the objects were tapping the power from power lines and telephone systems for their own purposes. I do not feel this is a valid theory.

Rather, I now believe that the UFO phenomenon is primarily electromagnetic in origin and that it possesses the ability to adjust beams of electromagnetic energy to any given frequency, ranging from ultra-high frequencies (UHF) radio signals like those of the astronauts, to very low frequencies (VLF) which can be picked up only by special equipment, to very, very low frequencies identical to the magnetic fields surrounding telephone wires or the outputs of public address systems in schools and churches.

I also believe that this same phenomenon is flexible to an unbelievable degree. It can create and manipulate matter through electromagnetic fields above and below the range of our perceptions and our own technical equipment.

The phenomenon is mostly invisible to us because it consists of energy rather than solid earthly matter. It is guided by a great intelligence and has concentrated itself in the areas of magnetic faults throughout history. It makes itself visible to us from time to time by manipulating patterns of frequency. It can take any form it desires, ranging from the shapes of airplanes to gigantic cylindrical spaceships. It can manifest itself into seemingly living entities ranging from little green men to awesome one-eyed giants. But none of these configurations is its true form.

The UFO sighting data confirm this theory, but we lack the necessary technology to prove it conclusively.

Energy and Illusion

Any high school student of physics can tell you that our reality is an illusion. The occultists have been saying this same thing for centuries. All matter is composed of confined energy. Tiny moving electrons and energy particles form atoms of varying weights and densities. These atoms are joined together to form molecules of specific substances. They are so tiny that the atom remained only a theory for many years. We cannot perceive the atom but now can prove scientifically that it exists and that it is made up of energy.

Atoms and molecules form larger structures, even though they do not touch. If we could reduce ourselves to the size of an electron in an atom, the next nearest atom would seem like a distant star. We are so much larger than the atom that a collection of atoms seems to form solid matter to us. This page seems solid to you, but it is made up of billions of atoms. So are you. If you try to poke your finger through this page, you will tear it. But you can easily poke your finger into a cloud of cigarette smoke because its molecules are farther apart.

We learned to reshape molecules long ago through chemical and physical manipulation. We can melt a bar of steel and mold it into a sword or a plowshare. We can cut down a tree and build a chair out of it—or a piece of paper. Such manipulations are primitive processes. But our industries and sciences have been built around them.

Now we are beginning to learn how to manipulate energy itself. We started by finding ways to peel electrons off atoms and release the basic energy hidden in the atom. We naturally applied this important discovery to melting cities and disintegrating human beings.

The chair you sit in is composed of billions and billions of molecules made up of atoms. Each cell of your body is also composed of millions of atoms. If the energy patterns or frequencies of the atoms of your body were radically different from the atoms of your chair, it is conceivable that they would intermix and you would sink right through the chair somewhat in the same way that your finger passes through a cloud of cigarette smoke.

Our reality is based entirely upon what we can perceive with our physical senses. If we can touch something and feel it, we say that it is real and exists. If we can see it, smell it, hear it, and taste it, then we know definitely that it exists. But actually you may be sensing only a small portion of the existing universe. At this very moment you are surrounded by a wall of electromagnetic waves from dozens of radio and television transmitters. You cannot see or sense these waves, but you can transform them into movements of air with a radio receiver. You have the instrumentation necessary to perceive waves that exist beyond the limitations of your sensual perceptions. There are other waves around you that you can't detect.

There are thousands of microscopic life forms in a drop of water. You can't see them, feel them, or taste them because they are too small. A teenaged boy with a cheap microscope can peer into that drop of water and invade the privacy of those microbes. But the microbes don't know he is there. They swim about in their liquid environment totally unaware that their tiny world is actually an insignificant part of a much larger, and very different, whole.

Our world may also be part of something bigger, something beyond our senses and abilities to comprehend.

That bigger something is undoubtedly made of energies, too. But energies of a different frequency, forming atoms radically different from the atoms of our own world. These energies could coexist with us and even share the same space without our becoming acutely aware of them.

The evidence we have outlined in this book does clearly point to this unperceived coexistence, and now we must come to terms with "it" or "them" or the Great Whatzit in the sky.

Secrets of the Spectrums

For thousands of years the occultists, spiritualists, and religionists have talked about and written about auras, frequencies, vibrations, and other planes of existence. Each group developed its own complex vocabulary for explaining and defining these things. Each tried to fit its theories into its own particular frame of reference. Thus, these "other planes" became the Valhalla where worthy spirits ascend upon death. The casual browser leafing through this mountain of literature is usually repelled by the nonsensical terminology and the abstract theories, yet, underneath all of the belief-ridden folderol, there lies a thread of truth that is now being verified by the many manifestations surrounding the UFO phenomenon.

I will try to demonstrate that the UFO entities are directly related to the entities and manifestations involved in religious miracles and spiritual séances. There are many thousands of published messages from both the ufonauts and the spirits, all of which employ the same techniques for burying information deep in simple-minded descriptions about life on other planets or other planes. One of the most important correlations is that many of these messages have discussed in depth the existence of another reality that is formed by energies operating on another frequency, or vibrationary level.

There has also been a great deal of discussion about light and rays of light. The lore of the "seven rays" goes back to the most ancient of times. The Bible's *Book of Revelation* repeats the number seven in many ways, and the Seven Sisters, or the Pleiades (seven stars in the sky), form an important part of this ancient lore. The color spectrum is also most important in the context of the overall picture painted by religion and occultism. God and Christ are "The Light" in most of this literature.

The "source" has made repeated attempts to explain all of this in terms that we might understand. On January 8, 1968, "Mr. Orion," of the Ashtar Intergalactic Command, passed this message along to a contactee: "The saucers which you speak of as such are in reality the space bodies of certain aggregates of consciousness. They exist duodimensionally; that is, they penetrate both the third and fourth dimensions simultaneously or can, if they wish, confine themselves to either one of these. Their purpose has been, and still is, for the time being, to interlace these two realms of consciousness which are seemingly separate. However, the time quickly comes when the veil is torn aside and what is One is perceived as One. It is at this moment that the saucers seen by the few will be seen by the many. It will appear that they have suddenly arrived in your skies in great number. In reality this is untrue. For in reality they are where they have always been, but man sees with new eyes."

Man's old eyes aren't very good. We can actually see only a very small part of the electromagnetic spectrum. Light waves are really visible vibrations of the spectrum, somewhat akin to radio waves. The different frequencies register as different colors on the cones in our eyes. You could say that our visual apparatus really consists of thousands of tiny radio receivers carefully tuned to a minute portion of the electromagnetic spectrum. We really can't see very much at all, but we can see enough to cope adequately with our immediate environment.

The accompanying chart is a rough outline of the basic electromagnetic spectrum. Cosmic rays—high-intensity, high-frequency rays of energy that radiate throughout the universe—occupy one end of the spectrum. They are followed by potent gamma rays, the energy forms that do so much damage when we set off our atomic bombs. Next we have x-rays, short waves which penetrate matter, ionize gases, and cloud up photographic film. These blend in with gamma rays on our scale.

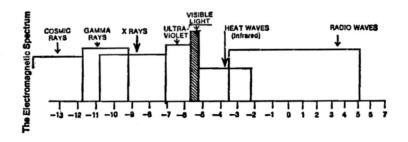

Ultraviolet rays come next, and they are tremendously important to the UFO phenomenon. These are also invisible but can burn the flesh and the eyes. A neglected part of the UFO evidence consists of the hundreds of sightings in which the witnesses suffered all of the symptoms of klieg conjunctivitis afterward. Actors performing on movie sets brightly illuminated by arc lights sometimes experience these same symptoms. The eyes redden, itch, and feel sore. This is caused by the ultraviolet radiation (also called actinic rays). These same rays give you a sunburn on the beach. If you don't cover your eyes when lying on the sand, you can burn your eyes from the sun's rays.

The many cases of skin burn and conjunctivitis following nighttime UFO sightings give absolute proof that ultraviolet waves are radiating from some of the objects. Stars, space satellites, and other natural or man-made aerial objects could not possibly produce this effect. I have interviewed many people shortly after their sightings when their eyes were still swollen and reddish from conjunctivitis. I suffered this ailment myself after a close sighting in 1967.

Visible light is sandwiched in between -5 and -6 on our scale. This is the only portion of the spectrum that we can see and utilize. These visible rays are divided into the basic frequencies of blue, yellow and red. When combined, they form white.

Beyond red there is infrared, the visible rays radiated by heat. Many UFO witnesses have complained of feeling oppressive waves of heat, even when the objects seemed to be many yards away. Concentrated infrared can also hurt the eyes. Infrared rays are shorter than microwave radio signals and longer than the waves of visible light. Man-made radio signals are last on the scale. These range from microwaves to UHF (ultrahigh frequencies) on one end, to VLF (very low frequencies) on the other.

The Van Allen belt, a belt of radiation circling the earth, and the atmosphere strain out most of the cosmic rays that are constantly bombarding us. The ultraviolet and infrared rays of the sun penetrate this barrier, fortunately, and plant and animal life have adjusted to absorb and utilize these energies.

Visible Light (Color Spectrum)

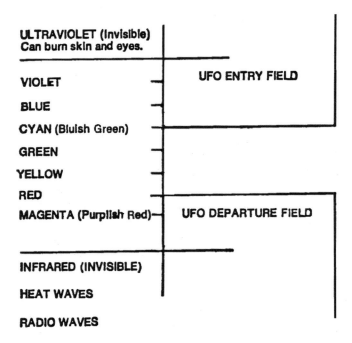

ULTRAVIOLET (Invisible)
Can burn skin and eyes.

VIOLET — UFO ENTRY FIELD

BLUE —

CYAN (Bluish Green) —

GREEN —

YELLOW —

RED

MAGENTA (Purplish Red)— UFO DEPARTURE FIELD

INFRARED (INVISIBLE)

HEAT WAVES

RADIO WAVES

If our eyes were tuned to see beyond the infrared rays, we could look at a telephone microwave relay tower and see a steady stream of brilliant reddish light pouring from it. If we were tuned in visually to the longer radio waves, we would see ourselves bathed in multicolored light (because of the many different frequencies), and it would be like living in the end of a rainbow.

We are surrounded by energies we cannot see. It is possible that some of these energies form objects, entities and even worlds that we can't see, either. But just because we can't see, hear, feel or taste them doesn't mean that they aren't there.

Let's recap this basic lesson in physics. (1) All solid matter in our environment (or reality) is composed of energy. (2) All energies are of an electromagnetic nature. (3) The human eye can perceive only a very small portion of the electromagnetic spectrum. (4) Electromagnetic waves of many different frequencies permeate the known universe. We live in a sea of such radiations, and the space through which our planet travels is an ocean of radiation.

In recent years, specially equipped satellites, and our radio telescopes, have discovered that space is filled with infrared rays of unknown origin. Invisible stars have now been detected with infrared devices. They are invisible because they do not issue rays within the limited frequencies of the visible light spectrum. Instead, their energies are being radiated in the higher frequencies of X-rays and the lower frequencies of radio waves. Thanks to the excellent work now being done by radio telescopes all over the world, we are rapidly learning more about these invisible objects. It is extremely unlikely that these radio signals are being deliberately broadcast to us by a superior intelligence.

Somewhere in this tangled mass of electromagnetic frequencies there lies an omnipotent intelligence, however. This intelligence is able to manipulate energy. It can, quite literally, manipulate any kind of object into existence on our plane. For centuries the occultists and religionists have called this process transmutation or transmogrification. Thousands of books have been published on this process, many of them serving as secret texts for alchemists and sorcerers. The early occultists understood, at least partially, that energy was the key to the whole. Because fire has always been a basic source of energy, many of their rites centered around candle flames and bonfires. Early religious rites involved the offering of sacrifices by fire to the unseen gods. In Biblical times, animals were consigned to the flames as offerings. In other cultures, human beings were sacrificed on pyres.

Essentially, fire breaks down the molecules of the substance being burned, freeing some of the energy contained therein and producing intense infrared radiation.

One well-known, heavily documented type of poltergeist (noisy ghost) manifestation produces mysterious fires. "Haunted" houses often burn to the ground eventually. Fires of undetermined origin erupt suddenly throughout UFO flap areas. Many pyromaniacs set fires because "a voice" in their head told them to do so.

Although I have had neither the means nor the time to study adequately and confirm this fire factor, my experiences in flap areas have led me to believe that the energies of these mysterious conflagrations are being utilized by the UFO phenomenon. There may be a definite relationship between the numbers of fires and the numbers of UFOs seen in a specific sector. A community suddenly beset with fifteen or twenty major fires within the short span of a week or two seems to produce more UFO sightings in that same period than a place with no fires. Either the UFOs are somehow indirectly causing these fires, or they are directly feasting upon the energies produced by the flames.

The Mystery of the Aura

You are a chemical machine made up of electromagnetic energy. Your brain is actually an electrical computer connected to all parts of your body by a wiring system of nerves. Constant chemical reactions are taking place throughout your body. The food you eat is being burned off continuously in the form of heat and energy. Although you can't see it, your body is surrounded by self-generated fields of radiation. The occultists have always called this radiation the aura. There have been many people—mediums and sensitives—who have claimed that they could actually see this human aura. Some amazing demonstrations and tests have been performed before large groups of witnesses in which sensitives were able to look at a stranger's aura, and by supposedly noting various shadings in that aura, they could accurately announce, "You have a scar on your abdomen, and there's a black cloud over your liver. You've been having liver trouble."

Special eyeglasses have been on the market for years so that almost anyone could see the aura. Because the human body does radiate infrared rays, the glasses do work!

In recent years, science has begun to take the aura seriously. The Albert Einstein Medical Center in Philadelphia has been conducting experiments with infrared devices for some time, with surprising results. They have, for example, photographed a man's arms and hands with the devices before and after he smoked a cigarette. The "after" shot showed how his arms had darkened because the nicotine had constricted the blood vessels and lowered the temperature in his limbs. Tumors and other disorders readily show up in these thermogram photos. (See *Scientific American*, February 1967.) These studies have confirmed the wild claims of the occult aura watchers.

The Biomedical Engineering Center at Northwestern University's Technological Institute has also been experimenting with an ultrasound system which has produced similar results. A hand dipped in water agitated by a special sound transducer device reveals blood vessels as green, blue or orange lines. It even works with metal. A spot of defective welding appears in varying colors, while a good weld is uniform.

What has the aura got to do with flying saucers? Perhaps a good deal. Many contactees have been told that they were selected because of their aura. Occultists have long claimed that each person is surrounded by an aura that reveals his spiritual state. An evil person has a black aura. A saintly type has a golden radiation. There are supposed to be blue auras, and white ones also, all with their own meaning. Here, again, the literature on auras is massive, and not all of it is nonsense.

A milkman was walking along a beach south of Sydney, Australia, early one morning in the summer of 1960 when he came upon a strange metal disk surrounded by a violet light and making a whining sound. Two men suddenly appeared, both dressed in space suits complete with transparent helmets. Their eyes were blue and had an Oriental slant. They allegedly addressed the milkman in perfect English, although their lips did not move. He said their voices seemed to come from square boxes on their belts. After warning the milkman that entities from Orion were preparing to take over the earth, they said that they had been able to contact him because of his aura. They promised to return and contact him again at some time in the future, stating that he "was going to be used for a certain job."

This witness told no one about his alleged contact for two years, but finally his story leaked out and he was investigated by Cohn McCarthy and other Australian ufologists. (A more detailed description of this case can be found in *The Scorriton Mystery* by Eileen Buckle.)

Because many animals have better vision than man, it is possible that the UFOs and the ufonauts may also have superior vision. They may be able to perceive frequencies of the electromagnetic spectrum that are invisible to us. Perhaps they can even see the entire spectrum and can clearly view not only our limited world, but the more vast invisible worlds that surround us.

There have been numerous confirmed radar sightings of UFOs that could not be seen by the naked eye. We also have the thousands of soft sightings in which the objects suddenly appeared and/or disappeared instantaneously in front of the witnesses. All of these events seem to prove that a large part of the UFO phenomenon is hidden from us and is taking place beyond the limited range of our eyes. We can only see the objects and the entities under certain circumstances, and *perhaps only certain types of people can see them at all.*

Thus, by all the standards of our sciences (and our common sense), the UFOs do not really exist as solid objects. They may be a constant part of our environment, but they are not an actual part of our reality. We cannot, therefore, catalog them as manufactured products of some extraterrestrial civilization sharing our own dimensions of time and space. They are extradimensional, able to move through our spatial coordinates at will but also able to enter and leave our three-dimensional world. If this is a true hypothesis, then they may also be operating beyond the limitations of our time coordinates. Our years may be minutes to them. Our future may be their past, and thus they have total knowledge of the things in store for us.

The Purple Blobs

Among the most neglected of all the soft sightings are the strange purple blobs, some so faint that they can barely be seen with the naked eye. Such blobs were frequently reported in earlier days of the saucer scare, but newspapers were soon diverted by the more intriguing hard sightings of seemingly solid disks. The purple blobs have been busy throughout the world, but the published sightings have become increasingly rare. People who see these things often dismiss them as some kind of illusion or natural phenomenon, or they feel they are not worthy of being reported.

Between 9:15 and 11:00 P.M. on the night of June 24, 1947, scores of people in Seattle, Washington, watched peculiar purple and light-blue spots of light dancing around the skies. That was the same day that Kenneth Arnold saw his famous flying saucers.

I have seen many strange blue lights and purple spots in my travels. The first time I was roaming around the hills behind Gallipolis Ferry, West Virginia, early in 1967, and when the spots first appeared, I thought my eyes were playing tricks. They were barely visible in the darkness and seemed to be small clouds of glowing gas. I climbed a steep hill, accompanied by two local teenagers, hoping to find a better vantage point to view a sector where many objects had been sighted previously. The purple spots were moving all around us; there were twenty or more. The sky was overcast, and at first I suspected the phenomenon might be caused by stars faintly shining through the clouds. But they seemed very close by, maneuvering around at treetop level. I blinked my huge flashlight at them and was startled when these things actually leaped out of the way of the beam.

When we reached the summit of the hill, I experimented further, aiming my light at spots that had remained perfectly stationary since we had first noticed them. The instant my beam struck them, these spots skittered across the sky, some of them darting 25 or 30 degrees before they paused again.

After much more experimentation, on other nights in other places, I concluded that the purple spots were part of the UFO phenomenon and were being controlled by, or possessed, some kind of intelligence.

Return now to our two charts of the electromagnetic and color spectrums. You will see that ultraviolet rays immediately precede the visible spectrum. The first visible frequencies are of purple or violet light.

Let us assume that UFOs exist at frequencies beyond visible light but that they can adjust their frequency and descend the electromagnetic spectrum—just as you can turn the dial of your radio and move a variable condenser up and down the scale of radio frequencies. When a UFO's frequency nears that of visible light, it would first appear as a purplish blob of violet. As it moves farther down the scale, it would seem to change to blue, and then to cyan (bluish green). In our chapter on meteors we note that they most often appear as bluish-green objects.

I have therefore classified that section of the color spectrum as the UFO entry field. When the objects begin to move into our spatial and time coordinates, they gear down from the higher frequencies, passing progressively from ultraviolet to violet to bluish green. When they stabilize within our dimensions, they radiate energy on all frequencies and become a glaring white.

In the white condition the object can traverse distances visibly, but radical maneuvers of ascent or descent require it to alter its frequencies again, and this process produces new color changes. In the majority of all landing reports, the objects were said to have turned orange (red and yellow) or red before descending. When they settle to the ground they "solidify," and the light dims or goes out altogether. On takeoff, they begin to glow red again. Sometimes they reportedly turn a brilliant red and vanish. Other times they shift through all of the colors of the spectrum, turn white, and fly off into the night sky until they look like just another star.* Because the color red is so closely associated with the landing and takeoff processes, I term this end of the color spectrum the UFO departure field.

The great mass of observational data fully supports these hypotheses. Our glowing objects change color, size, and form, and this fact indicates that they are comprised of energy which can be manipulated to temporarily simulate terrestrial matter. Such energies must be somehow collected together at the invisible frequencies, and then frequency changes are brought about to "lower" them into the visible spectrum. Once they become visible, they can then organize themselves into atoms and produce any desired form.

Barney and Betty Hill, the couple who were allegedly taken aboard a UFO in New Hampshire in 1961, first observed a brilliant moving "star." As it drew closer, the brilliance faded and it became a seemingly material flying saucer occupied by small men in uniforms. Brazil's Villa-Boas, who claimed he was taken aboard a UFO in 1957, first saw a reddish object which then became a grounded saucer. When it took off again, the object first surrounded itself with a red glow. The glow intensified, and the reddish object sailed off into the stars.

---

* Back in 1952, the late Danton Walker's syndicated newspaper column stated, "Confidential Air Force reports indicate that flying saucers remain stationary at night to get lost in the stars."

Those who have tried to investigate the UFO phenomenon in purely physical terms have speculated on the possible mechanics of such objects. The general consensus has been that the UFOs utilize an antigravity device which surrounds them with a magnetic field, and this magnetism ionizes the nitrogen in the air around the object, causing it to glow. On the surface, this has seemed like a plausible theory. But in reality it is not workable. A tremendous amount of magnetism would be required to produce the magnetic effects blamed on the objects, such as the stalling of automobiles. The Ford Motor Company, working with the UFO-investigating group at Colorado University, discovered that simple magnetism could not stall an auto engine encased in the protective steel body of a car. A field strong enough to accomplish this would also be strong enough to bend the car itself and possibly affect the passengers as well.

Continuous ionization of the air is also a difficult feat. It's more likely that the objects are composed of electromagnetic energy themselves. Witnesses are observing frequency changes rather than ionization. In some cases, the ground has been found radioactive after an object has landed. This might be the by-product of the gamma rays, which are one of the energy constituents of the objects, not just an effect of some mechanical process.

We also have a considerable body of testimonial evidence in which the objects were transparent, even though they appeared to be mechanical in some way. For example, at 7:30 P.M. on Friday, October 18, 1968, the McMullen family in Medulla, Florida, looked outside their home when their dog began to howl and bark. They reportedly saw a purplish red object hovering about 10 feet in the air. It was completely transparent, and two normal-sized men were visible inside it. A strong odor of ammonia was in the air. The two men were pumping a horizontal bar up and down. As they watched, the 30-foot sphere slowly ascended and flew off. A few minutes earlier, two other witnesses saw a bright light rising from the grounds of the Medulla school, just north of the McMullen home. There were also some mysterious explosions in the area during that period.

Was this transparent sphere a spaceship from another planet? Not very likely. The witnesses saw nothing inside it except the men and the bar. No machinery. No wonderful apparatus.

There have been many bewildering accounts of shell-like objects with no visible means of propulsion, no signs of any kinds of technology. Contactee Reinhold Schmidt's German-speaking ufonauts, who invited him aboard their saucer in Nebraska in 1957, didn't walk but glided across the floor of their spaceship as if they were on roller skates. Other sober and baffled witnesses have described how the UFO occupants seemed to fly from the ground to their waiting saucers. Still others have claimed that the ufonauts simply walked through the sides of their craft like ghosts. In story after story we have testimonial proof that the objects and their occupants are not made of normal substances.

The hard (seemingly solid) objects are another problem. Bullets have been fired at them and have ricocheted off. They sometimes leave imprints on the ground where they land. If they are the product of a superior intelligence with an advanced technology, they seem to be suffering from faulty workmanship. Since 1896 there have been hundreds of reports in which lone witnesses have stumbled onto grounded hard objects being repaired by their pilots. In flight, they have an astounding habit of losing pieces of metal. They seem to be ill-made, always falling apart, frequently exploding in midair. There are so many of these incidents that we must wonder if they aren't really deliberate. Maybe they are meant to foster the belief that the objects are real and mechanical.

In the foregoing I have tried to demonstrate how the soft objects seem to be directly related to the electromagnetic spectrum. This is hardly a new theory. Not only have the occultists, spiritualists, and religionists been telling us about frequencies, vibrations, and the color spectrum for centuries, but modern researchers such as Dr. Meade Layne worked all of this out years ago. Dr. Layne evolved a theory of "mat" and "demat" (materialization and dematerialization) of extradimensional objects. His findings were privately published and not very widely circulated.

Others, such as British ufologist Harold T. Wilkins, also worked this out and published books about it in the early 1950s. But the spectrum theory lacks the strong emotional appeal of the extraterrestrial thesis.

There is a rather curious entry in *Project Blue Book Report No. 14* (1955) on page 295. In the section showing how various sightings are classified, number 8 in Code 79-80 Final Identification is "Electromagnetic Phenomenon." This is crossed out (the report was reproduced by photo offset), and the now well-known classification of "Unknown" was substituted.*

---

* For a more detailed treatment of the material in this chapter, see *The Eighth Tower* by John A. Keel.

4
Machines from Beyond Time

"It was shaped like a disk about the size of a boxcar, with a domed top and square red and green windows," Mrs. Rita Malley recalled. "And it made a humming sound, something like the vibration of a television antenna in the wind."

Mrs. Malley, a pretty, young blond mother of two, was recounting her science-fiction-like experience of Tuesday, December 12, 1967. She was driving home along Route 34 to Ithaca, New York, with her five-year-old son, Dana, in the back seat. Around 7 P.M. she became aware of a red light that seemed to be following her.

"I was speeding slightly," she explained later. "So naturally I assumed that I was just about to be pulled over by the state police."

She glanced out of the window and discovered that instead of a police car she was being paced by an eerie illuminated flying object that was traveling along just above the power lines to the left of the car. At this same moment, she said, she was horrified to find that she could no longer control the automobile. She shouted anxiously to her young son to brace himself, but he remained motionless. "It was as if he were in some kind of a trance," she continued. "The car pulled over to the shoulder of the road by itself, ran over an embankment into an alfalfa field, and stopped.

"A white twirling beam of light flashed down from the object... and I heard the humming sound. Then I began to hear voices. They didn't sound like male or female voices but were weird, the words broken and jerky, like the way a translator sounds when he is repeating a speech at the United Nations. But it was like a weird chorus of several voices.

"I became hysterical," she admitted frankly. "My son would not respond to my cries. I knew the radio wasn't on. The voices named someone I knew and said that at that moment my friend was involved in a terrible accident miles away. They said my son would not remember any of this. Then the car began to move again, although still not under my control. We came up out of that field and over the ditch as if it were nothing, and then back onto the road."

She said she got control of the car again and jammed her foot down on the accelerator, speeding all the way home.

"I knew something was wrong the moment she walked into the house," her husband, John Malley, told reporters. "I thought maybe she had had an accident with the car or something."

The next day Mrs. Malley learned that her friend had been in a serious automobile accident the night before. She told her incredible story to local civilian UFO investigators, and later the Syracuse, New York, *Herald Journal* (December 21, 1967) published a brief outline without revealing her name.

For years now, apparently sincere people have been relating unbelievable experiences similar to Mrs. Malley's. Some of the UFO factions have battled to ridicule and suppress such contactee tales, fearing that they serve to discredit the situation. But they keep coming in, year after year, from every corner of the globe. Reporters and investigators who interviewed Mrs. Malley came away convinced that she was telling the truth as she knew it.

"Days later, when memories of the episode would flood her mind," the Syracuse *Herald-American* noted, "she would break down sobbing all over again."

Her story does contain several important details that have cropped up in many other little-known UFO encounters. A large percentage of these events seem to occur when a small child is present. In this case, the child went into a kind of trance. Such trances are frequently reported. The car itself was taken out of Mrs. Malley's hands. This seizure of control of mechanical objects—even of airplanes in midflight—is also a common factor. Mrs. Malley's extreme emotional reaction to the event, even days afterward, is still another key point. Finally, if her story is true, she was given absolute proof (to her) that the UFO not only knew her identity but knew of her relationship to a distant person and even knew that that other party was involved in an accident.

All of this is a pretty big pill to swallow for those who have not followed events like this carefully over a long period of time. In many eases, the ufonauts have convincingly demonstrated that they have total knowledge of the individual percipients and that they can even foretell their future.

There is a superabundance of historical documentation which plainly indicates that these objects and their elusive occupants have always been a part of the environment of earth and that they seem to know everything about us, are able to speak our languages, and are even familiar with the total lives of some—if not all—human beings.

So long as we adhere to the notion that we are dealing with random extraterrestrial visitors, none of these contactee stories makes any sense. So I ask you to place the UFOs into a terrestrial or ultraterrestrial framework. Think of them as you might think of a next-door neighbor who is hooked up to your party line. The pieces of this puzzle will begin to fall into place.

Of Prophets and Prophecy

Most theologians reject any suggestion that unidentified flying objects may be even remotely connected with religion, but many leading ufologists suspect that innumerable historical incidents branded as religious phenomena may actually be misunderstood UFO activity.

The Bible was completely suppressed for centuries during the Dark Ages, and then it was heavily edited and censored, whole sections being deleted altogether before the modern version was released. Scores of translators contributed to the muddle by altering meanings with high-flown poetry, and by subtly interjecting their own comments and opinions. As a result, the contents of modern translations vary widely, and many of the original meanings and descriptions of what were probably actual events have been mutilated beyond interpretation. Theologians recognize this and freely comment upon it. The late Pope John XXIII once made a wry remark about the confusion brought about by all these translations.

Try to shelve your own religious beliefs for a moment, and look at the Bible stories objectively. The prophet Elijah was well protected by balls of fire that came out of the heavens and consumed 100 soldiers and their captains (Kings II, Chapter 1). In Chapter 2 of the Second Book of Kings, Elijah leads Elisha into the desert where a fish-shaped object spitting fire from its tail descends from the sky to carry him away forever. (Most translations of the Bible have somehow managed to turn this object into a chariot of fire drawn by fiery horses.) Read this section carefully, and the implications are startlingly clear: Was Elijah somehow connected with an aerial race who protected him and who finally took him away?

Fireballs and thunderbolts from the angry skies apparently wreaked a lot of havoc in Biblical times. Some scholarly scientists have suggested that these accounts sound suspiciously like atomic explosions. A Soviet physicist, Professor M. Agrest, has even proposed that Sodom and Gomorrah were destroyed by an atomic bomb. Lot's wife, he asserts, did not turn into a pillar of salt but was reduced to a pile of ashes when she ignored a warning not to linger behind Lot's fleeing party. Furthermore, in an article in Moscow's *Literaturnaya Gazeta* in 1959, Professor Agrest offered the startling theory that ancient Baalbek was the Cape Kennedy of its day, serving as a launching platform for spaceships from another civilization. His "proof" consisted of the tektites and fused crystals found there. Such substances are the by-products of atomic explosions.

A "flying roll" measuring 15 feet by 8 feet is described in the Bible's Book of Zechariah, Chapter 5, and the children of Israel were said to have been led out of Egypt by a pillar of fire in the sky (Exodus, Chapter 13). According to the detailed Bible story, Moses not only held conversations with a brightly burning bush ("And the angel of the Lord appeared unto him in a flame of fire out of the midst of a bush; and he looked, and behold, the bush burned with fire, and the bush was not consumed" Exodus 3:2), but he was called to the summit of Mount Sinai after a "cloud" appeared and covered it. Moses climbed the mount and disappeared into "the midst of the cloud." He was gone for forty days and forty nights while his people waited below (Exodus, Chapter 24). Mount Sinai is actually just a high and rugged hill, and we might ask how Moses managed to survive alone on its summit for more than a month without food. Perhaps there was more to that "cloud" than the children of Israel suspected. When Moses finally returned, he brought with him orders for the construction of an ark to be filled with gold artifacts and left as a token to the Lord. Among the instructions were directions for building a "mercy seat" of pure gold measuring 50 inches long and 30 inches wide. Gold plays an important part in many Bible stories and it also seems to have an interesting role in the UFO mystery.

That "pillar of fire" not only led the Israelites out of Egypt, it also intervened and protected them from the pursuing Egyptian army (Exodus, Chapter 14). But the most graphic account of all is detailed in the first chapter of Ezekiel and is so well known and so frequently quoted that we need only mention here that Ezekiel claimed an encounter with four strange beings who got out of some kind of flying object. "Their appearance," he said, "was like burning coals of fire, and like the appearance of lamps."

In a paper presented before the American Rocket Society on November 15, 1962, Dr. Carl Sagan, a young Harvard astronomer, repeated some of Professor Agrest's speculations and urged that ancient myths and legends be reexamined for possible clues to an early visit by an extraterrestrial civilization. The Biblical story of Enoch, for example, relates how he dreamed of "two men, very tall, such as I have never seen on earth. And their faces shone like the sun, and their eyes were like burning lamps… They stood at the head of my bed and called me by my name. I awoke from my sleep and saw clearly these men standing in front of me."

These tall men took him into the sky and conducted him on a

tour of "seven heavens." When he returned to earth, he wrote 366 books about what he had seen and learned. Although *The Book of the Secrets of Enoch* has been widely published, the Bible grants him only a few lines of Chapter 5, Genesis.

Another book, a latter-day Bible, was created in the nineteenth century by a young man who claimed an experience similar to Enoch's, except that he did not go off to other worlds. It is the *Book of Mormon,* the Mormon Bible, and is purportedly a history of North America in Biblical times. Therein lies another remarkable story.

On Tuesday, September 23, 1823, a young man named Joseph Smith awoke in his bedroom in Palmyra, New York, to find a strange luminous being standing over his bed. This being, he said, was dressed in a white robe and had a brilliantly glowing face. He called the youth by name and told him where he would find some gold plates buried nearby. When the proper time arrived, the entity is supposed to have told him, he was to dig the plates up. Then the figure floated upward and vanished.

Sometime later the boy was crossing a field when, in his own words, "my strength entirely failed me, and I fell helplessly to the ground, and for a time was quite unconscious of anything." When he came to, he said the same "messenger" was standing over him and gave him further instructions about the gold tablets. He was to dig them up four years later.

So on Saturday, September 22, 1827, Joseph Smith went to the appointed spot and started digging. Sure enough, he actually found a stone box containing several plates of gold bearing a strange, neatly engraved writing. Later eleven of his friends and neighbors examined the plates and signed affidavits swearing that they had seen them and that they contained writing "which has the appearance of ancient work, and of curious workmanship."

Smith was not a well-educated man. He worked for years deciphering and translating the writing on these tablets, and when he was finished, he had an intriguing historical document that was, apparently, a history of North America in very ancient times—predating the Indians. This document became the Book of Mormon, for Joseph Smith founded the Mormon Church. The tablets later disappeared or were somehow destroyed, and Joseph Smith was brutally murdered by a hostile mob in Illinois in 1846. Today the Mormon Church has more than 2,500,000 followers.

Was Joseph Smith's strange nocturnal visitor a UFO type of entity? Was some strange psychic force at work there, trying to pass along information about those gold tablets?

Consider the prophet Daniel. Like Ezekiel, Daniel reported seeing "wheels as burning fire" (Daniel 7:9). He describes in some detail his encounters with an entity who came down from a "throne" in the sky and whose hair was "like pure wool." This being was dressed in a white robe with a gold belt and had a luminous face with two bright glowing eyes. He spoke to Daniel in a thundering voice that terrified the earthman. "And I Daniel alone saw the vision: For the men that were with me saw not the vision; but a great quaking fell upon them, so that they fled to hide themselves" (Daniel 10:5-9). "Yet I heard the voice of his words; and when I heard the voice of his words, then was I in a deep sleep on my face, and my face toward the ground."

Like Joseph Smith, and even like Dana Malley, Daniel apparently passed into some kind of hypnotic trance. Later he was given specific prophecies about contemporary problems, and they came true.

Angels and Spacemen

In his book *A Guest from the Universe,* Alexander Kazentsev theorized that the angels mentioned in the Bible might actually have been extraterrestrials. British ufologist Brinsley Le Poer Trench, author of *The Sky People,* supports this notion, as does Paul Misraki in *Les Extraterrestres.* They all cite the Biblical stories in Genesis in which Lot meets two angels and takes them into his home, where they feasted like ordinary men (Genesis 19:3). The Bible never describes angels as being winged creatures, although artists usually depict them that way. Indeed, the angels seem to have been manlike, though gifted with extraordinary powers. When they appeared before Abraham (Genesis 18:2), they were described as "three men" who ate and drank with him. Again and again "three men" play important roles in Biblical events. "Three men" repeatedly turn up in modern UFO events, too, and provide still one more puzzling aspect of the problem.

Misraki notes that the Church did not accept the spiritual nature of angels until the sixth century A.D. Before that, theologians considered angels to be physical beings. A few years ago the Reverend H. Wipprecht of Cobalt, Canada, stated that "the Bible's description of angels fits 'intelligent beings' from other planets." More aptly, the descriptions fit intelligent beings from this planet: beings that look like us but possess the peculiar special qualities of ultraterrestrials who share our world yet are a species apart from us.

We must also note that these "angels" were, according to the Bible, frequently concerned with the propagation of the human race. Abraham's elderly wife, well past childbearing age, is said to have given birth to Isaac after a visit from the three men (Genesis, Chapter 21). So we are told that these "men" possess the power of life and death. They are credited with the destruction of Sodom and Gomorrah, yet they restored Abraham's Sarah to fertility.

The Book of Revelation, the last section of the New Testament, is especially important to this study. At first reading it may seem to be filled with vague poetry and may defy interpretation, but if you take many of the passages *literally*, and avoid a symbolic or religious interpretation, new meanings will open up to you. For example, in Chapter 4 we are told that "a door was opened in heaven," and there is a description of the interior of a place occupied by creatures similar to those reported by Ezekiel, together with a throne apparently surrounded by glass ("And before the throne there was a sea of glass like unto crystal" [4:5]). Twenty-four beings in white robes sat around this "throne." "They had on their heads crowns of gold" (4:4). We must remember that the men who wrote the Bible had no knowledge of machinery or technology, and so they were forced to describe things in terms that were familiar to them. Those "crowns of gold" could have been helmets of some kind. In Chapter 10, John declares, "And I saw another mighty angel come down from heaven clothed with a cloud; and a rainbow was upon his head, and his face was as it were the sun, and his feet as pillars of fire." It sounds as if he were describing a brilliantly glowing sphere surrounded by vapors ("cloud") and colored lights ("a rainbow") and two beams of light or flame were jetting down beneath it ("pillars of fire").

A well-known astrophysicist, Morris K. Jessup, sought links between UFOs and religion in his book *The UFO and the Bible*. Were the flaming crosses and other objects seen in ancient skies really religious omens, he wondered, or were they actually machines from some alien civilization? Dr. Carl Jung, the celebrated psychiatrist, and astronomer Dr. Jacques Vallee also wondered if the historical reports of these objects might not have been distorted by interpretations created by the climate of the times Thus, in Biblical days when men were seeking some indication that there was a higher power, they almost automatically considered objects in the sky to be of religious import. During wartime, such objects were regarded with suspicion as possible weapons of the enemy. And in this present era, when space flight is the national goal of two major nations, there is a strong tendency to accept unidentified flying objects as extraterrestrial visitants.

Many of the Egyptian and Biblical accounts are supported by other histories written during the same period. Early Greek and Roman historians dutifully recorded many strange things seen in the sky. A light "so bright it seemed to be full day" descended over the temple in Jerusalem during the Feast of Unleavened Bread in A. D. 70, and Josephus describes a "demonic phantom of incredible size" that appeared in that same year on May 21. Before sunset on that date "there appeared in the air over the whole country [Jerusalem] chariots and armed troops coursing through the clouds..." Livy reported "phantom ships" in the sky in 214 B.C., and Pliny, the most notable of ancient historians, recorded several instances in which "three suns" were seen in the sky at one time. A "flaming cross" appeared over the heads of Constantine and his army in A.D. 312, and the army of Alexander the Great was thrown into a panic when two shining silvery "shields" spitting fire around the rims buzzed their encampment.

Scholars and researchers have now uncovered hundreds of ancient UFO accounts. Pick out any century and you will be able to find several good reports of disks, fireballs, and cigar-shaped objects in the sky. Historian W. R. Drake has unearthed references to "Magonia," a strange country that was a legend among the peasants of medieval France. They believed that the Magonians rode about in "cloud ships" and frequently raided their crops. Agobard, Archbishop of Lyons, wrote that one of these ships is supposed to have fallen from the sky around A.D. 840, and its occupants, three men and a woman, were stoned to death by the angry farmers.

Italian ufologist Alberto Fengolio uncovered another intriguing "touchdown" story, which is supposed to have occurred near Alencon, France, at 5 A.M. on June 12, 1790. A police inspector named Liabeuf was sent from Paris to investigate, and his final report has been preserved. The witnesses, a group of French peasants, told him that an enormous globe had appeared that morning, moving with a rocking motion, and that it crashed into the top of a hill, uprooting the vegetation. Heat from the object started grass fires, and the peasants rushed to put them out before they spread. The huge globe was warm to the touch.

"The eyewitnesses of this event were two mayors, a physician, and three other local authorities who confirm my report," Liabeuf wrote. "Not to mention the dozens of peasants who were present."

As the crowd gathered around the mysterious object, "a sort of door opened, and *there came out a person*, just like us, but dressed in a strange manner, in clothes adhering completely to the body, and seeing this crowd of people, this person murmured something incomprehensible and ran into the wood."

The peasants backed away from the object fearfully, and a few moments later it exploded silently and nothing was left but a fine powder. A search for the mysterious man was launched, "but he seemed to have dissolved in thin air."

Here, in 1790, we have a description comparable to the modern ufonaut reports of a man wearing a tight-fitting coverall type of garment.

(According to a story filed by the Lusitania News Service in April 1960, hundreds of villagers in Beira, Mozambique, East Africa, saw a whistling orange object land in a field, and "tiny little men" leaped out of it and ran into the forest just as the thing exploded violently. Those "little men" could not be found, either.)

The Zurich Central Library has an old drawing of the strange event that took place over Germany on April 14, 1561. A large number of "plates," "blood-colored crosses" and "two great tubes" staged an aerial dogfight on that date, enthralling and frightening the whole population of Nuremberg. Five years later a similar group of objects is said to have appeared over Basel, Switzerland. Some of them turned red and faded away, just as modern UFOs have been reported to do. A sketch of this incident is also in Zurich's Wickiana collection.

The late Charles Fort, an eccentric but indefatigable researcher, spent much of his life wading through yellowing newspapers and forgotten history books to ferret out Ripleyesque items. Without realizing it, he became the first ufologist, and his *Book of the Damned* and other works are treasure troves of unexplained aerial phenomena. He discovered that 1846, for example, was a most peculiar year. It rained blood-real blood according to the newspaper accounts of the day—in several areas around the world. And all kinds of odd lights and shapes were seen in the sky. Some very peculiar people also turned up in Europe at that time, prancing around the English countryside in silver uniforms, capes, and helmets, with red lights on their chests. These beings were human in size but seemed to possess the ability to leap great distances. So the British newspapers referred to them as "spring-heeled Jacks." Old Jack got plumb away from all those who turned out to search for him after each one of his puzzling appearances.

On Tuesday, October 3, 1843, a "remarkable cloud" passed over Warwick, England, and one Charles Cooper reported seeing three white, human-shaped figures in the sky. Another person, six miles away, is supposed to have also seen these flying beings. The sighting was added to the constantly growing "angel" lore.

A very important contact with ultraterrestrials took place in France in 1846, when a luminous being descended in a glowing sphere and passed along some prophecies that later proved to be very accurate. This case will be discussed in another chapter.

The whole nineteenth century was a busy one for unidentified flying objects. It was also the century in which man made his first faltering attempts to fly.

A French engineer, Henri Giffard, built the first controllable dirigible in 1852. Powered by a steam engine, it was 144 feet long and whizzed through the sky at a breathtaking seven miles per hour. Paul Haenlein, a German, built a gas-powered dirigible in 1872. And a Hungarian named David Schwartz constructed the first metal dirigible and took off from Berlin on November 13, 1897. He managed to fly several miles before a gas leak brought him down.

While these pioneers were struggling to go a few miles in their slow, clumsy, cigar-shaped machines, thousands of people around the world were reporting the presence of larger, faster dirigible-shaped objects. Astronomers, such as Trouvelot of the Observatory of Meudon, first claimed notice of the things in the early 1870's. They were high in the atmosphere, he said, and didn't resemble anything within his experience. Trouvelot described his August 29, 1871, sighting in *L'Annee Scientifique* and observed that one of a formation of objects appeared to descend "like a disk falling in water." This was the first description of the "falling-leaf motion" that appears in so many modern reports and has even been recorded on film.

Newspaper accounts of these aerial objects were frequent and widespread during the last three decades of the nineteenth century.

But the dam really broke in 1896-97 when giant cigars were reportedly viewed by thousands of people as they flew over many of the major cities on earth. Leading newspapers of the day carried extensive descriptions and drawings of them. Their mysterious journeys created the first important UFO flap and inspired H. G. Wells to write his classic novel, *The War of the Worlds*.

5
The Grand Deception

The "secret" of the flying saucers was exposed in 1896, not by the phenomenon itself but by the hidden patterns now revealed in UFO activity of a single week that November. The pattern was a classic of carefully planned confusion and deception.

Thanksgiving week 1896 marked the beginning of the great "airship mystery" in the United States. Strange luminous objects and cigar-shaped craft were first reported over California. The mayors of both Oakland and San Francisco went on record as having seen the things. All the descriptions as published by the San Francisco *Call*, San Francisco *Chronicle*, and other leading journals of the period fell into the now-familiar categories. Brilliant multicolored lights, bobbing and weaving as if they were on yo-yo strings, were seen over Sacramento. People in Oakland reported an egg-shaped vessel about 150 feet long with four rotor-like arms; a giant light mounted underneath. It lit up the ground below.

A San Jose, California, electrician named J. A. Heron claimed that the airship pilots enlisted him to make some repairs on the machine. He was taken to a desolate field north of San Francisco for the job and was rewarded by being taken on a flight to Hawaii. He said the craft made the 4,400-mile trip in twenty-four hours. Later his wife told reporters that he had been home in bed on the night of the alleged trip.

Another man, William Bull Meek of Comptonville, California, told reporters that the airship landed near his home and that he enjoyed a brief chat with the pilot—a bearded man who told him that the ship "had come from the Montezuma Mountains."

Crews on ships were seeing glowing spheres and saucer-shaped machines rising out of the water and flying away while the Wright brothers were still fussing with gliders. These ocean-bound disks and "wheels" apparently concentrated their activities around the coasts of Japan and China throughout the Gay Nineties, but they were also seen in Europe. News traveled slowly in those days, so it is unlikely that the witnesses in one area had ever heard of the identical sightings that had occurred thousands of miles away. As is still the case today, no newspaper or journalist made an effort to collect all of these reports and collate them into a whole.

In March and April 1897, the airship reports began to spread across the country but seemed to concentrate in the Midwest from Texas to Michigan, the same areas that still account for the largest number of reports.

We are indebted to Dr. Jacques Vallee, Lucius Farish, Charles Flood, and Jerome Clark who have spent many tedious hours examining dusty newspaper files and microfilm collections throughout the country in their search for the published accounts of the 1897 flap. They have unearthed hundreds of forgotten reports, many of them quite startling in content. A study of these reports reveals the same patterns that seem to be present today. Many of the local newspapers assumed that only one airship was involved and that it was the product of some secret inventor who was taking it out for a trial run across the country. But we find that many of the airship sightings took place on the same day in dozens of widely scattered areas, indicating that a whole armada of these objects must have been in the air at the time.

Quite a few of these accounts are as incredible as the reports of modern witnesses. Yet many of the 1897 witnesses were distinguished members of their communities and often signed sworn affidavits to back up their beliefs in what they had seen. There were a number of remarkable consistencies in the reports, and many detailed contactee stories.

Judge Lawrence A. Byrne was, to quote a reporter for the *Daily Texarkanian*, Texarkana, Arkansas, "known here for his truthfulness by his fellowmen." On April 25, 1897, that paper published this amazing story: " I was down on McKinney bayou Friday looking after the surveying of a tract of land and, in passing through a thicket to an open space, saw a strange looking object anchored to the ground. On approaching I found it to be the airship I have read so much about of late. It was manned by three men who spoke a foreign language, but judging from their looks, would take them to be Japs. They saw my astonishment and beckoned me to follow them, and on complying, I was shown through the ship."

The judge then explained "about the machinery being made of aluminum and the gas to raise and lower the monster was pumped into an aluminum tank when the ship was to be raised and let out when to be lowered." There is no further description in the account. The most interesting thing about this story is that the judge mistook the pilots for Japanese, perhaps meaning that they were small men with Oriental features similar to the men described in the controversial modern contact story of Betty and Barney Hill.

Can we assume that Judge Byrne was a reliable and responsible witness? One yellowing newspaper clipping doesn't offer much evidence. But his was not the only 1897 contactee tale. There were scores of others, although no one else reported meeting "Japs."

Most of the people who claimed to glimpse the airship pilots described them as being bearded. Michigan was very much involved in the 1897 flap, and the *Courier-Herald* of Saginaw followed the reports closely. On April 16 it ran this story: "Bell Plains, Iowa, April 16—The citizens of Linn Grove declare there is no longer any doubt among them of the existence of an airship. Yesterday morning a large object was seen slowly moving in the heavens in a northerly direction and seemed to be making preparations to alight. James Evans, liveryman; F. G. Ellis, harness dealer; Ben Buland, stock dealer; David Evans, and Joe Croskey jumped into a rig and started in pursuit. They found the airship had alighted four miles north of town, and when within 700 yards, it spread its four monstrous wings and flew off toward the north. Its occupants threw out two large boulders of unknown composition, which were taken to the village and are now on exhibition.

"There were two queer looking persons on board, who made

desperate attempts to conceal themselves. Evans and Croskey say they had the longest whiskers they ever saw in their lives. Nearly every Citizen in Linn Grove saw the airship as it sailed over the town, and the excitement is intense."

The *Argus-Leader* of Sioux Falls, South Dakota, together with many other papers, ran an account on April 15 datelined Springfield, Illinois. Two farmhands, Adolph Winkle and John Hulle, signed affidavits stating that the airship had landed two miles outside of Springfield to repair some electrical apparatus on board. The farmhands said they talked to the occupants, two men and a woman. They were told that the machine had flown to Springfield from Quincy (a distance of about 100 miles) in thirty minutes and would "make a report to the government when Cuba is declared free."

Two lawmen, Constable John J. Sumpter Jr., and Deputy Sheriff John McLemore of Garland County, Arkansas, signed affidavits on May 8, 1897, testifying that they had also conversed with the airship occupants. Their account was published in the Helena, Arkansas, *Weekly* World on May 13:

> While riding northwest from this city on the night of May 6, 1897, we noticed a brilliant light high in the heavens. Suddenly it disappeared and we said nothing about it, as we were looking for parties and did not want to make any noise. After riding four or five miles around through the hills we again saw the light, which now appeared to be much nearer the earth. We stopped our horses and watched it coming down, until all at once it disappeared behind another hill. We rode on about half a mile further, when our horses refused to go further. About a hundred yards distant we saw two persons moving around with lights. Drawing our Winchesters—for we were now thoroughly aroused to the importance of the situation—we demanded, "Who is that, and what are you doing?" A man with a long dark beard came forth with a

lantern in his hand, and on being informed who we were proceeded to tell us that he and the others—a young man and a woman—were traveling through the country in an airship. We could plainly distinguish the outlines of the vessel, which was cigar-shaped and about sixty feet long, and looking just like the cuts that have appeared in the papers recently. It was dark and raining and the young man was filling a big sack with water about thirty yards away, and the woman was particular to keep back in the dark. She was holding an umbrella over her head. The man with the whiskers invited us to take a ride, saying that he could take us where it was not raining. We told him we preferred to get wet.

Asking the man why the brilliant light was turned on and off so much, he replied that the light was so powerful that it consumed a great deal of his motive power. He said he would like to stop off in Hot Springs for a few days and take the hot baths, but his time was limited and he could not. He said they were going to wind up at Nashville, Tennessee, after thoroughly seeing the country. Being in a hurry we left and upon our return, about forty minutes later, nothing was to be seen. We did not hear or see the airship when it departed.

[Signed] John J. Sumpter, Jr.
John McLemore
Subscribed and sworn to before me on the 8th day of
May, 1897.
C.G. Bush, JP

As the airship sightings increased, another familiar phase began. The explainers and hoaxsters moved in. Professor George Hough of Northwestern University blamed Venus at first. But later he said, "Alpha Orionis has been roaming through its regular course in the firmament ten million years, and why it should have been settled upon in the last three weeks, and pointed out as the headlight of a mysterious aerial vehicle, is hard to explain." (Chicago *Tribune*, April 11, 1897).

An electrician named A. H. Babcock built a large box kite and sent it skyward on November 26, 1896, over Oakland, California, setting off a new rash of airship reports there. (San Francisco, California, *Chronicle*, November 27, 1896). And paper balloons filled with gas entertained others all over the country.

"Anything from Jupiter to the moon was picked out as an airship by the credulous people," the Portland, Oregon, *Oregonian* observed on November 25, 1896. "Early in the evening a fire balloon went sailing through the air, and the newspapers were overwhelmed by telephone messages from people in various parts of the city who thought they had discovered the mysterious airship."

Newspapers that weren't receiving any reports blithely made up some to fill the gap. The Hudson *Gazette* at Hudson, Michigan, ran a long piece that quoted every prominent citizen in the town ("It was quite a bit larger than the Republican majority in Hudson," said Plim Gilman). When the editor of the Adrian, Michigan, *Weekly Times and Expositor* received his copy of the *Gazette*, he ordered his Hudson correspondent to look into the matter. On April 17, the *Weekly Times and Expositor* printed (with relish, no doubt): "The sensational report of the airship having been seen by many reputable citizens of this place turns out to be a huge fake. Hudson did not propose to be behind the times, so one of our enterprising editors set his imagination to work and produced a half column sensation. The airship is very likely as filmy as the aforesaid article."

More bizarre explanations were offered, too. In discussing the "moving lights of fires... said to have been seen nightly on Saginaw Bay off Caseville during the past week," the Benton Harbor, Michigan, *Evening News* noted on April 1, 1897, that "the superstitious believe that they are produced by the ghosts of those who were lost with the steamer Oconto which was wrecked on Big Charity Island a few years ago."

A "wheel" fell out of the sky near Battle Creek, Michigan, and was retrieved by a well-to-do farmer named George Parks. Parks and his wife were crossing a field when they saw "a very bright object that appeared to be about 100 feet from the earth and swiftly approaching." As it flew low over them, emitting a humming sound, something fell to the earth and buried itself in the ground. Mr. Parks reportedly dug it up the next morning and "found it to be a large wheel made of aluminum, about three feet in diameter, and a turbine in shape." He kept the object as a memento and displayed it on his farm in Pennfield, Michigan (Detroit, Michigan, *Evening News*, April 15, 1897).

A Mrs. Wyngate "residing just over the line of Charleston township" was one of the witnesses who reported seeing a brilliant white light around 10 P.M. on the night of March 31. She said that "she distinctly heard human voices from above at the time of the occurrence" (Detroit *Evening News*, April 1, 1897).

Others around the country were also hearing voices in the sky. "I saw the airship last night at 10:30 P.M. over my barn," one Bid Osborne wrote to the Lansing, Michigan, *State Republican* (April 17, 1897). "About 800 feet long—big brute—row of Japanese lanterns all along top—large wide sail like a fantail dove—dark bay in color—and I heard voices from above—sounded like Jim Baird and Charlie Bicher—no fake—make affidavit."

Another man in nearby Pine Lake, Michigan, named William Megiveron, told the same newspaper that he was awakened by a tap on his window and the glare of light that at first blinded him. The *Republican* continues:

> On stepping out into the night, he was accosted by a voice from above, which told him that the light was from the airship; that during the afternoon the ship had been lying concealed behind a bank of clouds over the lake, and that a stray shot from the gun of some duck hunters had injured one of the ship's wings, and they were laying by for repairs. William then says that he was directed to prepare

four-dozen egg sandwiches and a kettle of coffee for the crew, and when prepared, the provender was hoisted on board with a scoop fully as large as a freight car and paid for in Canadian quarters. William further says that the aerial monster appeared about 300 feet above the lake, but only the outlines were visible on account of the brilliant searchlight which made everything below as bright as day and above as dark as midnight during a cyclone. He observed a red light at each end and thinks the ship was fully a half a mile long. All appeals to be taken aboard were met with a merry "Ha! Ha!" But William says he thinks the occupants hailed from either Kentucky or Milwaukee as they asked for a corkscrew. Bill said if he knew their address, he would have the whole crew arrested for violating the fish law, for the light reflected so strongly on the lake that it was no trouble for the occupants to pick out the biggest and best fish in the lake with a long-handled spear. Just before daylight, the ship sailed off toward the city. The whir of machinery was plainly discernible for several moments.

It sounds as if Megiveron were pulling somebody's leg, or maybe the editor of the *Republican* was doing it for him.

The editor of the *Daily Chronicle*, Muskegon, Michigan, may have been doing some leg pulling, too, with this next item, published on April 30. But there is also a chance that he may have taken a real report and added a few touches. It's difficult to decide:

Last night at 11:30 this town [Holton] received a visit from the wonderful airship. It came from the north and descended till it was about 200 feet from the ground, directly over the bridge. It was lighted with electricity and loaded with revelers who were making a good deal of noise.

The music was entrancing, the like of which never was

heard in this place. It wasn't long before everybody was on the street to look and listen, many in their nightclothes. Not a few thought the Judgment Day had come. It was about 300 feet long, tail about 40 feet. Its breadth and depth about 90 feet. It stayed fifty-five minutes. Its tail commenced whirling and it moved off toward Fremont. But just as it began to move, a grappling hook was let down and caught one of our most truthful citizens who was instantly hoisted on board and carried away. The truthful citizen came back on the 11:30 train from White Cloud and has been talking ever since about aerial navigation.

Such hoary tales provided comedy relief during the flap. The newspapers generally took the matter lightly when the stories first started to appear, making wry comments about the quality of the whiskey in the flap areas, etc. But as the reports poured in and the objects began to appear over the cities where the skeptical newspapers were based, the tone of the published reports grew more serious. Something strange was going on, and the more responsible newspapers began to wonder what it was really all about.

One of the most celebrated cases of the period, the story of Alexander Hamilton's cow, has been widely reprinted in practically every UFO book extant, and we will therefore just summarize it here. Hamilton claimed that he and his family saw a cigar-shaped object swoop down over his farm near Vernon, Kansas, sometime in the middle of April. "It was occupied by six of the strangest beings I ever saw," he declared. "They were jabbering together, but we could not understand a syllable they said."

He described the object as being 300 feet long with a transparent glass carriage underneath. "It was brilliantly lighted within, and everything was clearly visible. There were three lights: one like an immense searchlight and two smaller, one red, the other green. The large one was susceptible of being turned in every direction... Every part of the vessel which was not transparent was of a dark reddish color." A "great turbine wheel about 30 feet in diameter" revolved underneath.

As his little group watched, the machine began to buzz and rise upward. Then it paused directly over a three-year-old heifer, which apparently was caught in the fence. "Going to her," Hamilton said, "we found a cable about half an inch in thickness, made of the same red material, fastened in a slip knot around her neck, one end passing up to the vessel and tangled in the wire [fence]."

He tried to free the calf but couldn't. So he cut the wire and watched helplessly as the ship and calf rose slowly into the air and sailed away. The next day the branded hide, legs, and head of the animal were found on the property of Lank Thomas, who lived about four miles away.

Farmer Hamilton not only signed an affidavit, but he collected the town's most prominent citizens, including the local sheriff, justice of the peace, doctor, and postmaster, and had them all sign a statement testifying that they had known him for from fifteen to thirty years "and that for truth and veracity we have never heard his word questioned and that we do verily believe his statement to be true and correct." (Yates Center, Kansas, *The Farmer's Advocate*, April 23, 1897.)

This case is significant not only because of the detailed description of the transparency of the object, but because it was the first of a long line of cattle-rustling reports concerning UFOs. The theft and mutilation of dogs, cattle, and horses have become unpleasantly commonplace in flap areas.

Texas had more than its share of sightings during 1897, and many of them were concentrated in the region where John Martin had reported seeing a flying saucer in 1878. On April 22, 1897, Mr. John M. Barclay conversed, allegedly, with a man from an oblong machine with wings and brilliant lights "which appeared much brighter than electric lights." He had been awakened about 11 P.M. by his furiously barking dog, and when he looked outside, he saw the object hovering stationary about 15 feet above the ground. It circled a few times and landed in a nearby pasture. Barclay grabbed his rifle and went to investigate. When he was about thirty yards from the ship, he was met "by an ordinary mortal" who asked him to put his gun aside.

"Who are you?" Mr. Barclay asked.

"Never mind about my name; call it Smith," the man replied. "I want some lubricating oil and a couple of cold chisels if you can get them, and some bluestone. I suppose the saw mill hard by has the two former articles, and the telegraph operator has the bluestone. Here's a ten-dollar bill; take it and get us those articles and keep the change for your trouble."

Mr. Barclay reportedly asked him, "What have you got down there? Let me go and see it."

"No," the man said quickly. "We cannot permit you to approach any nearer, but do as we request you and your kindness will be appreciated, and we will call you some future day and reciprocate your kindness by taking you on a trip."

Barclay located some oil and the chisels, but he couldn't get the bluestone. He returned and tried to give the man back the ten-dollar bill, but it was refused. "Smith" shook hands with the Texan, thanked him, and asked him not to follow him to the object. Barclay asked him where he was from and where he was going.

"From anywhere," Smith answered. "But we will be in Greece day after tomorrow."

He climbed aboard the object, there was a whirring noise, and it was gone "like a shot," according to Barclay. The newspapers in Rockland, Texas, said that he was "perfectly reliable."

That same night "a prominent farmer" near Josserand, Texas, also had a confrontation with the airship pilots. Mr. Frank Nichols claimed that he was awakened around midnight by the whirring of machinery. "Upon looking out, he was startled upon beholding brilliant lights streaming from a ponderous vessel of strange proportions, which rested upon the ground in his cornfield." Like Barclay, he went outside to investigate.

Before he'd gotten very far he was met by two men with buckets who asked for permission to draw water from his well.

He told them to go ahead, and they invited him to visit their ship. There he said he conversed freely with six or eight individuals and apparently was shown the machinery, which "was so complicated that in his short interview he could gain no knowledge of its workings."

Nichols said that they told him that "five of these ships were built in a small town in Iowa. Soon the invention will be given to the public. An immense stock company is now being formed and within the next year the machines will be in general use." The motive power was supposedly "condensed electricity." Mr. Nichols, the newspapers said, was "a man of unquestioned veracity."

This "invention" story spread, as you will see, and appears to support the possibility of an unexpected hoax. But before we explore the hoax question, there are two more contact cases that deserve examination.

An apparently well-known and highly reputable man identified as "Ex-Senator Harris" said that he had been awakened at 1 A.M. Wednesday, April 21, 1897, by a strange noise, and he was astonished to see the celebrated airship descending on his property outside of Harrisburg, Arkansas. He stepped outside and was met by the craft's occupants, conversing with them as they busied themselves "taking on a supply of fresh well water." Senator Harris said there were two young men, a woman and an elderly man on board.

"The old gentleman," the Senator is quoted as saying (Harrisburg, Arkansas, *Modern News,* April 23, 1897), "wore a heavy set of dark, silken whiskers, which hung down near his waist. He had jet black eyes and a deep, firm expression."

Whereas the airship occupants did not seem especially informative in the other contact cases of the period, this elderly gentleman talked his head off. He seemed to be familiar with the newspapers in St. Louis, Missouri, and referred to a story which had appeared in the St. Louis *Republic* "about twenty-six years ago." Here's the way Senator Harris quoted him:

In that paper there was an account of a scientific invention made by a gentleman whose name I will not mention, by which the laws of gravitation were entirely and completely suspended. He was offered big sums of money for it by several syndicates in this country and also had large offers from Paris, London, and many other places. During the time he was considering offers he had the invention securely locked in a safety deposit vault in New York City. Before he had accepted any of the offers he was taken violently ill, and after lingering a few weeks died, leaving his invention in the vault. This man was my uncle, and he had partially confided the secret to me, but not sufficiently for me to do anything without the original invention. After the lapse of about nineteen years I managed to secure the original, and having plenty of money at my disposal and having devoted my time and talent during the past seven years to experimenting, I have an airship which is almost perfection, but I am not quite through experimenting, and so I continue to travel at night to keep from being detected. I will make an attempt to visit the planet Mars before I put the airship on public exhibition. Weight is no object to me. I suspend all gravitation by placing a small wire around an object. You see I have a 4-ton improved Hotchkiss gun on board, besides about ten tons of ammunition. I was making preparations to go over to Cuba and kill off the Spanish army if hostilities had not ceased, but now my plans are changed and I may go to the aid of the Armenians. To use this improved gun we only have to pour the cartridges into a hopper and press a button and it fires 63,000 times per minute. No, gravitation is not in my way. I place my wire around this 4-ton gun and hold it with one hand and take aim. Oh, I could place my anti-gravitation wire around the national Capitol building and take it by the dome and bring it over and set it down in Harrisburg as easy as I could an inkstand. Distance is almost overcome; why, we came over the suburbs of Dallas at 12:10, less than an hour ago, and we have traveled very slowly. I could take breakfast here, do my shopping in Paris and be back here for dinner without inconvenience, as soon as I get my new propellers completed.

He offered Senator Harris a ride in the craft, but Harris declined. So the man and his crew of three climbed back aboard, and the object rose into the night.

Now this whole tale sounds like another editorial concoction. There has never been any kind of gun that could fire 63,000 times per minute, and all of the talk about antigravity smells of a put-on. Yet the story contains some interesting ingredients. The interjection of the Cuban crisis that then existed, and which later led to the Spanish-American War, and the mention of the Armenians who were then being slaughtered by the Turks, falls into a familiar pattern found in all contactee stories; i.e., the total awareness of contemporary events. And if the story isn't a fabrication, then the bearded man chose, either by accident or design, a first-rate witness to tell it to—an ex-Senator. In the story he carefully planted the important points that the airship was a secret terrestrial invention that would soon be made public. Other contactees in other areas were repeating the same thing.

Our final contactee is that "well-known Iron Mountain railroad conductor," the redoubtable Captain James Hooton, who claimed to have seen the airship, talked to men aboard it, and who drew an elaborate sketch for the newspapers, which showed a cigar-shaped vehicle covered with vanes, wings, and propellers. "Those who know Mr. Hooton will vouch for the truth of his statement," the Arkansas *Gazette* of April 22, 1897, noted.

It seems that Captain Hooton was hunting near Homan, Arkansas (no date is given for the incident) when he heard a familiar sound, "a sound for all the world like the workings of an air pump on a locomotive." He walked in the direction of the sound and came upon an open field containing the magnificent airship.

There was a medium-sized-looking man aboard and I noticed that he was wearing smoked glasses [sunglasses]. He was tinkering around what seemed to be the back end of the ship, and as I approached I was too dumbfounded to speak. He looked at me in surprise, and said, "Good day, sir; good day." I asked, "Is this the airship?" and he replied, "Yes, sir," whereupon three or four other men came out of what was apparently the keel of the ship. A close examination showed that the keel was divided into two parts, terminating in front like the sharp edge of a knife; in fact, the entire front end of the ship terminated in a knife-like edge, while the sides of the ship bulged gradually toward the middle, and then receded. There were three large wheels upon each side made of some bending metal and arranged so that they became concave as they moved forward. "I beg pardon, sir," I said. "The noise sounds a good deal like a Westinghouse air brake." "Perhaps it does, my friend. We are using condensed air and aeroplanes, but you will know more later on." "All ready, sir," someone called out, when the party all disappeared below. I observed that just in front of each wheel a two-inch tube began to spurt air on the wheels and they commenced revolving. The ship gradually arose with a hissing sound. The aeroplanes [wings] suddenly sprang forward, turning their sharp edges skyward, then the rudders at the end of the ship began to veer to one side, and the wheels revolved so fast that one could scarcely see the blades. In less time than it takes to tell you, the ship had gone out of sight.

There are many fascinating details in Captain Hooton's narrative. Again and again in modern contactee stories we are told that the UFO occupants wear goggles or ordinary sunglasses, perhaps to hide distinctive Oriental eyes. Hooton was apparently told very little except that he would "know more later on." His description of the craft makes it sound like a Rube Goldberg contraption, but rotating disks have been described on modern UFOs, too. And some equally strange-looking objects have apparently been sighted.

Enough of these reports have now been uncovered so that we can safely assume that some of these airships did land and that, at least, bearded men were aboard them. Some researchers point to 1897 as proof that we were being visited by Martians or Venusians at that time. This not only seems unlikely; in view of these stories it seems impossible. No, there has to be another answer to all of this.

Analysis of the 1897 Flap

Working purely from newspaper accounts is not easy, particularly because the standards of journalism in 1897 left much to be desired. But we weeded out 126 accounts that seemed reliable, named witnesses, and appeared to be responsibly written. All of these sample cases were reported in April 1897, and came from fourteen states. Actually the spring flap began in March in several states and tapered off in May. There were mass sightings in Omaha, Nebraska, in March, and in April an airship passed directly over Chicago, Illinois, and was reportedly viewed by thousands. A few days before that sighting (April 9) the Chicago papers had carried articles ridiculing the reports that were coming in from other sections of the country. Maybe the bearded "inventor" decided to put on a show for the skeptical Chicagoans.

In my outline of the flap of March 8, 1967, in Chapter 1 of this book, you will note that case No. 16 was reported in Eldora, a small town of about 3,000 souls smack in the middle of Iowa. On April 9, 1897, they also had sightings in this unlikely place! In fact, if we compare the 1897 flap with the things that are going on now, we find that the sightings have been concentrated in many specific areas for many years. The area around Dallas, Texas, is one. Michigan is another. There was a well-publicized flap in Michigan in March 1966 around Ann Arbor and Hillsdale. There were sightings in Ann Arbor on April 17, 1897. Michigan had, in fact, 30.5 percent of all the sightings used in our 1897 study. There is still constant UFO activity in that state, despite the dearth of publicity.

In 1897, when people saw actual objects they described them as being cigar-shaped or being large dark forms with lights attached. No flying saucers turned up in the reports I have collected. But the night-time observations then were exactly the same as they are now: bright lights with colored lights flashing around them, often moving in an erratic fashion but apparently controlled. It is possible that the airship was nothing more than a decoy—a cover for the real activity that was taking place in 1897. Certainly these objects did not consist of one or two clumsy balloons shuffling across the country.

On the night of Saturday, April 17, 1897, alone, there were reported sightings in seven scattered towns and cities in Michigan. That same night, twelve towns in Texas, far, far from Michigan, had sightings, as did Waterloo, Iowa, and St. Louis, Missouri. There were hundreds, if not thousands, of people involved in some of these sightings. We cannot dismiss them all, nor can we explain them. Texas had more than 20 percent of all the sightings in 1897, and that state has had continuous sightings for the past twenty years.

Iowa, Illinois, Michigan, South Dakota, Texas, and Washington, D.C., had sightings on April 15, 1897. About 25 percent of all the 1897 sightings occurred at approximately 9 P.M.; 20 percent at 8 P.M.; 20 percent at 10 P.M.; 15 percent at midnight.

Others were scattered in the early-morning hours. Most of the reported landings took place at 11 P.M. or later. This time pattern still holds true today.

Obviously, the great 1897 flap had much in common with the sightings of 1968. In short, nothing much has changed.

We have no way of knowing how many sightings went unreported, or how many published reports have been lost or still remain undiscovered. New ones are coming to light all the time. Each new flap since 1964 seems to have begun somewhere in the

Midwest, in those mysteriously favored states, and spread out from there. Of course, because the activity seems to cluster in the more thinly populated areas, the reports are reduced to an unsatisfactory trickle. Despite all the collections of descriptions of lights and wheels in the sky, we suffer from a real shortage of geographical data and are only just now beginning to learn how to properly analyze what little "hard" data is available.

If the newspapers of 1897 had not been so willing to ridicule the sightings and the sighters and had not indulged in devising nonsensical and misleading sightings of their own, we might have been able to untangle some of this sooner. There was no one crying "Censorship!" in 1897, yet many skeptical editors probably chose to ignore the phenomenon altogether, just as many of their modern counterparts do. A great cigar equipped with a powerful beacon is supposed to have passed over Sistersville, West Virginia, on April 19, 1897, but when I visited Sistersville in 1967, I learned to my dismay that the old newspaper office—and all of its files—had been destroyed by fire in the early 1950s.* Incidentally, many of the 1897 reports refer to powerful beacons or searchlights with which the objects sprayed blinding light over the ground they passed. This is still another thing that turns up repeatedly in modern UFO reports.

I do not doubt that *someone* was carefully flying over the United States in 1897, paying great attention to special isolated areas. We can lay out on the map the actual courses of some of these objects

---

* Flying saucers were still being seen regularly in Sistersville in 1966-67. The town's leading attorney, Robert Wright, told me, "We've been seeing these things for months. In fact, since last summer they've been showing up here almost every Wednesday like clockwork. Everybody's been watching them... but not everybody likes to talk about them.. One Wednesday a few weeks back, my wife and I watched one of these things for an hour just over that hill." He pointed to a high ridge visible from his office window. "Then it seemed to split into three... and all three of them took off like a herd of turtles." Characteristically, the local press had not commented on the numerous sightings.

and find that they often flew an almost straight line over several towns on a given night until they reached a place where a landing was later reported. Meteorites and swamp gas don't fit into these patterns. But neither do Martians and Venusians.

Whoever was involved in these activities knew precisely what they were doing, and they set up a careful smokescreen to cover their real activities. They engineered much of the ridicule, confusion, and disbelief that followed in their wake. By applying the techniques of what we now call psychological warfare, they managed to deceive a whole generation and they're still doing it.

Patterns of Deception

The operators of the wonderful 1896 airship(s) followed a careful plan which becomes transparent now that we are able to apply hindsight to the huge pile of newspaper reports. Here is a summary of the staged events, pieced together from many newspaper clippings of the period.

Early in November 1896, *before* the California airship excitement had erupted, an impressive stranger visited the office of a prominent attorney in San Francisco named George D. Collins. This man, never identified in the numerous newspaper accounts, told Collins that he was the inventor of a marvelous new airship that operated on compressed air. He asked Collins to represent him and help him obtain a patent. The lawyer was shown detailed drawings of the invention and was duly impressed. The mystery man seemed intelligent and articulate, appeared to be in his late forties, was "of dark complexion, dark-eyed, and about 5 feet 7 inches in height and weighed about 140 pounds." He was described as being very well dressed and projected an aura of wealth.

A few days after the first airship sightings hit the San Francisco newspapers, Collins told reporters that he had met the inventor of the craft and that he knew all about the airship. Reporters were unable to locate the mystery man. However, he soon visited an even better-known legal adviser, one William Henry Harrison Hart, who had once run for the office of state attorney general.

Soon after the flap peaked, a statement signed by Hart appeared on page 1 of the San Francisco *Call* (Sunday, November 29, 1896): "I have not seen it [the airship] personally but have talked with the man who claims to be the inventor. I have spent several hours with him. He has shown me drawings and diagrams of his invention, and I am convinced that they are more adapted for the purpose for which he claims them than any other invention making such claims that I have ever seen…I asked the gentleman who claims to be the inventor what his desires were in regard to carrying on the business, and he stated that he did not desire any money; that he didn't ask or want anyone to invest in it; that he was not a citizen of California, and that he had come here to perfect and test his airship …I will admit that this is the first time to my knowledge that anybody had anything in California in which he did not want anybody to invest money."

According to Hart, the invention operated on gas and electricity, and the inventor expressed interest in using his machine to fly to Cuba and drive out the Spaniards. Some of the local newspapers apparently misquoted both Collins and Hart badly, and this probably led to Hart's issuance of a signed statement. By the end of November, Collins was so disgusted that he refused to see reporters or discuss the matter further.

The mysterious inventor had managed to single out two of the most respected men in California. They had, in good faith, served as his spokesmen, and their reports were widely circulated. The flap of that Thanksgiving week supported their stories, but the inventor never came forward to enjoy his triumph. He simply vanished after the sightings subsided.

The description of the mystery man—dark-complexioned, dark-eyed, slight in stature—bears a remarkable resemblance to the numerous descriptions of the airship occupants as published five months later during the wave of April 1897. Also, witnesses to some of the 1897 landings claimed that the occupants discussed the situation in Cuba. Some of the minor discrepancies in the published stories of Hart and Collins may have been journalistic errors or may have been based on understandable misinterpretations of the technical data offered by the inventor. Collins thought the objects operated on compressed air, while Hart said they ran on gas and electricity. Compressed air was a favorite with inventors in those days. Gasoline and steam engines and electric motors were primitive, heavy and inefficient. A few years previously, one man, John Keely of Philadelphia, had built a strange contraption that could bend bars of steel and do other things considered impossible for ordinary machines of the period. Detractors claimed that the Keely engine really operated on compressed air. Actually, compressed-air motors required large, heavy tanks and pumps, spent their energy very quickly, and would be completely impractical for use in any flying machines where weight was an important consideration. The only effective use of compressed air was in World War I torpedoes, which had to travel relatively short distances and were expendable.

A summary of the mystery inventor affair appears in *Mysteries of the Skies: UFOs in Perspective,* by Gordon I. R. Lore and Harold H. Deneault, Jr. UFO historian Lucius Farish has uncovered hundreds of other clippings and reports. When all of this material is carefully studied, it seems, in retrospect, that the "inventor" was actually some kind of front man for the phenomenon and that he had prior knowledge of the impending flap. He therefore planted his airship story convincingly with Collins and Hart, knowing that their reputations would carry it a long way. It did seem like a reasonable explanation for the sightings that occurred, even though none of the witnesses reported an object which fitted Collins' description of a winged aluminum craft exactly. And as I have already pointed out, the frequency and distribution of the sightings indicated that several objects were actually in operation at one time.

In hundreds of modern UFO events we have repetitions of this tactic, which I call the press-agent game. In these events, small, dark-skinned, dark-eyed gentlemen appear in an area immediately before or immediately after a flying saucer flap. These cases are not widely known and have been poorly investigated because the hard-core cultists have found it impossible to reconcile such seemingly normal beings with "extraterrestrial visitants."

Striking examples of the press-agent game can be found in the religious and occult lore, going back thousands of years. Weeks before the birth of Christ, three dark-skinned men with Oriental features arrived in King Herod's court. They were obviously men of wealth and breeding, just like our mystery inventor. The various records say that they generated great excitement with their revelation that a very special child would soon be born somewhere in Judea. By making this appearance before King Herod and spreading this story, they made certain that the impending birth would be recorded in the court records and preserved for the ages. After successfully carrying out this mission, the trio "from the East" proceeded to Bethlehem, where they created another stir and focused attention on the Christ Child. Then, instead of returning to King Herod to report, as they had promised, they "went home by another way."

If these men had come from India or even farther away, it would have taken them many months or even years to travel by sea and land to Jerusalem. This would have taken considerable planning and expense and would have demanded that they have advance knowledge of the event. If they had been mortal men, they would almost certainly have created a similar stir when they arrived home in India or wherever, and it is likely that some written record of their story would have been preserved. There seems to be no such record.

Like our mystery inventor, they appeared in the area of the action prior to the event. They visited the most important personage they could find. They circulated their story. And then they vanished.

Our UFO mystery men usually travel in threes, also, and have become popularly known as the three Men in Black. They usually wear somber clothing, have olive complexions, and in most cases, high cheekbones and Oriental eyes.

According to Hart, the 1896 inventor had "three assistants

with him, all of whom are mechanics."

The secret inventor was a tremendously successful ploy in 1896, and it was reused again with many added embellishments in 1897. The story was carefully sustained through a series of landings and occasional planted messages.

Saturday, April 17, 1897, two boys were playing in Chicago's Lincoln Park when they spotted a package wrapped in brown paper resting high in the limbs of a tree. Daniel J. Schroeder, twelve, shinnied up the tree and retrieved it. When they unwrapped their prize, they found a pasteboard box "containing the remnants of a luncheon," and attached to the box there was a beautifully engraved card on which was printed the following inscription: "Dropped from the airship Saratoga, Friday, April 16, 1897." The card was folded and had "an embellished front page." In the upper corner were printed the words "air ship" and below them was a gilded ensign of a boy standing on a pair of outstretched wings. It was made of fine cardboard and looked expensive. Besides the printed words on the first page, this memo was written in blue pencil on the inside: "9:41 P.M.—Due northwest, 2,000 ft.; 61 N. Lat., 33 Long. Descending. Dense fog. Drizzling 'spods.'" If this message was not a complete hoax these figures would have placed the *Saratoga* over Greenland.*

The Sioux Falls, South Dakota, *Argus-Leader* commented hopefully on April 21: "There were no names or other useful information on the card, but it is expected that by it the persons operating the aerial navigation scheme may be located. The lunch box was either dropped from the airship and lodged in the branches of the tree or was placed there to hoax people.

"Many persons looked at the strange find yesterday. It was not generally denounced as a hoax, because as some observing men pointed out, anyone who had fancy airship cards printed was going

---

* Greenland is the world's only source of natural cryolite, important in the manufacture of aluminum, a substance that plays an important role in the UFO mystery.

to unnecessary expense to carry out a joke, while the package could just as well have been placed in some busy thoroughfare."

Who, indeed, would go to such elaborate lengths to pull off another airship joke? Perhaps the Chicago prankster—if a prankster was responsible—was trying to outdo another prankster in Appleton, Wisconsin, who had planted a similar note only two days before.

The Grand Rapids, Michigan, *Evening Press* of April 16, 1897 carried this article: "Appleton, Wisconsin, April 15—Many persons in this city declare that they saw an airship pass over the city last Sunday night. Last night on the farm of N. B. Clark, north of the city, a letter was picked up attached to an iron rod eighteen inches long sticking in the ground. The letter, which was not signed, is as follows:

"'Aboard the airship *Pegasus*, April 9, 1897—The problem of aerial navigation has been solved. The writers have spent the past month cruising about in the airship *Pegasus* and have demonstrated to their entire satisfaction that the ship is a thorough success. We have been able to attain a speed of 150 miles an hour and have risen to a height of 2,500 feet above sea level.

"'The *Pegasus* was erected at a secluded point ten miles from Lafayette, Tennessee, and the various parts of the machine were carried overland from Glasgow, Kentucky to that point, being shipped from Chicago, Pittsburgh, and St. Louis. We have made regular trips of three days each from Lafayette to Yaukon, and no harm has come to the *Pegasus* thus far.

"'Within a month our application for the patents for a parallel plane airship will be filed simultaneously at Washington and the European capitals. The ship is propelled by steam and is lighted by electricity, and has a carrying power of 1,000 pounds.'"

So now there were *two* airships—the noble *Pegasus* and the *Saratoga*. This second note confirmed what the contactees claimed they were being told—that it was a secret invention and soon patents would be filed and the whole world would know. Even today it would be difficult to build a steam-powered lighter-than-air-craft.

For steam you need lots of water—well, apparently the airship crews were draining wells all around the country—but you also need lots of fuel: heavy coal or wood with which to heat the water. And if your airship can lift only 1,000 pounds, you wouldn't be able to carry much of either. No, the story has the smell of dead fish to it.

The very day after the Grand Rapids *Evening Press* published the above, a new message from the airship turned up—in Grand Rapids. A man named C. T. Smith, an employee of a furniture company "who has always been considered honorable and truthful," was on his way to work at 6:15 A.M. when he found a piece of stiff wire about five inches long. At one end was attached "one of the iron combination stoppers and bottle openers commonly used to open beer bottles," apparently as a weight, and on the other end an envelope was fastened. "From the Airship Travelers" was scrawled on the outside, and it contained a piece of notepaper bearing a new message written in purple indelible pencil. It read:

> To whoever finds this:
> [We are] 2,500 feet above the level of the sea, headed north at this writing, testing the airship. Afraid we are lost. We are unable to control our engine. Please notify our people. Think we are somewhere over Michigan.
> Arthur B. Coats, Laurel, Mississippi
C. C. Harris, Gulfport, Mississippi
C. W. Rich, Richburg, Mississippi
April 16, 1897. 9 P.M.

The Grand Rapids paper added:

> That the airship is a wonderful reality is now assured, and that it passed through the vicinity of the corner of South

Division and Williams streets is a fact that is founded
upon the most irrefragable proof [that is apparently where
the note was found]. Mr. Smith, who found the letter,
positively avers that he is not a drinking man and never
owned a beer stopper in his life.

Three of the night men employed by the Wallin Leather
Company are very sure they saw the airship last night.

In Omaha, Nebraska, preparations were under way for a
large Transmississippi Exposition, so it was only logical for the
great airship inventor to bid for attention there. On April 13, the
secretary of the Exposition received the following tidbit in his
mail:

To the Exposition Director:

My identity up to date has been unknown, but I will come
to the front now; *i.e.,* if you will guarantee me 870,000
square feet of space. I am the famous airship constructor
and will guarantee you positively of this fact in a week. The
airship is my own invention and I am an Omaha man. I
wish it to be held as an Omaha invention. It will safely carry
twenty people to a height of from 10,000 to 20,000 feet.
I truly believe I have the greatest invention and discovery
ever made. Will see you April 17, 1897 at the headquarters.

[Signed] A. C. Clinton

Perhaps Mr. Clinton was aboard the ill-fated, out-of-control
craft that sailed over Michigan into limbo. In any case, he didn't
show up on the seventeenth, but several UFOs and airships were
busy in five states that night.

Aside from bottle openers and half-eaten lunches, a number of
other odd objects were dumped by the mysterious airship pilots. A
half-peeled potato fell overboard above Atchinson, Kansas, and a
Canadian newspaper dated October 5, 1896, was dropped at the

feet of Daniel Gray, a farmer, in Burton, Michigan. Gray said he had been working in his field on Friday, April 23, when he heard a rumbling sound in the sky and saw a dark object rushing past. The paper fluttered down from it and "was dry and well preserved and suffered little, if any, injury in its flight from the heavens." (Saginaw, Michigan, *Globe*, April 26, 1897)

All of these things could have been simple hoaxes, of course, but in forthcoming chapters we will describe some uneasily similar incidents that have happened in more recent years. Part of my research in the past four years has been devoted to a reexamination of the alleged UFO hoaxes, and I am now convinced that many of these hoaxes were actually engineered deliberately—and successfully—to discredit the UFO phenomenon.

Let's review briefly some of the salient points in this chapter:

(1) It is obvious that a great many unidentified flying objects were present in our skies in 1897.

(2) It is also obvious that they were manned by at least three different types of beings: (a) the regular types, some with beards and including women, as reported by several of the contactees of the period; (b) the Oriental type, the "Japs" as reported by Judge Byrne; (c) the unidentifiable creatures described by Alexander Hamilton.

(3) It sounds as if some of them, the stranger types, made a real effort to hide from witnesses who stumbled upon them accidentally.

(4) The occupants of these craft knew a great deal about us, were able to speak and possibly write our languages. If they were just fresh in from Mars, this would have been very unlikely.

Allow me now to do some educated speculating based upon my experiences with more recent situations. Let us assume that an unknown group of well-organized individuals, some of them quite alien from us in appearance, speech, etc., found it expedient to conduct a large-scale "survey" of the midwestern United States in 1897 by air. Because no aircraft existed in the United States at that time, they knew that they might attract undue attention, and *attention was the one thing they did not want.* They didn't want us even to know that they existed, and if we became conscious of their aircraft, we would automatically become aware of them. So they had to devise a plan by which this "invasion" would go relatively unnoticed, or at least seem harmless.

In 1897, everyone had at least heard of lighter-than-air craft. Crude dirigibles had already been flown in Europe, and pictures and drawings had appeared in American newspapers and magazines. So the obvious ploy for the people I call ultraterrestrials would be to construct a few craft that at least resembled dirigibles and make sure that they were seen in several places by many people, such as Chicago. These decoys would get a lot of publicity, and from then on everything that anyone saw in the sky would be classed as "the airship," even if it were shaped like a doughnut and had a big hole in the middle.

Such a plan had to go further, however, because the aerial activity was going to be most intense in some areas. Some kind of explanation for the mystery airship had to be tendered. This could best be done by staging deliberate landings in relatively remote places and contacting a few random individuals, telling them the "secret invention" story, and letting them spread the word. To add support to it, notes would be dropped occasionally confirming what the contactees were saying, and even a few ordinary artifacts such as half-peeled potatoes and foreign newspapers could be added to the stew.

Because some—or maybe most—of the ultraterrestrials looked very much like us, they would be assigned to occupy the decoys. The other objects, the *real* vehicles to be employed in this operation, would carefully remain aloof.

To lend further confusion to the situation, some of the contactees would be told ridiculous things that would discredit not only them but the whole mystery. Knowing how we think and how we search for consistencies, the ultraterrestrials were careful to sow inconsistencies in their wake. And they staged some outrageous stunts, such as singing loudly as they flew over Farmersville, Texas, on April 19, or playing a phonograph or other instrument over Fontanelle, Iowa, on April 12. When the startled townspeople reported hearing an orchestra playing in the sky, newspapers whooped and heaped ridicule on the story.

Was there an airship or wasn't there? Thousands saw it and became convinced, but millions read all of these conflicting tales and remained skeptical. Obviously, to the uninformed reader of 1897, there was only one airship and it was experimental—it was always breaking down somewhere. But what were those great, multilighted forms hurtling back and forth across the sky every night? Oh, just the airship.

Where were they going? Where were they coming from? Well, they were built by a secret inventor in Nebraska—or Tennessee—or Iowa—or Boston. Take your pick. That inventor kept his secret well. He never filed for his patents. Like a gentleman, he waited until Count Zeppelin took off in his first rigid airship on July 2, 1900, and flew 3.5 miles at 18 mph before his steering gear failed.

Recently a great British authority, Charles H. Gibbs-Smith, MA, FMA, stated: "Speaking as an aeronautical historian who specializes in the periods before 1910, I can say with certainty that the only airborne vehicles, carrying passengers, which could possibly have been seen anywhere in North America in 1897 were free spherical balloons, and it is highly unlikely for these to be mistaken for anything else. No form of dirigible [i.e., a gasbag propelled by an airscrew] or heavier-than-air flying machine was flying—or indeed could fly—at this time in America."

But if there was no secret inventor, and if there's no such thing as unidentified flying objects, then who or what was buzzing Eldora, Iowa, in 1897? And why have they chosen to go back there again and again ever since?

If I lived in Eldora, I'd sure as hell demand that somebody find out.

6
Flexible Phantoms of the Sky

The Wednesday phenomenon is quite evident in the historical events as well as in the contemporary sightings. A disproportionate number of UFO events seem to be concentrated on Wednesdays and Saturdays, particularly the landing and contact cases. The frequency of the Wednesday/Saturday events immediately removes the phenomenon from a framework of chance or coincidence. After I discovered this basic pattern in 1966-67, other researchers checked it with their own data and verified it. Historian Lucius Farish uncovered a number of early statements and cases which further indicated that this Wednesday phenomenon had been observed and reported upon long ago.

In *Myth and Legend of Ancient Israel* by Angelo S. Rappaport, the following statement appears: "Concerning 'demons:' They lodge in trees, caper bushes, in gardens, vineyards, in ruined and desolate houses, and dirty places. To go alone into such places is dangerous, and the eves of Wednesday and Saturday were considered dangerous times. Agrath [daughter of the she-demon Makhlath] commands hosts of evil spirits and demons and rides in a big chariot. Her power is paramount on Wednesdays and Saturdays, for on these days Agrath, the daughter of Makhlath, roves about in the air accompanied by eighteen myriads of evil spirits."

Not only do our unusual events show a decided preference for Wednesdays and Saturdays, but the early cases contain many of the same features found in the modern events. Blinding searchlights were frequently described in the reports of the nineteenth century, and such searchlights remain one of the consistent features of the modern sightings. The arc light had been invented in the nineteenth century, but searchlights utilizing it required considerable power either in the form of many heavy batteries or a powerful generator driven by a steam or gasoline engine. This kind of equipment would add too much weight to any known aircraft of the period and would have been completely impractical. The only available lights in the 1890s and early 1900s were dim incandescent lights, and they would not have produced the blinding glare so often described in these reports. The few automobiles of that time used kerosene or gasoline lanterns as headlights. It was not until the middle 1960s that airliners and military planes began regularly to employ powerful strobe lights and new, more brilliant landing lights. The landing lights are, of course, used only during takeoffs and descents. The strobe lights are now often mounted on the tops and bottoms of the fuselage and flash off and on with a brilliant white glare. They are easily recognizable and seldom mistaken for the prismatic UFO lights. There has also been some recent experimentation with searchlights mounted on helicopters. Let's compare a searchlight story of 1875 with a more recent one.

Harold I. Velt's *The Sacred Book of Ancient America* quotes from a contemporary account by J. J. Cornish:

> On account of working at daily labor this baptism was performed on Wednesday, late in the evening of December 29, 1875, an intensely dark night. After our prayer meeting Mrs. John Taylor and Miss Sarah Lively were baptized by me in the River Thames in London, Ontario, Canada* when suddenly there came a very beautiful light from heaven, which rested on all—both members and nonmembers— brighter than the sun at noonday... It came down with a sound like a mighty rushing wind. We could hear it far above in the distance, and as it reached the place where we stood we were enveloped in the brightest and most

---

* London, Ontario, has been the site of many interesting UFO events in the past twenty years.

beautiful light I ever saw—the glory of the Lord. The light was round, straight up and down, like a shaft from heaven to earth, and just as bright on the inside edge as it was in the center, and so far as we could see it was just as dark on the outer edge as it was a mile away... After baptism and dismissal the light did not go out, but gradually went up until it vanished from our sight...

Here we seem to have had a directed and controlled beam of electromagnetic energy (which is what light is) that did not reflect on the area outside of the immediate beam. This is commonly described by UFO witnesses. The witnesses to the Presque Isle, Pennsylvania, landing in 1966 reported that the angular object which settled onto a beach was projecting several beams of concentrated light in all directions. The peculiar thing about these beams was that they seemed to go out from the object and extend to different lengths, not fading into the darkness but terminating suddenly like poles or rods of light. Some of these beams were said to have darted into the forests on the edge of the beach as if they were "looking for something."

In April 1966, Robert Howard was visiting some friends on a farm outside Sinclairville, New York, when a UFO showed up at 8:30 P.M. on a Sunday evening. Howard and several others stepped outside to watch what they described as "a saucer-shaped object about 12 feet in diameter, with flashing red lights set in its edge." It settled in a nearby swamp. Howard headed across the fields toward the object while more people gathered. The thing appeared to be beaming a very narrow stream of brilliant white light into a nearby woods. As Howard neared it, he says it bobbed to the right and took off over the treetops. For days after the incident his right eye was puffy, bloodshot, and watery.

Cherry Creek, New York, only a few miles from Sinclairville, was the site of an alleged landing on Thursday, August 19, 1965. Presque Isle in Erie, Pennsylvania, is just south of this area.

The UFO wave in Australia and New Zealand has been

most intense, and another interesting "light beam" story was investigated there by researcher Dr. Paul Zeck, a psychiatrist, in 1967. The witness, a prominent businessman named A. R. Spargo ("an employer of a large labor force"), was driving alone near Boyup Brook in Western Australia when the incident reportedly occurred. It was about 9 P.M. on the night of Monday, October 30, 1967. Suddenly his car stopped, and his lights and radio went dead. A brilliant beam of light seemed to be focused upon him. It came from "a mushroom-shaped craft, 30 feet or more in diameter, hovering above the treetops at an estimated 100 feet above the ground." The object itself was glowing with an iridescent bluish light. The beam seemed to be coming from the underside at an angle of 40 degrees.

"I seemed to be surrounded by the beam," Spargo said. "It was two to three feet in diameter, and brilliant on the outside. Yet I could see up it, and there was no glare or anything inside the tube... I had the most extraordinary feeling that I was being observed through the tube. I couldn't see anyone—I could just make out the shape of the glowing craft. I felt compelled to look up the tube. But I didn't feel any fear, and I don't remember thinking of anything in particular.

"After about five minutes it was switched off—just like someone switching off an ordinary electric light. The color of the craft seemed to darken, then it accelerated very swiftly and disappeared toward the west at terrific speed."

The next thing he knew, he was speeding along the road. He had absolutely no recollection of starting up the car and driving off again. Later he discovered that his watch—an expensive Omega chronometer—was unaccountably five minutes slow. He decided to report the incident to the authorities and voluntarily submitted to a psychiatric testing. His story was published in the *West Australian*, November 1, 1967, but his name was not used.

Unearthly beams of light, sudden automobile failures, disturbing lapses of time and memory: all of these are commonplace minor elements in our UFO mystery.

But let's go back to the puzzling historical sightings so that we may gain a better view of the overall picture.

The Flap of 1909

There were, of course, many observations of unusual aerial objects between 1897 and 1909. Thanks to the efforts of Lucius Farish and his colleagues we have an impressive sampling of these early reports to work with. The reliability of some of the newspaper accounts can certainly be questioned, but the tongue-in-cheek journalistic jokes are quite transparent, at least to someone who grew up in the newspaper business.

A minor airship flap broke out in California in 1905. On Wednesday, August 2, 1905, J. A. Jackson, "a well-known resident of Silshee," was out at 1:30 in the morning when a bright light appeared in the sky and headed for him. According to the account published in the Brawley, California, *News* (August 4, 1905):

> He watched it closely until behind the light there appeared the form of an airship, apparently about 70 feet in length, with a searchlight in front and several other lights aboard, The mysterious machine appeared to be propelled by wings alone and rose and fell as the wings flapped like a gigantic bird. Apparently there was no balloon attachment as is usually the case with airships.
>
> Mr. Jackson, being close to the home of W. E. Wilsie, woke him up in time to see the lights of the machine before it disappeared…The same night, H. E. Allatt, postmaster at Imperial, was awakened from sleep by a bright light shining into his room. There was no moon, the light was thought to be a fire, and Mr. Allatt rose to investigate, but no fire was found. Looking at his watch, the time was discovered to be 1:30 o'clock, and it is believed that the brilliant light was caused by the searchlight from this mysterious airship.

Other witnesses in the same area reported seeing strange lights maneuvering over some nearby mountains, And one group said they had seen "a titanic white bird" at a distance of about five miles. "As it was clearly impossible, even in the desert air, to see a bird at that distance, they, too, have been pondering the case and come to the conclusion that what they saw was the airship making its way over the desert," the newspaper remarked.

Winged objects, things with tail fins and propellers, had been reported during the 1896-97 wave, too. The "flapping wings" is a rather unique feature, however, and perhaps the bobbing-falling-leaf motion created some kind of illusion. There is no way of reaching a final assessment on most of these early cases.

Based upon my study of modern sightings versus published reports, it is very possible that many people on the West Coast were seeing UFOs throughout the early 1900s but that very few of these ever made their way into print. The spotty clippings that have been uncovered to date do suggest a continuing flap of unsuspected proportions.

The year 1908 brought a minor flap to Tacoma, Washington, and the same area of the Puget Sound that would play an important part in the Maury Island "hoax" (a sighting which preceded Kenneth Arnold's by three days) thirty-nine years later. On Saturday, February 1, 1908, and again on the next night between the hours of 7 and 9, a brilliant reddish object "two or three times as bright as Jupiter" passed over Kent, Washington, and was seen by many. Some described it as being cigar-shaped. A story in the Tacoma, Washington, *Daily Ledger* (February 4, 1908) added, "During the same week, on clear nights, colored lights were displayed at high altitudes, and on one occasion a rocket was discharged high in the air, it is asserted." The light was viewed by the populaces of many of the towns along its route. Some newspapers suggested that it was a Japanese spy craft of some sort. (The Russo-Japanese war had taken place three years earlier, and the "Yellow Peril" was a popular topic of racial bigots on the West Coast.)

On June 30, 1908, the now-famous "meteor" exploded over Siberia.

The next summer, in mid-July 1909, residents in the thinly populated Blue Mountains of New Zealand began to see a "cigar-shaped or boat-shaped" object cruising their skies. One account from the Otago, New Zealand, *Daily Times* described it this way: "It did not appear to be very long but was very broad.... It flew over and past the school grounds, turned around, and went back the way it came. It was flying along very easily and had no trouble in turning." Unusual flying lights were reportedly observed in the same areas at night.

On Friday, August 6, 1909, "ten hitherto skeptical workmen" saw a "cigar-shaped balloon with a carriage suspended below. It had a powerful white headlight and changed altitude steadily several times." The mystery airship of 1896-97 had returned! This time it was halfway around the world from Europe and the United States. We have found no mention of the New Zealand sightings in the American press of the period and assume that the news did not travel far. The airship itself did travel very far, however.

Late in August 1909, the Russian correspondent of the London *Daily Mail* filed a dispatch about "an unknown controllable airship" that had appeared over the city of Reval, making two wide circles before disappearing in the direction of Finland. The event was said to have caused great excitement.

A month later a machine "of great size, elliptical-shaped, and equipped with wings of some kind" passed over the Castle Forest near Gothenburg, Sweden, at an altitude of 300 feet. The time of the sighting was 6 P.M. That morning another object—or possibly the same one —flew over the Swedish city of Osthammar at an altitude of 300 feet, coming from the northeast and disappearing in a westerly direction. The date was Friday, September 24, 1909.

Gothenburg was revisited at 8:30 P.M., Thursday, December 2, 1909, when an "illuminated balloon" appeared high in the sky and moved swiftly toward the sea. The Stockholm newspaper *Dagens Nyheter* noted: "Suddenly a rocket of some kind was thrown from the gondola into a garden named Redbergs Park. This took place a few minutes before the balloon went out of sight."

The events of 1909, 1913, and 1934 are crucial to our overall understanding of the phenomenon. They provide vital links in the long and tangled chain that we are trying to unravel. These early reports are especially meaningful because they were written as human interest items and routine news stories long before the appearance of the UFO controversy or before any government had issued a denial. The people of Sweden were completely unaware of the sightings in New Zealand. And Americans had not heard of either group of events. Skeptical explanations of mass hysteria simply cannot be applied to these early reports. Some mechanical-like object—or group of objects—was circling the globe at a time when the number of known existing dirigibles could be counted on one hand and only a few crude airplanes, homemade and of very limited range and capabilities, could be found. In fact, the development of the airplane was very slow until World War I came along and it became necessary to make improvements in design quickly.

The first European airplane flight (Santos-Dumont) took place in 1906 in Paris. Except for one or two experimental models, all of the planes of 1909 were fashioned after the Wright brothers' model, with the pilot sitting on the fore edge of the lower wing, his feet dangling in space, and a modified automobile engine coughing and sputtering behind him. It was almost a tradition for these machines to crash after flying a few miles at low altitude. Lieutenant Thomas E. Selfridge earned the unhappy distinction of being the first man to die in an airplane crash in 1908 when he was a passenger on a plane piloted by Orville Wright which went out of control and plummeted to earth from an altitude of 75 feet. Wright was badly injured, too.

In 1910, there were thirty-six licensed pilots, and they outnumbered the available airplanes.

So all of the known pilots, planes, and dirigibles of 1909 were accounted for. They were not buzzing New Zealand and Sweden. Someone else was.

This someone else next visited the New England states in

December 1909.

A New "Secret" Inventor

The story of the Massachusetts flap of 1909 is another jigsaw puzzle that we have pieced together from dozens of newspaper clippings. The sightings of that December were widely published all over the United States. Thousands of witnesses were involved, and the objects described possessed all of the UFO characteristics of the 1896-97 flap. But there is a rather odd fly in this ointment: a self-proclaimed inventor from Worcester, Massachusetts. He became the focus of many of the newspaper stories, and he seems to have been surrounded by considerable mystery.

The early newspaper accounts suggest that unidentified flying machines might have been sighted with some regularity before journalists really paid any heed to them.

First, we have an interesting coincidence. One of the first published sightings—perhaps the very first—of the flap appeared in New York and Long Island newspapers on the same day that our mystery inventor held a press conference in Worcester and revealed his marvelous discovery to the world.

A Long Island lifeguard, William Leech, was among those who claimed that they heard an airplane engine passing directly overhead in the darkness while on patrol off Long Island. They could not see the object but seemed certain that the sound had come from the sky, not from the water or the island. This report wouldn't mean much ordinarily, but even while Mr. Leech was talking to New York reporters about the incident, our mystery man was shooting off his mouth in Worcester for the first time.

His name was Wallace E. Tillinghast, and he was the vice president of the Sure Seal Manufacturing Company in Worcester. According to the newspapers, he was a man of eminence and reputation and was the holder of several patents. He claimed that he had invented, built, and tested an airplane "capable of carrying three passengers with a weight limit of 200 pounds each, a distance of at least 300 miles without a stop to replenish the supply of gasoline, and if necessary, at a rate of 120 miles per hour."

On September 8, 1909, he said, he had flown his machine around the Statue of Liberty and then had soared to Boston and back to New York without landing.

The newspapers continued: "Another part of this trip is still more wonderful. Mr. Tillinghast says that when near Fire Island [off the coast of Long Island], one of the cylinders of the flier ran irregularly, so the motor was stopped, with the machine 4,000 feet in the air, and sailed forty six minutes, while two mechanics repaired it in midair, the engine being started again when the airplane was near enough to land to be seen by a member of the lifesaving crew patrolling the beach."

Presto, we have an explanation for Mr. Leech's story! Or have we? Before we can review the flap of Christmas week, 1909, we must dissect the remarkable story of Mr. Tillinghast. It bears many interesting resemblances to the tales of San Francisco's mystery inventor. Unlike Lawyer Collins' well-dressed, well-spoken, middle-aged client, Mr. Tillinghast was located by numerous reporters. He was interviewed. His wife was interviewed. He was well known in Worcester, held a responsible position there, and had no discernible motivation for making up outrageous claims. Rather, he had everything to lose.

As soon as the sightings of the mystery airplane broke in the newspapers, he stepped forward and offered an explanation that was taken very seriously by the nation's press. Although all of the known airplanes of the period were tiny open biplanes, Mr. Tillinghast described his invention as being a monoplane weighing 1,550 pounds, with a wingspread of 72 feet and an engine of 120 horsepower. It could take off in a small area of about 75 feet, he said, and could travel at the unheard-of speed of 120 miles an hour—2 miles per minute. Sage scientists were then mumbling behind their Ph.D.s that no man could ever travel faster than 60 miles an hour without suffering tremendous pressures and getting his brains scrambled. Racing car driver Barney Oldfield was taking that chance, however. The fighter planes of World War I eventually managed to hit speeds of 125-150 miles an hour. As for the 72-foot wingspan, American bombers of the 1950s, such as the Douglas B-66, had spans ranging from 75 feet to 185 feet (the B-52). Most modern fighters have a span of 30-50 feet. The Douglas DC-9 transport plane (two-engined) has a wingspan of 87 feet 6 inches.

In short, Mr. Tillinghast's machine was larger than anything that could have been successfully flown in 1909. It would have probably required much more than 120 horsepower to lift it, and a craft of this size could hardly have taken off in the space of 25 yards. Nor is it likely that any plane, then or now, could have glided for forty-six minutes at the low altitude of 4,000 feet while mechanics tinkered with a recalcitrant engine.

These facts brand Mr. Tillinghast a liar from the outset. But why? More important, why did he choose to issue this lie at the very moment when a massive UFO flap *was about* to inundate the New England states?

He declared that he had made "over 100 successful trips, of which 18 have been in his perfected machine. His latest airplane is so perfect and adjusted so correctly that upon being taken from the shop it immediately made uninterrupted trips covering 56 miles." (Portland, Oregon, *Journal*, December 23, 1909)

The same day that William Leech told his story to the New York press and Mr. Tillinghast made his revelations to reporters in Massachusetts, a man near Little Rock, Arkansas, many hundreds of miles to the southwest of New England, reported seeing an unusual light in the sky.

According to the Arkansas *Gazette* (December 15, 1909): "A. W. Norris of Mabelvale, road overseer of District No. 8, is of the opinion that an airship passed over his residence at about 10 o'clock Monday night [December 12]. Mr. Norris states that he was standing in his doorway when a strange light appeared, apparently about 300 feet above him, traveling south at a rapid rate of speed and disappearing a moment or two later in the darkness. He said that the light had the appearance of a searchlight similar to those used on automobiles, and it rose and fell like a bird in flight. The night was cloudy, which precludes the possibility of the light having been a star or any atmospheric phenomena."

Our strange aerial lights were apparently back in Arkansas, keeping their usual 10 P.M. timetable. We can't blame this one on Mr. Tillinghast.

Things were relatively quiet for the next few days. After his initial press conference, Mr. Tillinghast withdrew and refused to issue further statements. He was supposedly laboring in his secret laboratory, preparing for the enormous wave of sightings that occurred Christmas week, beginning on Monday, December 20.

Shortly after midnight on the morning of December 20, those residents of Little Rock, Arkansas, who were still awake were amazed to see a very powerful beam of light probing across the southern sky. The Arkansas *Gazette* (December 20, 1909) said it was "a cylindrical shaft of light, which, arising from the southeast horizon, stretched athwart the firmament far to the east." The editor consulted astronomers and could find no explanation for the phenomenon.

At 1 A. M. people around the harbor of Boston, Massachusetts, saw "a bright light passing over." "Immigration Inspector Hoe ... came to the conclusion that it was an airship of some kind" (*New York Tribune*, December 21, 1909).

The next night, Tuesday, December 21, the real flap began. At 1:15 A.M. residents of Pawtucket, Rhode Island, saw "two red lights proceeding southward... All were able to make out the outline of the flying machine against the background of the stars" (*New York Tribune*, December 22,1909).

At 5:20 P.M. on Wednesday, December 22, a brilliant light appeared over Marlboro, Massachusetts, its powerful "search-light" sweeping the sky. Then it slowly proceeded to Worcester, some sixteen miles distance, where it hovered above the city for a few minutes and then disappeared for two hours. Finally it returned and circled four times above the city, "using a searchlight of tremendous power. Thousands of people thronged the streets to watch the mysterious visitor."

The newspaper reports on this sequence of events are voluminous. Reporters immediately dashed to Mr. Tillinghast's home in Worcester, where they found the "inventor" absent. His wife told them, "My husband knows his business. He'll talk when the proper time comes."

The following night everyone in New England was out scanning the skies. They were not disappointed. Strange flying lights seemed to be everywhere. They were seen over Boston Common, and throngs in Marlboro, South Framingham, Natick, Ashland, Grafton, North Grafton, Upton, Hopedale, and Northboro witnessed them. Because the lights moved against the wind, balloons were ruled out as an explanation. Something carrying a searchlight that "played from side to side" passed over Willimantic, Connecticut.

Here is a summary from the Providence, Rhode Island, *Journal* (December 24, 1909):

> As on Wednesday night, the light was first reported passing over Marlboro about 6:45 o'clock. The light, which was at a height so great as to make impossible a view of its support, disappeared to the southwest in the direction of Westboro and Worcester.

> It was traced from North Grafton, not far from Worcester, through Grafton, North Grafton, Hopedale, and Milford, and then after being lost sight of reappeared in Natick about 7:30 o'clock, going in the direction of Boston. Observers are positive that it was a searchlight. At 7:45 it was seen from Boston Common, by the testimony of several persons, among them men who were at a prominent clubhouse on Beacon Hill.

> At Northboro and Ashland, early in the evening, the population turned out en masse to watch the light pass overhead.

> Observers at several points report that while the light was

generally steady, occasionally it flashed, and once or twice it disappeared entirely.

That night Mr, Tillinghast was not "aloft." Reporters found him and extracted this statement from him:

> I was out of Worcester last night. Where I was is my own business. It may be that I flew over the city, but that is my own business, too.
>
> When I said recently that I had flown from Boston to New York and returned, I said nothing but what was true. I have an airship which will carry three or four persons and will make the speed I claimed for it—that is, about one hundred twenty miles an hour.
>
> When I get ready, I shall speak fully and not until then.

The Mysterious Shed

An unnamed "staff correspondent for the United Press" was reportedly arrested for trespassing when he tried to get to the bottom of the Worcester mystery. Following up rumors, he visited the estate of John B. Gough, six miles outside of the city, and there he discovered a shed more than 100 feet long concealed in a dense woods.

The widely published UPI dispatch revealed the following:

> Fourteen men in the employ of the Morgan Telephone Company of this city were at work there on some secret occupation. Paul B. Morgan, head of the telephone company, is a close friend of Wallace E. Tillinghast, who is supposed to be the inventor of the mysterious flying machine... Morgan has been interested in aviation for several years, and two years ago he spent $15,000 trying to perfect a machine invented by a Swedish aviator. The Swedish invention, however, proved unsatisfactory and

was abandoned… John D. Gough, on whose estate the shed was found, is an old-time temperance lecturer and is friendly with Tillinghast and Morgan. His place is near West Boylston.

The secrecy maintained at the Gough estate and the careful manner in which the shed discovered today is being guarded lends new weight to the belief that a marvelous ship has been constructed. The correspondent was taken before the justice summarily today, and the swift manner in which he was prosecuted for trespassing is believed to have been employed as a warning to others who might attempt to invade the secrecy of the airship plant.

There were many more sightings of brilliant lights apparently under intelligent control over Rhode Island, Connecticut, and Massachusetts on December 24, and the "searchlight" was frequently described by the many witnesses.

Reporters from New York and Boston converged on Worcester and tried to interview Mr. Tillinghast, but he fell silent again. All they could learn was that "Mr. Tillinghast is a businessman of good standing in Worcester. He is an experienced mechanic and has invented several devices which are the foundation of the company of which he is vice-president. He has made a specialty of airships for eleven years, he says."

The Providence, Rhode Island, *Journal* remarked: "Tillinghast is absolutely incommunicado. The notoriety that has followed him since the mysterious lights were seen has seriously interfered with his business and with his homelife. He has not been permitted an hour's peace. At his office there are constantly two or three persons who want to know something. At the door of his place of business and at his home he is closely watched by mysterious men. When he is home, his telephone rings constantly. As his wife has only recently recovered from an illness, the constant clangor is not conducive to his good nature."

"... closely watched by mysterious men!"

A member of the Aero Club of New England, J. Walter Flagg, managed to obtain an audience with the elusive inventor, and he later told reporters that Mr. Tillinghast had not only repeated his claims of the September flight to Boston and back to New York, but that "he had done far more wonderful things." These "far more wonderful things" were not defined.

The good citizens of Worcester were understandably upset by all of the furor, and a committee from the local Board of Trade was organized to confront Tillinghast and demand proof of his claims. He responded through a spokesman, one William Hunt. On December 30, Hunt told reporters in Boston that the marvelous Tillinghast machine would be publicly displayed at the Boston Aero Show planned for the week of February 16-23, 1910.

Sightings in the New England states ceased. The ten-day wonder became a memory. So far as we have been able to learn, no Tillinghast machine was displayed at the Aero Show. He slipped back into oblivion, and the contents of that 100-foot shed on the Gough estate were never revealed.

On the basis of what we know, we can draw some parallels between the 1896 flap in San Francisco and the 1909 events in New England.

Just before the San Francisco wave, an impressive mystery man visited lawyer Collins, a prominent attorney, and made a seemingly rational claim. He had invented a wonderful new airship and wanted Collins to handle the patent problems. When the UFO flap broke in the area a few days later, Collins, in good faith, told the press that there was no mystery. His client had perfected an airship and was probably testing it in the San Francisco area.

The wave came and went. The "inventor" disappeared. No patents were ever filed. The great new invention was lost to humanity, and tinkerers like the Wright brothers and Count Zeppelin were obliged to perfect crude machines that were in no way as remarkable as the objects seen in California.

In the summer of 1909, a new airship flap began in New

Zealand and northern Europe. And an even bigger wave was planned for New England that December. The planners had enjoyed considerable success with their California "mystery inventor" ploy and therefore decided to use the same gimmick again on a somewhat more sophisticated level.

Here is my theory. Sometime in the fall of 1909, Mr. Wallace E. Tillinghast, one of the most prominent and reputable members of his community with a track record as an inventor, was approached by a man or a group of men who offered to take him for a ride in a marvelous new "secret" aircraft. Mr. Tillinghast was a man of science, and he was far too curious to reject such an opportunity. He went to an isolated field and climbed aboard the machine he found there. His hosts kept their promise and flew him around the countryside, perhaps even to Boston and back.

When they landed again, the pilots of the machine offered a proposition to Mr. Tillinghast. They struck a bargain (which they had no intention of keeping), and perhaps they offered him a large interest in the profits from their flying machine, provided he did exactly as they ordered during the next few months. They explained that they needed a responsible, respectable man to front for them while they ironed the bugs out of their invention. They appealed to his ego, saying that they were interested only in giving their airship to the world, and they didn't care if he took full credit for it. After the machine was fully tested, they promised, they would turn it over to him, and he could make all the arrangements for manufacturing more of them. He could also claim full credit for inventing it. They, the real inventors, would happily remain behind the scenes.

Mr. Tillinghast accepted the proposition, visions of glory dancing in his brain. The machine had been proven to him. He was convinced of the reality of the trip he had taken. When reports of mystery airplanes started to filter into the press in early December, his mysterious friends called upon him and told him that it was time to disclose the existence of the invention. Tillinghast dutifully appeared before the reporters, revealed that he had already made a number of flights, and that the invention would be fully unveiled at an appropriate time in the near future.

We can only guess at the contents of the shed on the Gough estate. Perhaps it was completely unrelated to the whole business. Or perhaps it housed special communications equipment supplied by the Morgan Telephone Company for the real "airship inventors." Mr. Morgan also had a known interest in aviation. He might have also been approached by "them" and was involved in the same deal as Tillinghast.

Whatever the case, thousands of people throughout New England observed UFO-type phenomena that Christmas week, and most believed that they were watching the wonderful invention of a local man. The objects flew orderly patterns over specific geographic points and performed maneuvers, which automatically ruled out convenient natural explanations. Morgan and Tillinghast were never given the promised model to back up their earlier claims. Like so many of the modern UFO contactees, they were used.

The 1910 Sightings

"Three huge lights of almost uniform dimensions" appeared over Huntington, West Virginia, early on the morning of Friday, December 31, 1909. A farmer named Joseph Green thought they had fallen on his land, but a thorough search failed to find any trace of them.

Then at 9 A.M. on Wednesday, January 12, 1910, thousands of people saw an unusual flying machine passing directly over Chattanooga, Tennessee, at great altitude. The chugging of an engine was clearly heard. That same night an airship passed over Huntsville, Alabama, traveling at high speed, according to the reports.

At 11 A.M. the next morning "a white dirigible balloon" reappeared over Chattanooga, heading from south to north. It was again seen the following day at noon, this time coming from the north and heading southeast.

The most interesting sightings of 1910 took place directly over New York City that summer. They are significant because of their similarity to the sightings of Scandinavia in 1934, which we will discuss shortly.

At 8:45 P.M. on Tuesday, August 30, 1910, "a long black object" flew low over the island of Manhattan, accompanied by the sound of an engine. Hundreds of people stared upward in amazement as the object approached Madison Square and the Metropolitan Life Insurance Company tower. The New York *Tribune* (August 31, 1910) reports: "The vague bulk, as it came into nearer view, took on the semblance of a biplane. It swung past the tower, then turned and described one graceful circle after another around the illuminated structure, its outlines standing out clear in the lights from many windows."

It flew off toward the Flatiron Building and then returned again to Madison Square, where it circled again, swooping down so low that "it seemed to brush the top of the trees."

The next night (Wednesday) it came back again at 9 P.M. and performed the same maneuvers, circling Madison Square in view of hundreds of people lounging in the park on that warm summer night. "Persons who saw the flying mystery differ as to the number of lights it carried. Some say it carried two red lights, others lean to the three-green theory." The few known pilots in the New York area had not been aloft that night. It was unlikely that any pilot of the period would have even considered attempting a night flight to perform hazardous low-level maneuvers directly over the city. In fact, pilots avoided Manhattan even in the daytime.

The identity of the mystery flier of 1910 was never determined. The description of a long black biplane does not fit any of the flimsy craft then performing Sunday demonstrations in fields and meadows on Long Island and in New Jersey.

South Africa: 1914

There was a good deal more to the flaps of 1909-10, but we can't hope to cover everything here. The year 1913 also produced a series of important sightings all over the world, and a European ufologist, Edgar Sievers, has done extensive research into the wholesale UFO sightings that took place from Cape Town to Pretoria in 1914. The powerful "headlight" of a cigar-shaped object is supposed to have sprayed over the plains of South Africa nearly every night that summer. One farmer reported coming upon a landed aircraft on the veld near Greytown, Natal. Two of its occupants, he said, were pailing water from a stream. Sievers dug into the old records and found there were no airplanes of any kind in South Africa at that time. Only three or four flimsy, short-ranged biplanes existed on the entire continent.

From New Zealand to Boston, from Arkansas to Sweden, from Russia to South Africa, our mysterious aviators plied the globe. All of this happened long before any known nation had truly conquered the air, fifty years or more before the advent of the high-flying U-2 spy planes and the man-made satellites.

Were these unknown "biplanes" and "dirigible balloons" space probes from some distant planet, or were they machines operating from hidden bases or a "hidden world" much closer to home?

7

Unidentified Airplanes

Conventional prop-driven airplanes with discernible wings and tails are an integral part of the UFO mystery. Although international law requires all aircraft to bear identifying markings and license numbers on their wings, tails, and fuselages, none of these mystery airplanes bothers to comply. They are usually a dull gray or black and display no insignia of any kind. Often they are seen flying very low at night in UFO flap areas, and the pilot's cabin is usually brightly illuminated. Customarily, conventional planes flying at night do not have brightly illuminated cockpits because it would interfere with the pilot's night vision.

These pirate aircraft have been busy all over the world since 1896. At 2 P.M. on the afternoon of Monday, July 22, 1968, one of them appeared in the clear skies over the airports of San Carlos de Bariloche, outside the city of Bahia Blanca, Argentina. It circled the field lazily at an altitude of 200 feet, apparently preparing to land. Innumerable witnesses, including pilots, police officers, and airport employees, paused in whatever they were doing and watched. The arrival of an airplane at a busy airport in broad daylight was hardly an earth-shaking event—but there was something very odd about this one. Something very odd, indeed.

All of the witnesses later agreed that the plane had an unusually long fuselage and that its delta wings seemed far too short to support a craft of its size. Furthermore, it moved very slowly—too slowly to stay aloft. One of the fundamental rules of aerodynamics is that the shorter an airplane's wings are in comparison to its overall size, the faster it must go to maintain lift.

The airport control tower made an effort to contact the plane by radio but received no reply. Then a green light was flashed at it, signaling permission to land. The giant machine continued to lope around the field. When it reached the end of runway 28, it suddenly rolled over on its axis, completing a 360-degree turn in remarkably little space. Astonished viewers on the ground studied it through binoculars and could find no markings or insignia except for three small black squares and one large one on its fuselage. None of the airport employees could identify the make or design of the plane. They had never seen anything like it before, even though they were familiar with everything from Constellations to U-2s. It seemed to glide rather than fly and made only a slight hissing noise. After a few minutes, it picked up speed and shot away to the southeast.

Argentine authorities were never able to identify this stranger or explain the incident. The newspaper *La Razon* carried the story on July 25, 1968, and it was investigated by Miss Edith Greinert for England's *Flying Saucer Review*. The Bahia Blanca sector of Argentina was beset by a wide variety of UFO sightings, landings, and alleged contacts throughout 1968.

Whole formations of unidentified delta-winged craft have been seen over the United States. At least one case was given careful study by the U.S. Air Force. *Project Blue Book Report No. 14* lists as "unidentified" the following incident: "A naval aviation student, his wife, and several others were at a drive in movie from 2115 to 2240 hours [9:15 to 10:40 P.M.] on Sunday, April 20, 1952, during which time they saw nine groups of objects fly over. There were from two to nine objects in a group, and there were about twenty groups. The groups of objects flew in a straight line except for some changes in direction accomplished in a manner like any standard aircraft turn. The objects were shaped like conventional aircraft. The unaccountable feature of the objects was that each had a red glow surrounding it and was glowing itself, although it was a cloudless night."

A government official in Washington, who must remain anonymous for obvious reasons, recently told me about a sighting he had made while living on Long Island in 1957. His dog had started to bark and howl one night, he said, and he stepped outside in time to see a huge delta-winged aircraft passing swiftly overhead in total silence. It was surrounded by an eerie reddish glow. He had never seen anything like it before and decided to call the local Air Force base. He reported what he had observed, and the next day an officer called him and asked for additional details, admitting that several other people had reported seeing the same thing. (Except for a few experimental types, delta-winged aircraft were very rare in the 1950s.)

UFO enthusiasts and their organizations are largely concerned with unusual configurations, such as disks and flying sausages, but the Aerial Phenomena Research Organization (APRO) has received one especially intriguing "mystery airplane" report that they have investigated as thoroughly as possible. The witness voluntarily submitted to a lie detector test, answering questions conceived by trained psychologists. His name is William Hertzke, a rancher in Calgary, Alberta, Canada, and he passed those tests. A full chapter is devoted to this case in the book *UFOs over the Americas* by Jim and Coral Lorenzen.

One morning in October 1965, Mr. Hertzke was horseback riding in a pasture on the Circle Jay Ranch near Calgary when he saw what looked like a small airplane parked on the ground. It was a silver-gray color with swept-back (delta) wings. He estimated that it was about 16 feet long, with a wingspan of about 12 feet, and the fuselage was 4 or 5 feet deep. He rode over to it and examined it cautiously.

The exterior, he reported, was irregular "like a waffle." A transparent plastic-like dome covered the cockpit. Through it he could see complicated instruments, a 14-inch "TV screen," and two small, transparent glasslike bucket seats. There were no visible motors, propellers, or jets, and no insignia or identifying marks of any kind. He saw no sign of life around the object, and his work schedule did not permit him to return to it again later for another look.

Hertzke's description, which is much more detailed than we can present here, is most extraordinary. Although the object had

a conventional tail and delta wings, its interior and its waffle-like*
exterior placed it in a class by itself. Apparently it was built for very
small pilots, and it flew on some unknown principle that did not
require jets or propellers. (Incidentally, conventional sailplanes and
gliders have exceptionally long wings, while this object had very
short ones.) If you were to glimpse this kind of aircraft passing
slowly overhead, you probably wouldn't even give it a second glance.

Mystery "Cargo Planes"

There are several other types of mystery airplanes operating
in North America. Giant craft resembling standard AF "Flying
Boxcars" are frequently reported in UFO flap areas, often
performing hazardous hedge-hopping maneuvers. One group of
witnesses on the outskirts of Gallipolis, Ohio, told me that they
had been seeing mysterious flying lights in their hills and fields
for thirty years. They also remarked, without any prompting on
my part, that "big cargo planes" came over the hills a couple of
times each month, and "sometimes they're so low we think they're
going to crash." These "cargo planes" are multi-engined and a dull
gray color. The area does not lie on the direct route between the
distant Ohio AF bases and the Charleston, West Virginia, airport.
Furthermore, hedge hopping over the treacherous hills and
mountains of Ohio-West Virginia would be foolhardy.

In his report to the Armed Services Committee Hearing on
Unidentified Flying Objects (April 5, 1966), an engineer named
Raymond Fowler outlined his investigation into the sightings
around Exeter, New Hampshire, and stated: "On my first two visits
to the Carl Dining field [where UFOs had been sighted previously]
on the morning of September 11, 1965, I saw a low-flying C-119

---

*   There have been many UFO sightings of objects described as having a
roughened or stippled exterior. Obviously any kind of lumpy or irregular surface
would present considerable drag and greatly reduce the potential speed of the
object. Modern airplanes are made with as smooth a surface as possible. Even
exposed rivet heads can cut down speed appreciably.

Flying Boxcar pass over the area on both occasions."

During my own extended field investigations people in many scattered areas far removed from AF bases described flying boxcars to me. They were nearly all seen at very low levels, sometimes performing intricate and hazardous maneuvers. For a long time I suspected that the Air Force was sending special instrument-laden planes into flap areas to take photographs and perform various tests. But eventually the circumstantial evidence mounted, and I had to discard this plausible theory for an implausible one, *i.e.,* that aircraft *resembling* C-119s were being deployed in flap sectors, but they weren't related to the Air Force.

Smaller planes of the single-engine type are also frequently observed at low altitudes, sometimes flying back and forth in search patterns over places where UFOs have been seen to alight. As usual, these little planes are gray and unmarked. They have been reported in Texas, Florida, and West Virginia by competent witnesses, some of whom have studied them with binoculars. Like their larger counterparts, they fly at night with their cabins fully illuminated, and they have often been seen hedge hopping in rainstorms and blizzards at night when no private pilot in his right mind would even consider taking off. This inclement-weather flying is a historical pattern.

In March 1968, experienced UFO watchers in Point Pleasant, West Virginia, told me of seeing a formation of low-flying UFO-type lights over Highway 62 at night in a raging snowstorm. Directly behind the lights there was a small single-engined plane, keeping close on their heels despite the high winds and billowing snow.

The year before, early in April 1967, I had pursued a peculiar flying light from the TNT area, an abandoned World War II ammunition dump, north of Point Pleasant to the steep hills behind Henderson, West Virginia. I joined a cluster of people on a hilltop just as a twin-engined plane circled and flew directly at us at treetop level. As it drew closer, *it cut its engines* and glided over our heads—an idiotic maneuver when flying the treacherous updrafts surrounding the steep hills and valleys. The cabin was brilliantly illuminated, and the pilot was visible. Because it was about 9 P.M. and pitch-dark, this seemed doubly stupid. Here we had a pilot who was flying at treetop level over very dangerous terrain, yet he deliberately cut his engines and blinded himself by turning on his cabin lights!

I sprang into a car and dashed across the Ohio River to the little airfield at Gallipolis, Ohio, to see if the mad flier had landed there. The field was deserted, and none of the parked planes had a warm engine. In any case, few sensible private pilots care to indulge in low-level night flying, and few would be willing to risk their licenses by performing stupid and dangerous stunts over populated areas.

The Mystery Planes of 1934

A Swedish researcher, Mr. Ake Franzen, has recently been going through the Stockholm newspapers of the 1930s, piecing together the many fragments of the forgotten Scandinavian flap of 1932-38. He has uncovered more than ninety detailed reports thus far and has tediously translated them into English for us. They form a startling picture.

Beginning in 1932, large unmarked airplanes began to appear over northern Sweden, Norway, and Finland. They were always described as gray. They frequently appeared during raging blizzards and circled towns, railroads, forts, and ships at sea. Very often these planes would cut their engines while they circled. Many of the descriptions were of huge, multi-engine machines. One group of five witnesses declared they had seen a giant plane with eight propellers. In several accounts, groups of three planes were sighted at one time.

There were almost no private planes operating in Scandinavia at that time. The giant China Clipper was still under development in the United States, and the clumsy Ford trimotor had cornered the market and was being used by the few commercial airlines then operating. In 1926, Admiral Byrd and Floyd Bennett had flown a Fokker trimotor from Spitsbergen, Norway, to the North Pole. Their flight had received considerable publicity in Scandinavia at the time, and photos of their plane had been widely published. Six years later, when the mystery planes began to appear, many of the witnesses compared the craft to Byrd's Fokker.

The Swedish government took these reports most seriously. In 1934, no less than twenty-four Swedish Air Force biplanes were sent to the isolated, thinly populated sections where the "ghost fliers" were being reported. A thorough search by land, sea, and air was held. Conditions were so hazardous that two of the Swedish planes crashed during the search.

I will try to summarize some of the main events of this flap. Our sources are the following newspapers: *Dagens Nyheter, Stockholms-Tidningen, Vasterbottenskuriren, Norrbottens A Ilehanda, Hudiksvalls Tidningen,* and the *New York Times.*

A dispatch published on January 22, 1934, described some early sightings:

> Piteå. The permanent curate in Lângtrask has reported that he has been seeing mysterious airplanes in the area for the past two years. Last summer the ghost flier passed over the community twelve times, following the same route each time, southwest to northeast. On four different occasions the plane appeared at very *low* altitude, but no marks or insignia were visible.
>
> Once the plane's altitude was only a few meters above the parsonage. For a few seconds two persons were visible in the cabin. The machine was grayish in color and single-winged.
>
> The curate had not reported this earlier because he thought the flier had been reported by the coastal population.

Published reports are scanty until December 1933, but, as with the 1909 New England reports, we are led to believe that there had been many sightings before that. Our first item briefly describes a sighting on Christmas Eve: "December 24, 1933. Kalix—A mysterious airplane appeared from the direction of the Bottensea about 6 P.M. Christmas Eve, passed over Kalix, and continued westward. Beams of light came from the machine, searching the area."

On December 27, 1933, the *New York Times* devoted almost a full column to the audible appearance of a "mystery airplane" directly over New York City during a fierce snowstorm. At 9:30 A.M. on December 26, people throughout Manhattan heard the sound of an airplane apparently circling overhead in the blinding storm. An NBC newscast mentioned it, and reports were soon telephoned in from all points of the island. The *Times* stated:

> A check of the various calls indicated the flier had gone as far as 72nd street, circled above Central Park, and then proceeded north to the vicinity of 231st Street and Sedwick [sic] Avenue, the Bronx. For a time no further reports came in, but about 2:25 P. M. the sound of the motor was reported over Riverside Drive and 155th Street ...All fields in the Metropolitan district reported there had been no flying during the day, and no stray plane had dropped down from the snowy skies.

The planes of 1933 were simply not capable of operating under such severe weather conditions, nor is it likely that any known plane could have remained aloft for five or six hours in a blizzard. But this one seems to have done so. It was never identified.

There was a similar incident over London, England, in February 1934 (*New York Times*, February 4, 1934).

In Scandinavia, the ghost flier stepped up his activities immediately after Christmas (just as the 1909 flap had occurred during Christmas week). It was seen flying back and forth over the Norwegian border, with reports coming in from Tarnaby, Sweden, and Langmo Vefsn, Norway. On December 28, 1933, the Swedish Flying Corps No. 4 was ordered to Tarnaby to begin an investigation.

A minor mystery developed when Lieutenant Georg Engelhard Wanberg of the artillery regiment in Gotland, Norway, set out on skis from Tannas for a trek to Storlien, which would take him through the heart of ghost-flier country. He was never heard from again. Search parties, including planes from the Norwegian Air Force, looked for him in vain. On January 4, 1934, a group of three men started out to find him. They failed to return on schedule, and new rescue parties were organized to look for them. The trio had vanished.

Even the *New York Times* was licking its chops over the growing mystery. On January 10, 1934, the *Times'* Stockholm correspondent reported:

> The Swedish Air Force has already lost two airplanes, without loss of life, in efforts to locate the base of the strange plane. Concern is now felt for Lieutenant Wanberg who disappeared on foot on Christmas, and for a party of three skiers forming a rescue party. Military headquarters reported today that the search for the four along the Norwegian border had been fruitless.

The three missing men turned up suddenly at the New Styl Station on January 12. The newspapers did not explain their overlong period of absence. No published interviews with them have been located.

Lieutenant Wanberg's tent was found on January 17, and his frozen body was discovered two or three miles from the campsite. Although fierce blizzards had been raging in the area, he had left his skis and all of his equipment in his tent and had gone into the mountains on foot to meet his death. There were no further published reports or explanations of this sequence of events.

What impelled an experienced skier and outdoorsman to abandon his equipment and head into the mountains on foot?

We'll never know.

While Lieutenant Wanberg was wandering around the mountains of northern Norway, the ghost flier was busying himself over three countries. Approximately one-third of all the published reports of January-February 1934 were of sightings made on Sundays. The Swedish officials openly referred to the ghost flier as "the Sunday flier." Several landings were reported in scattered areas. These all took place on Wednesdays. Traces were found in the snow at some of these landing sites, suggesting that the mystery planes were equipped with skis.

There were many mass sightings involving the populations of whole villages and cities. The planes frequently flew over during snowstorms, sometimes circling low over villages and projecting powerful searchlights at the ground.

Let's run down some of the many correlative factors in these incidents (compiled from the previously named newspapers):

1. Sunday, December 31, 1933. Mr. Olof Hedlund, "a reliable man with a good reputation," saw "a large gray airplane, bigger than any Army plane" circle the Sorsele railway station three times at 3:45 A.M. "It was single-winged and enclosed, like a passenger plane, and was equipped with pontoons or some sort of skis... No marks or insignia were visible." (It was a night of the full moon. Clear skies.) "The engine stopped during the turns over the village."

2. Wednesday, January 10, 1934. At 6 P.M. people in Tarna saw a brilliant object at an altitude of 1,000 feet. Turned and headed toward Arjeplog. Fifteen minutes later people in Arjeplog heard airplane engines and left their homes to watch it pass.
Then, at Rortrask, northeast Norsjo, the plane appeared, and witnesses "observed the engine stop three times as it passed directly over them... The machine was flying so low that the whole forest was bathed in its light."

3. Wednesday, January 10, 1934. Trondheim, Norway. "Two landings of the ghost fliers were reported from northern Norway Wednesday evening. One machine landed near the island of

Gjeslingen, outside Rorvik, and the other at a place called Kvaloj in the area Namndal. The report from Gjeslingen says that the people there saw a great beam of light and heard the sound of a strong engine. The machine landed and remained on the water quietly for an hour and a half. Its light went out after it landed."

A Norwegian cruiser, the *Eagle*, was sent to the area, but the plane was gone when it arrived.

4. Sunday, January 21, 1934. "At 6 P.M. Sunday evening a crowd of people in Bengtsforsen, Jämtland, saw a very bright light in the sky. It was the size of a half-moon and traveled very fast. The roar of an engine was heard during the sighting. In Indal, west of Bengtsforsen, a light appeared after 6 P.M. A large crowd heard it and watched as the light circled the area for ten minutes before vanishing in the west."

To the dismay of the Swedish military authorities, these planes chose to circle railways and forts (particularly the fort at Boden) and other strategic areas. Many of the sightings were of lights only, often described as blinding, and the old familiar "searchlight" was described in one account after another.

When a large gray airplane chose to circle low over the Norwegian freighter *Tordenskiold* outside of Tromso, Norway, on Tuesday, January 23, 1934, it projected a blinding beam of light onto the ship's deck "lighting it up like daylight." Captain Sigvard Olsen said the pilot was visible in the illuminated cabin and that he wore a hood and big eyeglasses or goggles.

The known part of the flap really began in earnest on Saturday, January 6, with many simultaneous sightings throughout Sweden. There were other peaks on Monday, January 8; Wednesday, January 10; Saturday, January 20; Sunday, January 21; Tuesday, January 23; Thursday, January 25; Tuesday, February 6; and Sunday, February 11. Published reports in February declined sharply as the military authorities moved into the flap areas and began in-depth investigations. These investigations were apparently most thorough, for the Swedish, Finnish, and Norwegian defense

departments took a very dim view of the whole situation. Their air
territories were being invaded. From the sighting data it is apparent
that many airplanes were involved, not just one or two. Most of
these planes were larger than ordinary military planes, and they
were able to operate in foul weather over treacherous mountainous
territory. Such an operation called for well-equipped bases staffed
with mechanics and linked to supply lines to provide the necessary
fuel, spare parts, and logistical needs. Despite a thorough search
by the armed forces of three countries, no such bases were ever
discovered.

Aircraft carriers were still being developed, and the ones then
available could handle only a few small biplanes. In 1942, the
United States modified the carrier *Hornet* to transport General
Doolittle's twin-engined B-25s to the coast of Japan, where they
launched their raid against Tokyo. But the B-25s could not land
again on the carrier and had to fly on to China.

Hitler had just come into power in 1933, and the Luftwaffe did
not yet exist. The Soviet Union did not have the planes or, more
important, the motivation for such a senseless series of maneuvers
over Scandinavia. Besides, the risks of an international incident
were tremendous. If one of these planes had crashed and had been
found to be the property of any foreign power, the overflights
would certainly have been regarded as an act of war.

For some peculiar reason, the *New York Times* suggested that
Japan was the culprit. But none of the Scandinavian newspapers
even mentioned Japan in connection with the ghost fliers. Japan
was having trouble with China at that time and would have had
neither the capability nor the motivation for the operation.

For a time early in the flap, the Swedish newspapers toyed with
theories about liquor smugglers flying around the North. But the
official investigations completely ruled out the smuggler theory.

As with the waves of 1896-97 and 1909, the 1934 flap featured
random low-level flights of recognizable objects and hundreds of
flights of high-altitude lights carrying out seemingly intelligent
maneuvers. The mystery airplanes were the "hard" objects used to

provide a frame of reference for the more numerous "soft" objects being deployed throughout the northern latitudes. Witnesses saw and reported definite airplanes carrying red, green, and white lights. When brilliant red, green, and white lights were seen at higher altitudes, it was assumed that they were attached to ghost fliers hidden by distance.

The ghost fliers were capable of astounding maneuvers. The airplanes could cut their engines at low altitudes, sometimes only 100 feet or so in the air, and circle not once but three or four times without power. Try this in a conventional airplane, and you'll end up in a box.

On April 30, 1934, Major General Reutersward, commanding general of upper Norrland, Sweden, issued the following statement to the press:

Comparison of these reports shows that there can be no doubt about illegal air traffic over our secret military areas. There are many reports from reliable people which describe close observations of the enigmatic fliers. And in every case the same remark has been noted: No insignias or identifying marks were visible on the machine …It is impossible to explain away the whole thing as imagination. The question is: Who are they? And why have they been invading our air territory?

When all of the well-described ghost-flier sightings of 1934 are laid out on a map, their route becomes clear. They seemed to have followed a great arc week after week, circling southward into northern Norway, sweeping across Sweden, and heading north again over Finland. If they were following such an arc, the upper part of the circle had to lie somewhere in the Arctic Ocean, perhaps in the vicinity of the very thinly populated island of Spitsbergen. An alternate route could have brought them from northern Greenland. There have been many interesting sightings in Greenland. (In Chapter 1 we discussed a major event in which a formation of objects was picked up on radar as they swept westward over Greenland.)

The hundreds of UFO flights seemingly emanating from the Arctic regions and following routes south have helped reinforce the popular theory that flying saucers are coming from a hole in the North Pole. The Aerial Phenomena Research Organization has advanced the theory that the objects enter the earth's polar regions from space in order to avoid the intense radiation belts that are concentrated in space above the temperate zones.

Radio Signals from Nowhere

Enigmatic radio signals were widely received throughout Sweden and Norway during the flights of the ghost fliers. These also became a topic of discussion in the press.

A widely published dispatch datelined Umea, Sweden, January 11, 1934, noted: "Members of the headquarters of the Air Force are of the opinion that the mystery airplanes are equipped with wireless transmitters and radio navigational aides… The airplanes are part of an extraordinary organization."

An item in the *Hudiksvalls Tidningen*, January 1, 1934, states:

Radio listeners in Umea have been receiving conversations on their loudspeakers containing information about the ghost fliers, indicating that their intelligence service is modern …The conversations are on the wavelength of a popular gramophone program in Umea and discussed a meeting at a special point. The broadcast concluded with a discussion of which radio station should be used the next time.*

---

* Reporters investigating the claims of New Jersey UFO contactee Howard Menger, in 1956-57, allegedly discovered that he had a peculiar radio transmitter in a tent on his farm. This transmitter did not project a beam of its own but "hitchhiked" on the signals of conventional AM stations in the area.

At 6 P.M. on Thursday, January 25, 1934, a workman named Hjalmar Hedstrom reportedly picked up the following message on "a lower wavelength" in Norrbyskar, Sweden: "The sea is calm; two degrees warmly; therefore you can go down on the water and catch what you shall have... Returning quarter to eight for further message." There was also a statement on wind direction and position, all in broken Swedish, but Hedstrom couldn't remember all of it.

Another radio listener, in Hedesunda, picked up an identical message that same day. And additional messages were received at the appointed hour of 7:45.

Some messages came over the 900-meter band. Others were received between 230-275 meters.

A majority of all the 1934 sightings took place at 6 P.M., no matter where the locale. The flap died down in March 1934, but there were periodic reports throughout the 1930s. Here's one datelined Harstad, Norway, November 21, 1936:

> Reports of a mysterious light have arrived from several different places. The Norwegian Telegraphic Agency correspondent learned of the sightings during an interview with the Sixth Division. An inquiry into the reports is being conducted by the county constabulary. The division has also received a message about mysterious lights seen Tuesday evening outside Tromso.
>
> There is every reason to believe that the observations are real. During the last sighting in upper Norway many people received mysterious radio signals.

This Swedish report suggests that someone in the Umea sector was utilizing a similar device in 1934, using the output of a regular radio station to power "pirate" signals.

The ghost fliers returned to Scandinavia in 1936, following the same routes and patterns of the 1934 sightings. They were again accompanied by baffling radio signals. The *New York Times* correspondent, who had tried to blame Japan in 1934, now accused Germany of broadcasting the signals. But none of the Scandinavian newspapers mentioned Germany in connection with the planes or the radio signals.

When a brilliant glowing object pursued a railroad train across the Midwest in 1937, the *New York Times* (August 15, 1937) quoted astronomers who explained the incident as being caused by Venus.

I hardly need mention that the populations of northern Scandinavia are very familiar with the northern lights and other routine atmospheric and astronomical phenomena. It is unlikely that they would pay too much attention to something that seemed to have a natural explanation.

We have two widely separated reports from 1937 that deserve notice here. On Thursday, February 11, 1937, the crew of the fishing boat *Fram* started out from Kvalsvik, Norway, at 9 P.M. Just outside of Kvalsvik there is a cape with high hills separating it from the mainland. As the Fram circled this cape, they discovered a very large airplane resting on the water. Thinking the plane was in trouble, the captain changed his course and headed for it. Red and green lights were glowing on the machine, but as the boat approached, the lights were suddenly extinguished. Then the plane was quickly enveloped in a cloud of smoke, and it vanished!

At noon the next day, Friday, February 12, 1937, an unknown aircraft appeared over Vienna, Austria, and circled the city. This event was unusual enough to be widely noted in the European press. Apparently the identity and origin of the plane were in doubt for some reason.

Scandinavia: 1946

On June 10, 1946, objects "resembling German V weapons" passed over Finland. Within a few short weeks UFO-type lights, cylindrical objects, and unidentified winged machines were being seen by thousands of people throughout Norway and Sweden, with the greatest concentrations taking place in the bleak, sparsely populated north country. The European press played up the stories. "Ghost rockets" had replaced the ghost fliers of 1934. They were seen over Greece, far to the south, and over the mountains of Switzerland, weaving expertly through the valleys and canyons. They were tracked on radar. They were photographed. (One picture of an arrow-shaped streak of light taken near Stockholm was published in the *London Morning Post,* September 6, 1946.) They were measured at speeds of from 400 to 1,000 miles per hour. Some of them seemed to explode in midair. Some released fragments of metal that proved to be common slag.

The British and Scandinavian newspapers openly accused the Soviet Union of testing new rocket weapons in the skies of northern Europe. Moscow denied it. In September, bright green fireballs were seen over Portugal. "Flying projectiles with a tail of flame" flashed over Casablanca. Great glowing things hurtled out of the skies over Oslo, Norway, and exploded with deafening noises. On Wednesday, July 3, 1946, a mysterious explosion shook central Scotland at 9 P.M., blowing out windows and killing one man (apparently by concussion). No source or explanation for the blast was found. Swedish authorities collected more than 2,000 ghost-rocket reports. General James Doolittle flew to Stockholm to join in the investigations, even though this flap was barely mentioned in the American press. London was shaken by a series of explosions that no one could account for.

At the end of August 1946, the lid came down. The *Daily Telegraph* of London reported on August 22: "To prevent technical information from being obtained from the firing of rockets over Denmark, the Danish government has asked newspapers not to name areas where the missiles have been seen."

On August 31, 1946, the *Telegraph's* correspondent in Oslo revealed: "The discussion of the flight of rockets over Scandinavia has been dropped in the Norwegian newspapers since Wednesday.

On that day the Norwegian General Staff issued a memorandum to the press asking it not to make any mention of the appearance of rockets over Norwegian territory but to pass on all reports to the Intelligence Department of the High Command...In Sweden the ban is limited to any mention of where the rockets have been seen to land or explode."

In a brief fifty years, we had gone from mystery inventors to spies and smugglers and then on to Russian secret weapons. Because none of these explanations was ever proven valid, and because the phenomenon continued despite all our explanations, we seemed to have only theories left—the arrival of Martians and Venusians. Already the erstwhile members of the Fortean Society, fans and followers of the late Charles Fort, were warming up in the bullpen. They had the answer even before they knew what all the questions were. You see, it worked out this way: In 1945, we dropped our atom bombs on Japan. The bombs sent a blast of energy into space, where it was detected by the sensitive instruments of superintelligent beings on other worlds. Said beings were terribly concerned that poor, bumbling man had discovered the secrets of atomic energy. So an expedition to the earth was formed to investigate. However, some superintelligent navigator made a slight error. Instead of leading his spaceships down to troubled Japan, he missed by a wide margin and ended up in Scandinavia instead. Sorry about that.

Mystery Helicopters

The thousands of sightings of phantom dirigibles and mysterious airplanes from 1896 to 1938 provide us with a substantial body of evidence which indicates that the phenomenon is actually flexible and that it tailors itself to adopt acceptable forms for the time periods in which it operates. All of this raises a very sticky question for the believers. Did all of these things really exist? Or were all of these thousands of reports merely examples of mass hysteria, journalistic jokes, and misinterpretations of some natural phenomenon?

You can't have both. Either a very large percentage of all these reports are honest and valid—or they are *all* pure poppycock.

If I were writing a book on, say, the Civil War, I would go to these very same sources—old newspapers, historical records, letters of the actual participants—and I would produce a book that would be accepted by scholars and historians with little or no questions asked. But flying saucers have been dragged down by the amateur theorists and thrown into disrepute by the believers in extraterrestrial visitants. Their efforts have produced skeptics who have found the obvious flaws in the beliefs and have therefore decided that all UFO data are equally invalid.

If a farmer of the 1860s fought in the Civil War and left behind a packet of scrawled letters describing his experiences, historians would pounce on those letters and quote them over and over again in scholarly tomes. But if this same farmer saw an unusual object in the skies over California in 1875 and reported it to the local newspaper in the form of a letter, that printed letter would become a source of controversy today. Skeptics would dissect every word and debate the man's frontier semantics.

We must stop asking: Can these things be? And begin asking: Why are there these things?

Misguided souls might make up stories about wonderful spaceships from Mars. But would they make up stories about seemingly conventional airplanes and helicopters? Yes, we have phantom helicopters, too!

On Tuesday, October 11, 1966, a brilliant flying light bobbed over the Wanaque Reservoir in New Jersey. There had been many unusually close sightings in the area prior to this one, but this incident had an added twist. A formation of mystery helicopters turned up minutes after the object left.

"This thing was so bright that it blinded me so bad I couldn't find my car," Wanaque police sergeant Ben Thompson, one of the many witnesses, told Dr. Berthold Schwarz. "It was all white, like looking into a bulb and trying to see the socket, which you can't do …I was totally blinded by that light for about twenty minutes."

Within fifteen minutes after the glowing object departed, a formation of seven helicopters appeared and circled low over the area. They were accompanied by ten or twelve jet airplanes. Lines of cars were parked all around the reservoir, filled with eager UFO watchers. They knew a helicopter when they saw one. But they were all baffled by this unexpected group of choppers. Police sergeant Robert Gordon discussed his own bewilderment: "I've never seen seven helicopters at one time in this area before in all my life … And I've lived here for forty years."

Science writer Lloyd Mallan investigated the Wanaque incidents, and he checked with all the local Air Force bases, airports, and even the Pentagon. All denied knowing anything about these planes and helicopters. The Civil Aeronautics Board was baffled, too. No one could throw any light on the mystery. Nor did it seem plausible that the Air Force could have acted so quickly, particularly because no one ever formally reported any of the Wanaque sightings to the Air Force directly. There are those, of course, who believe that the Air Force lies about everything connected with UFOs. But there aren't seven helicopters available instantly and at one time at the McGuire Air Force Base in New Jersey and the Stewart Air Force Base in New York, the two closest bases. Nor could slow-moving, short-ranged choppers have made it from those two points in fifteen minutes.

The people at Wanaque were convinced they saw helicopters and jets that night. Were they all lying? If so, why? If not, then who was flying these machines, how, and why?

The North Vietnamese are pitifully short on aircraft, especially helicopters. Nevertheless, late in June 1968, a formation of inexplicable lights appeared over the Ben Hai River, and one nonexistent "helicopter" was reportedly shot down. Robert Stokes, *Newsweek*'s Vietnam correspondent, was there. Here's his report (*Newsweek*, July 1, 1968):

It was 11 P.M. and U.S. Army Captain William Bates sat in front of a radio set at his regimental headquarters at

Dong Ha. Just then, a Marine forward observer came on the air reporting that he had spotted, through his electronic telescope, thirteen sets of yellowish-white lights moving westerly at an altitude of between 500 and 1,000 feet over the Ben Hai River which runs through the middle of the DMZ. Bates immediately checked with authorities at Dong Ha to see whether there were any friendly aircraft in the area of the reported sightings. He was told there were not. Then he checked with the counterbattery radar unit at Alpha 2, the northernmost allied outpost in I Corps. Within minutes, the answer came back from Alpha 2's radar tracker: The "blips" were all around him, 360 degrees.

By 1 A.M., U.S. Air Force and Marine jets were scrambling at Pa Nang in pursuit of the unidentified objects. Forty-five minutes later a Marine pilot radioed that he had just shot down a helicopter. But when an Air Force reconnaissance plane, equipped with infrared detectors which pick up heat, flew over the area, it could find no evidence of burning wreckage. All it could confirm, the plane reported, was a "burned spot."

These objects were tracked on radar "nearly every night" over the Demilitarized Zone that June. They were never identified, and there was little reason to believe that they were actually Vietcong aircraft. If they were, the North Vietnamese stopped using them very abruptly, and they haven't been heard from since.

A few weeks after this series of incidents, the mystery helicopters turned up in the state of Maryland. At 8:20 P.M. on the night of Tuesday, August 19, 1968, an oval object with a center band of red and white flashing lights hovered above the Rosecroft Racetrack near Phelps Corner, Maryland. One of the many witnesses, Mrs. Gwen E. Donovan, reported that she also saw at least seven helicopters circling the object. "It struck me as funny," she said, "because I have never seen so many in the sky at one time."

Is the U.S. Air Force secretly chasing flying saucers in lumbering helicopters? We do frequently scramble jets to pursue "unidentifieds," but I've talked with a lot of AF personnel and have never even come across any rumors about the use of helicopters.

Helicopters are expensive machines, and they're difficult to fly. The World War II predictions that there would be "a helicopter in every garage" never came to pass because of this. A UFO-chasing operation would demand that several helicopters were readied and fueled at all times, and that properly trained pilots were on constant alert and available to fly them. I've snooped around AF bases looking for evidence of such an operation—and have drawn a complete blank.

I can only conclude that these unidentified helicopters fall into the same category as the ghost fliers of 1934 and the tiny aircraft of Calgary. They are part of the UFO activities, not part of our UFO-chasing operations.

Do Flying Saucers Really Exist?

Thousands of UFO photos have been taken since 1882. Many of these are of indistinct blobs and streaks of light, but many are of apparently solid machines of some sort, with windows, fins, and other clearly discernible features. There's just one problem. With very few exceptions, no two UFO photographs are alike. I have received hundreds in the mail and have been shown hundreds more in my travels. Because photos are too easy to fake and too hard to authenticate, I usually avoid getting involved in an in-depth investigation of the pictures and their photographers. I have yet to personally handle two exactly similar photos taken in two different areas.

During these past three years I have conducted thousands of investigations in person, by telephone, and by mail, and while many of the descriptions of the luminous, flexible "soft" objects are exactly the same, I have rarely heard two independent witnesses describe separate seemingly solid "hard" objects in the same terms. I have been told about tiny "buzz-saw" devices, whirling "chains" over strip mines in Ohio, and gigantic gondola-shaped machines with "rows and rows of windows" hovering above the Kittatinny Mountains of northern New Jersey. There seem to be as many different kinds of objects as there are witnesses. Yet I have managed to reassure myself again and again that the witnesses were reliable and were describing the objects to the best of their abilities.

Because the witnesses seem to be telling the truth, we must assume that UFOs come in myriad sizes and shapes. Or no real shapes at all. This leads us to the old psychological warfare gambit once more. If the phenomenon has built-in discrepancies, then no one will take it seriously. If people in Brazil, Iowa, and Australia all gave exactly the same descriptions, then the scientific and military establishments would have to take the subject far more seriously.

Project Blue Book Report No. 14 tackled this problem. Air Force teams ran 434 "unidentified" reports through a computer, hoping to come up with a basic model. They ended up with 12 very different basic objects. From the thousands of reports compiled since then, it is obvious that there may be 1,200 or 12,000,000 different types. The 12 objects described in *Report No. 14* have rarely been seen since 1955.

So there may not be any types at all!

Our UFO catalog now contains flying cubes, triangles, hexagons, doughnuts, spheres, objects shaped like giant metal insects, and transparent flying jellyfish. We've got UFOs with wheels, with wings, with antennas, with pointed domes, flat domes, no domes at all. We've got objects of every color of the spectrum. There have been giant, multi-windowed "cigars" spitting blue fire from their tails ("Obviously a spaceship—a mother craft," the cultists tell us). We've got wheel-less automobiles cruising along deserted backroads a few inches above the ground. And we have unmarked airplanes and unidentified helicopters and jets flitting about flap areas. We have just about everything except a basic assembly-line model that has appeared consistently in many years and in many places.

In other words, we have thousands upon thousands of UFO

sightings that force two unacceptable answers upon us:

1. All the witnesses were mistaken or lying.

2. Some tremendous unknown civilization is exerting an all-out effort to manufacture thousands of different types of UFOs and is sending all of them to our planet.

The governments of the world have seized upon variations of the first explanation. The UFO enthusiasts accept the second.

I do not accept either one.

Instead, I propose a third alternative. I think that some "hard" objects definitely exist as Temporary Transmogrifications. They are disk-shaped and cigar-shaped. They leave indentations in the ground when they land. Witnesses have touched them and have even been inside of them. These hard objects are decoys, just as the dirigibles and ghost planes of yesteryear may have been decoys to cover the activities of the multitudinous soft objects. My real concern is with these soft objects. They hold one of the keys to the mystery.

There are countless sightings of objects that changed size and shape in front of the viewers or split into several smaller objects, each going off in a different direction. In some cases, this process was reversed, with several small lights converging together to form a single large one, which then went dashing off. Over and over again, witnesses have told me in hushed tones, "You know, I don't think that thing I saw was mechanical at all. I got the distinct impression that it was alive."

Researchers such as John Bessor and Ivan T. Sanderson have openly discussed the possibility that some UFOs may, indeed, be living creatures. It's a mixed bag. You can take your choice. Every belief can be supported to some degree, but in the final analysis, when you review all of the evidence, none of them can be completely proven beyond a reasonable doubt.

8
Charting the Enigma

At approximately 8:15 P.M. on Monday, April 25, 1966, a brilliantly illuminated object flashed across the Canadian border and sailed majestically southward over the northeastern United States. It was seen by millions of people along the Atlantic seaboard. Astronomers and amateur photographers took excellent color pictures of it, some of which were later published in *Life, Newsweek,* and newspapers all across the country. It was so bright that it lit up the countryside like daylight as it arced gracefully overhead.

It was quickly explained as a meteor. The explanation made sense to those who saw it, and so the whole incident was forgotten.

However, I spent many months collecting reports of this object and assembling the whole story. Thousands of actual unidentified flying objects are erroneously explained away as meteors every year. Usually no one bothers to collect these meteor reports, lay them out on a map, and study them properly. Astronomers seem least interested of all.

Meteors and comets are vitally important to our study of unexplained aerial phenomena. They reveal patterns which indicate that they follow precise routes year after year and even operate on a predictable timetable. This certainly suggests an intelligent plan of some sort. This plan is part of a larger one. I must stress once again that we cannot understand the broad spectrum of UFO events until we have studied each of the smaller parts.

The newspapers had quite a bit of fun with that 1966 meteor. It came right on the heels of the enormous nationwide UFO flap of March-April. Two men in Hector, New York, said that after the object passed over, they found rocks in their fields which were warm and "felt funny" when they touched them. The rocks were turned over to the sheriff in Watkins Glen, New York, for examination. Mrs. Joseph Powlis was one of the thousands who watched the thing from New York City. She said, "I thought it was a jet—a Roman candle-like thing." A woman in Baltimore, Maryland, described it as "orange and blue and red, and it left sparks—oh, it was lovely." A man in Asbury Park, New Jersey, called the *Press* office and declared, "I could see a head peering out of a porthole."

In Pikesville, Maryland, a state trooper told reporters that there had been reports of plane crashes in sixteen counties. "In the old days," he chuckled, "everyone would have said, 'Oh, what a beautiful meteor,' but now everyone is hoping that little men from Mars are landing."

On a highway near Towanda, Pennsylvania, Robert W. Martz and a friend saw the object scoot overhead. Simultaneously, their automobile engine stalled, and the headlights went out. Both men complained of feeling a wave of heat as they watched "a very awesome, huge flaming body which lit up a large area, visible for a few seconds. Then the second view was of a dark object. The huge flames went out like turning off an electric bulb for a few seconds. There was a dim light in four portholes, and then all darkness. It looked like it was 250 feet in front of us and 250 feet up, and it could go at terrific speed."

Something dropped out of the sky that night onto the grounds of the Salvation Army Camp near Upland, Pennsylvania. A group of boys watched a strange blue light descend into the woods, and John Wesley Bloom was the first to reach it. It smelled like burning rubber, was about two feet long, a foot high and a foot wide when they first saw it, the boys reported. Young Bloom claimed that something got into his eyes and blinded him. His friends had to help him home. His mother later told reporters that his face "was red and his eyes were swollen" and she placed cold compresses on his eyes. The next day there was a crimson blotch on his cheek.

The Upland object burned itself out. The next day searchers found a small coal-like lump at the spot. Dozens of other youngsters substantiated the story, according to a lengthy report published in the Delaware County *Times* on April 27, 1966. But Dr. I. M. Levitt, director of the Franklin Institute's Feis Planetarium, declared, "I just don't believe it. Meteorites do not continue to burn when they reach earth."

Dr. Thomas C. Nicholson, chairman of the Hayden Planetarium, said that the object "was probably ten thousand times brighter than the brightest star seen at night." He estimated that it must have weighed "several hundred pounds."

However, Dr. Fred L. Whipple, director of the Smithsonian Astrophysical Observatory in Cambridge, Massachusetts, disagreed with his colleague and announced that "it must have been less than the size of a football."

Although many of the witnesses claimed it moved slowly across the sky—slow enough so that photographers were able to snap pictures of it—one scientist estimated that it was traveling at thirty-five miles per second. It disappeared over the Atlantic after coursing across the Carolinas.

Thousands of miles away, in the far-off Soviet state of Tashkent, a Soviet scientist named Galina Lazarenko was awakened at 5:23 A.M. on April 26, 1966, by a brilliant flash of light.

"The courtyard and my room were brightly lighted up," she said later. "It was so bright that I could clearly see all the objects in my room."

Simultaneously, an engineer named Alexei Melnichuk was walking down a Tashkent street when he heard a loud rumble followed by a blinding flash.

"I seemed to be bathed in white light that extended as far as I could see," he recalled. "I was forced to shield my face with my hands. After a few seconds, I took my hands away from my face, and the light was gone."

Moments later the great Tashkent earth fault shuddered and buckled, and a tremendous earthquake struck, killing ten and leaving 200,000 people homeless. As the dazed and terrified residents staggered into the rubble-strewn streets, they saw strange "glowing spheres floating through the air like lighted balloons."

There is a nine-hour time difference between our Atlantic seaboard and Tashkent. Furthermore, Tashkent is at exactly the same latitude and longitude as the northeastern United States, precisely on the opposite side of the earth. We were watching that "meteor" cruising overhead at *exactly the same time* that a brilliant and inexplicable flash of light was announcing the impending disaster in Tashkent. These correlations are exact. Our "meteor" and the Tashkent earthquake occurred simultaneously on opposite sides of the earth!

What kind of coincidence was this?

An hour before the Tashkent quake, a schoolteacher living near the fault said that her dog began to howl, and that when the quake began, the dog ran to the door before each shock struck. Scientists have long been puzzled by the apparent ability of animals—particularly dogs and horses—to sense impending disasters.

Is it possible that unidentified flying objects may have some tenuous relationship to natural disasters? Many baffling cases seem to point to such a relationship, particularly in Europe and South America. Dr. Martin D. Altschuler contributed an interesting paper on earthquake-related UFOs to the Colorado University *Scientific Study of Unidentified Flying Objects*. He cited several Japanese cases in which spheres of light, powerful beams of light, and assorted fireballs appeared before, during, or after Japanese earthquakes. He suggested that these phenomena resulted from friction—the slippage of rocks, which is as far-out an explanation as visitors from Mars. If static electricity does build up from the slippage of rocks in fault zones, we should easily be able to detect it and thereby predict forthcoming quakes. Alas, this is not the case.

Large numbers of UFOs were reported over Algeria shortly after the tragic quakes of September 9 and 26, 1954 (1,100 dead; 2,000 injured). When a very heavy quake shook eleven counties in England on February 11, 1957, five "tadpole-like objects" were reported over the towns of Leicestershire and Nottinghamshire. The former was the epicenter of the quake. The descriptions of the witnesses hardly sound like descriptions of electrical phenomena produced by rocks rubbing together.

Flying saucer sightings have been numerous and spectacular around the great San Andreas Fault in California since 1896.

Another "meteor" was followed by earth tremors when it zipped in over the Gulf of Mexico early on the morning of Wednesday, March 27, 1968. It was first sighted by the crew of the tanker *Alfa Mex II* who described "two or three objects in the center of a bright ball of fire." The crew of the Mexican warship *Guanajuato* also reported seeing a flaming object, and the men of both ships said the waters of the Gulf were churned into fountains of spray after the object passed. This could mean that whatever it was, it was exerting a direct gravitational pull.

At 2:10 A.M. that morning, residents in Veracruz, Mexico, about twenty-five miles from the ships' positions, were awakened by a deafening rumbling noise.

"Before I had a chance to realize what was happening," Senora Angelita de Villalobos Arana, forty, told investigators, "it was as bright as day—and the terrible noise kept on... I felt cool, then cold. The light got brighter."

Within minutes, the streets of Veracruz were filled with hysterical people. They thought the end of the world had arrived as the sky filled with unearthly light and the ground trembled. The strange "meteor" loomed over the scene, seemed to dip toward the ground, then rose again and shot off.

Mr. Ernesto Dominguez, head of the Mexican Department of Meteorology of Veracruz, conducted a careful investigation and collected all of the reports.

"This probably was not a meteorite," he stated in his official summary. "We cannot say for sure just what it was. We do know that it did not fall to earth or collide with the earth.

"Its trajectory was curved. Imagine a jet or a spaceship suddenly going out of control and plunging down directly toward earth. Then—as if control was regained suddenly—the object or objects suddenly veered away from the earth, only moments before collision point, and went out over the Gulf of Mexico. But I think it did not fall into the sea. It could have gone upward.

"A meteorite would hardly do such a thing."

These peculiar "meteors" and green fireballs have been turning up in increasing numbers for the past fifteen years. They usually look like the astronomer's concept of meteors and comets, with a long tail dangling behind, but their maneuvers and the many physical effects accompanying their passage rule out a simple natural explanation. They are far more numerous than the intriguing flying saucer-type reports of metallic circular objects. In fact, the reports of mysterious lights and unlikely meteors form the major body of our neglected "soft" sightings. Furthermore, they pop up year after year in the same isolated, thinly populated areas. Natural meteors could hardly be so selective. And meteors don't change direction or angle of descent.

The object seen and photographed over the Northeast in April 1966 had a long corkscrew-like tail. This is a commonly reported feature. There are innumerable historical references to this same identical phenomenon. A member of the North Jersey Highland Historical Society recently came across an interesting meteor report published in *The Journal of Thomas Hughes*, the daily diary of a British officer who served with General Burgoyne during the Revolutionary War. On page 76, he stated: "November 21, 1779. A strange meteor was seen in the south, just as the sun went down. It appear'd like a ball of fire and left a long trail of light-something like the turnings of a corkscrew-visible for near an hour."

A meteor visible for "near an hour"!

Our nonconforming "meteors" appear repeatedly in places like Nebraska, Michigan, Canada, New Mexico, and Arizona. Professor C. A. Chant of the University of Toronto made a study of a train of meteors that roared across Canada on the night of Sunday, February 9, 1913. Unlike natural meteors, the fiery red objects traveled slowly across the sky in a straight horizontal line. They glided majestically out of the northwest and soared away to the southeast.

"Other bodies were seen coming from the northwest," the

professor wrote, "emerging from precisely the same place as the first one. Onward they moved at the same deliberate pace. In twos or threes or fours, with tails streaming behind them they came... They traversed the same path and headed for the same point in the southeastern sky..."

Very odd meteors, indeed!

The year 1913 was just one of the recently rediscovered UFO flap years, with all kinds of strange objects being reported in the sky.

The late Morris K. Jessup, a professional astrophysicist, was especially interested in the fireball-comet-meteor reports and studied them extensively. In his book, *The UFO Annual* (1956), he described many of the meteor reports of 1955 and had this to say:

We are having an influx of fireballs, and these have had an unusual amount of attention because of their number, brilliance, and the Kelly-green color of some of them. There does, indeed, seem to be something queer about them... For the record, it might be stated that the green fireball flurry did not originate in the United States, but apparently in Sweden [1946]. This was a few years ago and essentially before the greatest intensity of interest in UFO or saucers. They were then thought to be Russian rockets or missiles; and to this day we cannot prove that they were not Russian. In the United States the green fireballs made their debut in New Mexico and were thought to be associated with atomic energy experiments. Now, however, they have spread over much of North America and, frankly, we don't know what they are nor why, nor from where.

Odd "Meteor" Patterns

Toward sunset on the evening of Wednesday, April 18, 1962, a giant reddish object appeared over the northern part of New York State, apparently moving down from Canada in a southwesterly direction. Air Force radar locked onto the object and carefully followed it across a dozen states as it sped westward. Then, at 7:30 P.M., a brilliant flash followed by deep rumbles and earth tremors occurred in southwestern Nevada. Shortly afterward an unidentified circular object landed near a power station outside of Eureka, Nevada, and the lights went out for thirty minutes.

Lieutenant Colonel Herbert Rolph of the North American Air Defense Command Center at Colorado Springs, Colorado, faced a throng of excited newsmen that night. He admitted that NORAD's radar had tracked the object all the way across the United States and added, "A meteor can't be tracked on radar—but this thing was!"

What are these "things," and why don't we know more about them? The real problem lies in the scientific attitude. Because the objects do resemble meteors in appearance, astronomers have automatically dismissed them as such and apparently have never made a concerted effort to study these piles of reports filled with embarrassing contradictions. If the "thing" passes over at a high altitude, glows and hauls a tail, then it must be a meteor, according to their reasoning.

Biologist Ivan T. Sanderson went through the trouble of collecting and analyzing the many reports of another "meteor" in 1965. Late on the afternoon of December 9 (Thursday) of that year, sirens screamed and lines of police cars, jeeps, and army trucks converged on a thickly forested area about thirty miles south of Pittsburgh, Pennsylvania. Cordons were set up as teams of men from an unidentified military unit plunged into the woods with Geiger counters and other instruments.

"We don't know what we have here," an Army spokesman told the gathering cluster of reporters and curiosity seekers. "But it looks as if there's an unidentified flying object in these woods."

That was the first, last, and only official statement issued on the luminous blob which had sailed silently over several states, executed a deft 25-degree turn over Ohio, and then plummeted or crashed into a forest outside of Pittsburgh. It first appeared over

Michigan and was apparently high enough to be seen in Indiana, then it scooted across Lake Erie, passing over the tip of Ontario, Canada, and seemed to alter its course in the Ohio sector, shifting toward Pittsburgh. Sanderson estimated that it was traveling about 1,425 miles an hour and that it was less than 50 miles high. The slowest speed ever recorded for a genuine meteor was 27,000 miles an hour.

Most of the numerous witnesses scattered in the flight path of this one described it as a brilliant orange sphere.

Not only do our "meteors" refuse to obey the laws and regulations set down for them by our learned astronomers, but they also have an unnerving habit of traveling in formations with a military-like precision.

Northern Texas had its first big UFO flap in 1897, and the darned things have been hanging around the Panhandle State ever since. During the summer of 1951, the citizens of Lubbock, Texas, were enthralled by the aerial lights that were visiting their city night after night. These glowing somethings flew in perfect V formations and were photographed by a young man named Carl Harton on Saturday, August 25, 1951. His series of pictures were widely published and became known as the Lubbock lights. Although the Air Force took the sightings and the pictures very seriously at the time, they later attempted to explain them away as merely being the reflection of the city lights on the bellies of birds flying overhead. Think about this one for a minute. Mr. Hart's little Kodak must have had a most remarkable lens, for it is unlikely that such minor "reflections" would pick up on film at all.

The Great Circle Route

The state of Nebraska has a long and complicated history of UFO sightings. During the heavy but little-publicized flap of July-August 1966, some very definite patterns emerged. On Tuesday, July 5, 1966, at 10 P.M., a group of four witnesses reportedly viewed "a large octagon-shaped object with colored lights... The lights dimmed and brightened, and the object swooped twice over a field and then went back into the air." This took place about three miles northwest of Norfolk, Nebraska.

On the ninth and tenth of July, there were sightings in North and South Dakota, the states north of Nebraska. On July 11 there were several sightings in Iowa, the state bordering Nebraska on the east. The South Dakota sightings took place in the southwest corner of the state, close to the northwest corner of the Nebraskan border. If we had been able to collect this data fast enough, we could have successfully predicted that a flap was due in Nebraska, and statistically the odds were that it would take place on a Wednesday night at 10 P.M.

Shortly after 10 P.M. on Wednesday, July 13, 1966, a blazing object hurtled across the skies, heading southward from the northwest. About 10:10 P.M. scores of people in Muny Park, Cozad, Nebraska, saw "a very bright object with multicolored smaller bright stars trailing it."

If it had remained on that course, it would have angled straight across Kansas, and all of the later Kansan reports would have described a northwest to southeast course. However, a flood of reports from Kansas, including sightings by policemen, attorneys and many others, described the "meteor" as passing from northwest to northeast. This meant it had to be skirting the Nebraska-Kansas border.

There was a particularly heavy concentration of reports from Central Nebraska from small communities such as Scotia, Ord, Burwell, Comstock, Arcadia, and North Loup. All of these were consistent, describing the object as passing from southwest to southeast. Another cluster of sightings was reported from the Omaha area on the eastern tip of the state. These all stated that the object was going from southwest to southeast.

A larger picture can be drawn from this. The "meteor" came from the northwest, perhaps from Wyoming or South Dakota; it then executed a turn somewhere south of Cozad, bringing it over Kearney, Nebraska, and moved along the Nebraska-Kansas border toward Missouri-Iowa. Then it turned again and headed northward toward Illinois.

The sheriff of Warren County, Illinois, was sitting in front of the police station in Monmouth, Illinois, that night when he observed a fiery orange ball arcing across the sky toward the northeast. A few minutes later he received an excited phone call from a Galesburg, Illinois, woman who said she and her three children had been driving along the U.S. 34 bypass when they saw a green light seemingly skirting the treetops. A white-colored fire seemed to burst from it, she reported, and it appeared to dive toward the ground in the northeast. Thinking that a small plane might have crashed, she stopped at the nearest farmhouse and called the sheriff. He rushed to Monmouth Park, the area of the sighting, but found nothing. Eight other persons in the region called radio stations and newspapers to report similar sightings. All agreed that the object was green with a red ring around it and trailed a short red tail. One other person besides the sheriff reported seeing an orange object. Everyone reported that it first appeared in the southwest and traveled northeast.

What lies to the northeast of Illinois? Michigan, of course.

A few minutes after 11 P.M. Michigan time (10 P.M. Nebraska time), Jack Westbrook and Charles Frye of Willis, Michigan, were walking across Rawsonville Road when Mr. Frye exclaimed, "Look at that!"

Both men saw what appeared to be a silver disk with one red and one white light on it. They estimated that it was no more than 1,000 feet high. The object moved forward swiftly, stopped, seemed to reverse itself, circled around, moved up and down, and finally shot out of sight. They said they watched it for about seven minutes and heard no sound.

"This is not a swampy area," the Ypsilanti, Michigan, *Press* noted when it recounted the sighting on July 15. "And the only possibility of reflection would be from the microwave relay tower which has three red lights, but the object went over the top of it when it left."

Were all the Nebraska, Illinois, and Michigan sightings of

completely different objects independent of one another? This remains a possibility, of course, but once more we are confronted with surprising and unlikely coincidences involving correlations of time and geographical movement. It is highly possible that a UFO—or a group of UFOs—passed from Wyoming, crossed Nebraska, and then turned northward into Illinois and Michigan.

Charles Tougas of the Meteorite Recovery Project at Lincoln, Nebraska, was the man the press turned to for the answer. He said that special cameras had recorded the event, and he estimated that the "meteor" had appeared somewhere near McCook, Nebraska, and had plummeted to earth somewhere outside of Phillipsburg, Kansas, a few miles to the southeast. A search for it was launched at Phillipsburg, but the object was never found. If the "meteor" had enjoyed such a very brief lifespan and had traveled such a very short distance in the western part of the state, it is very unlikely that it would have been so clearly seen in the Omaha sector hundreds of miles eastward and that all of the witnesses would have described it as moving to the southeast. And it certainly would not have turned up in Illinois—still farther to the northeast.

The "meteor" explanation simply does not work in this case. There are too many ifs and too many unnatural coincidences.

All of the descriptions were uniform. A newsman in Brewster, Nebraska, described it as being "the size of a basketball; the white fore end changed colors, going from blue to green, trailing a long tail." A young witness on a ranch near Scotia said it was "round like a basketball, with a brilliant band of orange light encircling it." He said it crossed the southern skies and was visible for about half a minute. Witnesses in York, Nebraska, said it was green, while one report from near Pleasanton, Nebraska, described it as being a "bright, whitish-yellow light." Brilliant white lights were mentioned in a scattering of reports, but the overall consensus was that it was green or "blue-green with a red band around it." Viewers in Kansas thought it was green.

Only two groups of witnesses reported hearing any sound. Both were located in the central Nebraskan cluster. People driving near Arcadia said they saw "a flashing red light" and heard "more than one explosion." George Bremer of Ord reported the same thing. (Viewers of that 1913 "meteor" chain in Canada said that the objects produced a heavy rumbling sound, indicating that they were low enough in the atmosphere to displace the air as they passed.)

One week prior to the Nebraska flap, a "green object with a long white tail" appeared over Muskegon, Michigan, traveling a horizontal path from east to west. It was seen by police officers and other reliable witnesses. The date was Wednesday, July 6, 1966. The time, 11 P.M.

At 10 P. M., Monday, July 11, a round blue object was observed over Lake Erie by witnesses in Ashtabula, Ohio, facing in the direction of Michigan. Some noted that it seemed to have a long tail. One person described it as "a round ball of bright blue light with an outer rim of pale gold." It appeared to descend westward.

When we drew a great circle on a map of the United States, looping through Nebraska and curving up through Monmouth-Galesburg, Illinois, to Michigan, we found that the other end of the curve cut across the northeastern part of Wyoming. A quick review of our clippings and general report data revealed that *that very section of Wyoming* had a UFO flap a few days before the Nebraskan "meteor" arrived. Extensive UFO activity was also reported farther to the northwest around the Glacier National Park in Montana that month. (Great Falls, Montana, has been the site of many UFO spectaculars for the past twenty years.) Brilliant, fast-moving lights appeared in Glacier National Park nightly on precise schedules, passing from the northwest to the southeast. This course would have carried them to the Wyoming flap area and, if extended along a perfect curve, would have continued to Nebraska to the McCook-Cozad sector.

So the plot thickens once again. Our Nebraska "meteor" of July 13 was merely part of an overall flap involving several states, and all of the sightings fitted neatly into a near-perfect circle beginning in northwestern Montana, looping through the Central States, and curving upward through Illinois and Michigan and back into Ontario, Canada, with a bit of overlapping into Ohio, Pennsylvania, and the western tip of New York State—all active flap areas. If we continue the same circle into Canada, we find that the uppermost part of it would rest in the densely forested and sparsely populated regions of northern Manitoba and Saskatchewan. Both of these provinces had long UFO flaps in 1967-68.

Thousands of sightings can be fitted into the "great circle route," and often the dates are staggered so that it does appear that the phenomenon moves systematically from point to point along the route. We were, therefore, not surprised to receive clippings from Canada concentrated along the same circle. For example, on Wednesday, August 7, 1968, Harold Howery, a businessman from Hanna, British Columbia, was driving west from the village of Reveistoke late at night when a circular object suddenly descended about 60 feet in front of his car, swaying from side to side like a pendulum. It was one large light, he said, of a light-blue shade. There was no noise, and his car didn't stall. The object hovered for a few moments and then flew off southward. Southward from Reveistoke would have taken it into the area of the Glacier National Park in Montana.

Circles and Straight Lines

The brilliant French researcher Aimé Michel made a careful study of the French sightings of the 1950s and discovered that the objects often pursued a straight course across France. Sighting reports could be aligned along these routes, and in some cases, the speeds of the objects could be calculated, and other data could be extracted. This finding sent ufologists all over the world scurrying to their maps, and many attempts were made to try to figure out a worldwide route. But eventually it was learned that the straight-line theory was limited and unworkable on a worldwide scale.

France is a small country compared to the United States, and so the distances traveled are much shorter. I made many efforts to work out similar straight-line routes and discovered that UFO sightings within a given area during a specific period of time were confined to sectors with a radius of about 200 miles. The objects sometimes do follow a straight course within these sectors, but they vanish (or no reports are received) outside of the 200-mile boundary.

At first I termed these sectors base areas, but this was misunderstood by many UFO enthusiasts, and soon after my first article on UFO base areas appeared, teenagers everywhere were out scouring the countryside looking for underground UFO hangars. So I adopted the term "windows" as a good substitute.

Every state in the United States has from two to ten "windows." These are areas where UFOs appear repeatedly year after year. The objects will appear in these places and pursue courses throughout the 200-mile limitation. These window areas seem to form larger circles of activities. The great circle from Canada (not to be confused with the traditional geographic Great Circle) in the northwest through the Central States and back into northeast Canada is a major window. Hundreds of smaller windows lie inside that circle. Another major window is centered in the Gulf of Mexico and encompasses much of Mexico, Texas, and the Southwest.

Many windows center directly over areas of magnetic deviation such as Kearney, Nebraska; Wanaque, New Jersey; Ravenna, Ohio. In the 1950s, teams from the national Geological Survey Office quietly flew specially equipped planes over most of the United States and mapped all of the magnetic faults in the country. You can obtain a magnetic map of your locale from the Office of the Geological Survey, Washington, D.C. 20242. If you have been collecting UFO reports in your home state, you will probably find that many of those reports are concentrated in areas where magnetic faults or deviations exist.

UFOs seem to congregate above the highest available hills in these window areas. They become visible in these centers and then radiate outward, traveling sometimes 100-200 miles before disappearing again.

So if you are eager to see a genuine example of our phenomenon, pick a good Wednesday or Saturday evening, visit the highest ground in the area closest to you that has a magnetic fault, and watch the sky around 10 P.M. The best times are the last two weeks in March and the first two weeks in April, all of July-August, the last two weeks in October, and the first weeks in November and December.

Explanations and Contradictions

After having reached a series of conclusions and theories in 1966-67, I was naturally obliged to test them out and determine their validity. So a good part of my research in 1968 was devoted to such experimentation. There was no national UFO furor in 1968. In fact, public interest in the subject declined sharply.

The decline of UFO publicity in 1968 did not mark a decline in sighting reports, however. On the night of March 3-4, 1968, thousands of people in more than twenty states watched weird lights in the sky from 8 P.M. to 4 A.M. One group of men working on the Ohio River near Ravenswood, West Virginia, reported to me that they watched a series of large, luminous globes circle and go through the familiar falling-leaf motions for two hours that morning between 2 and 4 A.M. People driving north on the New Jersey Turnpike from Washington to New York told me that they observed a formation of unusual aerial lights continuously for more than an hour. Innumerable other sightings on that date trickled in from all over the country for months afterward.

The Colorado University report devotes several pages to this minor March flap. Project Blue Book received a total of seventy-eight reports for that night and explained them as being the disintegration of a Soviet satellite—Zond IV—re-entering the atmosphere. Dr. William K. Hartman of Colorado University noted that this alleged rocket re-entry occurred in an area inhabited by 23,000,000 people, so those 78 reports represented a microscopic percentage of the total number of probable observers. Only thirty of those reports were deemed detailed enough for study and analysis, meaning, no doubt, that they occurred somewhere around the same time as the rocket reentry. Such reentries are usually visible for no more than five minutes. The objects quickly burn out in the atmosphere, a process that most often requires less than two minutes. This particular re-entry took place at approximately 9:45 P.M. on Sunday, March 3, 1968, so it could not possibly explain the numerous sightings made before and after 9:45-9:50 P.M.

Dr. Hartman thus attempted to explain thousands of sightings by analyzing thirty that conformed to the rocket re-entry thesis.

This same explanation has now been used by the Air Force for several other flaps, including the worldwide flaps of the summer of 1967. In July 1968, Walter Sullivan, the *New York Times* science editor, published a review of the March 3 sightings, using the rocket explanation and quoting the National Investigation Committees on Aerial Phenomena as claiming that there had been a sharp decline in UFO reports and no significant flaps for two years. Apparently NICAP had not heard of the massive waves in Pennsylvania, Georgia, and New York State in the fall of 1967.

All hell broke loose in South America again in 1968, with innumerable landings, low-level sightings over major cities, and a wide variety of contacts. There was so much UFO news in June 1968 that some newspapers in Argentina had to relegate the story of Senator Robert Kennedy's tragic murder to the inside pages, their front pages being devoted to flying saucers.

Spain also experienced a monumental UFO wave throughout the summer of 1968. Hundreds of people reportedly saw strange formations of flying objects over Malaga, Madrid and the Balearic Islands. On September 8, 1968, a Spanish Air Force jet pursued a glowing pyramid-shaped thing over Madrid for sixty-five minutes, finally losing it at 50,000 feet. It was tracked on radar and photographed.

On the night of Sunday, September 15, another one of our strange "meteors" appeared over the New England states, following the usual northwest to southeast course down from Canada. That week an enormous new flap erupted in the busy Ohio-West Virginia sector. Mrs. Mary Hyre, the Associated Press stringer in

Point Pleasant, was inundated with hundreds of phone calls and sighting reports. She wrote only one newspaper article on the flap. In a telephone conversation that fall, she told me, "I've discovered that the less I write about these things now, the more people tell me what they've seen. Most of them don't want any publicity at all, and if they think I'm going to write up their story, they shy away from telling it."

In Nova Scotia, four boys reported seeing a black circular object dive out of the sky and disappear into the waters of the Cornwallis River dike on the afternoon of September 15. A professor from the National Research Council's meteorite committee interviewed them, and the story appeared in the Halifax, Nova Scotia, *Chronicle-Herald* on September 18. The boys said the object first hovered in the air, "oscillating like a spinning top," before it dipped down into the water. They estimated it was about 15 feet across and 6 feet high. It made no noise, and the water didn't even splash when it submerged.

Elsewhere in Canada, a wave of low-level sightings, landings, and creature appearances took place in the villages around Montreal, Quebec, that week. Canadian researcher Gene Duplantier collected the many reports and prepared a comprehensive summary for his magazine, *Saucers, Space and Science*. Other close sightings occurred on September 13, 16, and 17 in assorted areas in the province of Ontario.

On Wednesday, November 20, 1968, another train of strange lights traversed the British Isles, going from north-northwest to south-southeast. These were formations of multicolored objects with short tails in their wakes. They appeared at approximately 7 P.M. and were seen that night in northwestern Europe as well. One of the many witnesses, Commander V. J. Chown of Woodford, Essex, said the lights appeared "to be assembled as if around an invisible tube, rather like the old *Graf Zeppelin* in shape." He was impressed by the way the objects remained in rigid formation "just like warships." The Royal Observatory at Hurstmonceux watched the lights and identified them as the Russian rocket Cosmos 253 re-entering the atmosphere. Dr. Bernard Finch checked with the Russian embassy in London, and they flatly denied this.

The January Flap

Early in the fall of 1968, I issued a cautious prediction to ufologists around the country, alerting them to the possibility of a new wave of sightings early in January 1969. I had run a thorough study of the flaps of January 1966 and 1967, and had found that January was a neglected flap month. Most researchers concentrated on the months of March-April and July-August. Few were aware of the many other cycles and time patterns involved in the phenomenon.

The January cycle can be traced as far back as 1934, when there was a major wave in Scandinavia. The neglected November-December cycle began in 1896 and was repeated in 1909.

Type 1 Sightings—January 1967
(by states)

Sunday, January 1: No data
Monday, January 2: Tennessee
Tuesday, January 3: California*
Wednesday, January 4: No data
Thursday, January 5: Colorado; Oklahoma; England
Friday, January 6: West Virginia; Vermont
Saturday, January 7: No data
Sunday, January 8: Connecticut; England
Monday, January 9: California; Colorado; Kentucky; Michigan*
Tuesday, January 10: North Carolina; Kentucky
Wednesday, January 11: Michigan; Mississippi; Missouri; Wisconsin
Thursday, January 12: Colorado; Kansas; Michigan; Minnesota; Missouri
Friday, January 13: Kansas*; Missouri

Saturday, January 14: Arkansas; Indiana; Pennsylvania; Australia

Sunday, January 15: Connecticut; Kentucky***; Mississippi

Monday, January 16: Florida; Kentucky**; Kansas*; Oklahoma; Michigan**; Mississippi**; Iowa; North Carolina**; West Virginia

Tuesday, January 17: California; Connecticut; Idaho*; Indiana*; Kansas; Missouri; Nebraska; Oklahoma

Wednesday, January 18: California; Indiana; Kansas; Kentucky; Michigan; Pennsylvania**; Ontario, Canada

Thursday, January 19: Illinois; Mississippi; West Virginia; Washington; Canada**

Friday, January 20: Idaho**; Colorado; Illinois; Missouri; Pennsylvania; West Virginia

Saturday, January 21: California; Kansas*; Michigan; Texas

Sunday, January 22: California; Hawaii

Monday, January 23: North Carolina**; Pennsylvania

Tuesday, January 24: Indiana; Missouri; Oregon; Washington; West Virginia

Wednesday, January 25: Connecticut; Kentucky; New York

Thursday, January 26: California

Friday, January 27: Arizona; Iowa; Canada

Saturday, January 28: Kentucky; Missouri; Ohio

Sunday, January 29: Kentucky

Monday, January 30: Alabama; Connecticut**; Missouri; New Jersey; Oklahoma; Pennsylvania; Canada; England

Tuesday, January 31: New Hampshire

*   Small flap with several sightings.

**   Large flap with many reports throughout the state.

***   Power failure in area during sighting.

Sightings occurred simultaneously in several different widely separated states on the same dates, and no known natural phenomena (meteors and the like) could be applied as a possible explanation. A rocket test in Florida at 4:30 A.M. on January 16 accounted for a very small percentage of reports of sightings made at that time.

My prediction for 1969 was quite specific, for I expected the flap to begin in the Midwest along the perimeter of the great circle and radiate outward into the traditional flap areas of Ohio, Canada, etc. I also calculated that the flap would be preceded or followed by one or more "meteors" in the window areas.

On Tuesday, January 2, 1969, hovering globes of light were seen in three Missouri cities—Joplin, Webb City, and Carterville. These were the usual nonstars performing circular and falling-leaf maneuvers.

At 8:30 P.M. on Tuesday, January 9, a single bright light was observed following the Mississippi River along the border between Missouri and Iowa. The object reportedly paced an automobile from an estimated altitude of 400 feet. It sped ahead, stopped, hovered, and changed to an amber color before darting off.

A deputy sheriff in Green County, Missouri, reported seeing a bright, star-like object at 9:30 P.M. on Sunday, January 12. Other witnesses said the object hovered, moved in circles, and then hovered again.

The beginning of the January 1967 wave also occurred in this region along the Mississippi, although the major sightings of that period were concentrated farther south around Cairo, Illinois, where the Mississippi links up with the Ohio River.

During the first two weeks in January 1969, additional reports started to trickle in from Ohio. Unusual low-flying objects were sighted around Middletown, Ohio, and fireballs were seen by hundreds in the Cleveland area as they seemed to plunge into Lake Erie.

Back in Florida, residents of Jacksonville Beach were puzzled by "mystery clouds" which emitted sounds "like someone walking on pebbles." Police Chief James Alford heard it and ordered Captain Harold Bryan to follow the "cloud." He pursued it to the edge of the Atlantic, where it slowly dissolved into nothingness.

Strange nonstars were also bobbing around the skies of northern New Jersey again. On Wednesday, January 15, a professional man there was awakened by an odd mechanical beeping sound outside his bedroom window. No vehicles, police cars or UFOs were around. But simultaneously his wife, who was attending a civic meeting some miles away, thought she saw an unusual aerial light in the sky.

Random reports slowly built up in Ohio and Illinois. Then, on Sunday, January 26, a "brilliant flash of light" appeared in Wisconsin, following the predicted northwest to southeast course from Canada into Illinois and Iowa. A policeman in Appleton, Wisconsin, said he sighted an orange fireball trailing a plume of blue flame at 12:55 A.M. It seemed to pass directly overhead, he stated. A two-second power failure accompanied the sightings, and witnesses reported "balls of fire dripping from high tension wires."

Seven minutes later pilots at Chicago's O'Hare Airport observed "a smoking orange fireball." One man said he saw two brilliant flashes in succession. Although it took this object seven minutes to travel the 200 miles or so from Appleton, Wisconsin, to Chicago, Illinois, authorities said it was either a meteor or space debris. Take your pick. Man-made satellites travel from west to east (to take advantage of the earth's rotation), not from north to south.

Sightings-January 1969

Here are a few of the other January 1969 sightings that have been received. I am listing only the geographical location, time(s) of sightings, and sources. All these newspaper accounts named witnesses. Some of these objects were viewed by whole communities.

Friday, January 3: Togo, Minnesota; 8 P.M.; Togo, Minnesota, Cook *News Herald* (January 9, 1969).

Monday, January 6: Auburndale, Florida; 6:30 P.M.; Winter Haven, Florida, *News-Chief* (January 7, 1969).

Greenwood, South Carolina; 7 P.M.; Greenwood, South Carolina, *Index-Journal* (January 7, 1969).

Barnwell, South Carolina; no time listed; Barnwell, South

Carolina, *People-Sentinel* (January 15, 1969).

Portage-la-Prairie, Manitoba, Canada; 8-10 P.M.; Portage, Manitoba, *Leader* (January 9, 1969).

Tuesday, January 7: Barnwell, South Carolina; 7 P.M.; repeat of previous night; Barnwell, South Carolina, *People-Sentinel* (January 15, 1969).

Thursday, January 9: Keokuk, Iowa; 8:30 P.M.; Keokuk, Iowa, *Gate City* (January 11, 1969).

Bowling Green, Ohio; 8:30-9:30 P.M.; Bowling Green, Ohio, *Daily Sentinel-Tribune* (January 11, 1969).

Barrington, Cary, Algonquin, and Fox River Grove, Illinois; many witnesses viewed reddish objects throughout the evening; Chicago, Illinois, *Tribune* (January 10, 1969).

Saturday, January 11: Phoenix, Arizona; 10P.M.; Phoenix, Arizona, *Republic* (January 13, 1969).

Monday, January 13: Sault Sainte Marie, Michigan; various witnesses saw object bearing red and green lights from 10:45 P.M. to 1:30 A.M.; Sault Sainte Marie, Michigan, *Evening News* (January 14, 1969).

Thursday, January 16: Coos Bay, Oregon; 6:45 P.M.; Coos Bay, Oregon, World (January 18, 1969).

Portland, Oregon; 7 P.M.; green object traveling from northwest to southeast; Portland, Oregon, *The Oregonian* (January 18, 1969).

Friday, January 17: Jerseyville, Illinois; 12 noon; daylight sighting of circular object; Jersey County *Democrat-News* (January 23, 1969).

Saturday, January 18: Charleston, South Carolina; 7:15 P.M.; Charleston, South Carolina, *Evening Post* (January 20, 1969).

Monday, January 20: Columbia, Mississippi; 8-8:30 P.M.; Columbia, Mississippi, *Columbian Progress* (January 23, 1969).

On the evening of Thursday, February 6, a nauseating, unexplained fog crept over the south side of Houston, Texas. Forty-eight hours later a blinding blue-white fireball thundered across Arizona on a northwest-southeast course and traveled at least 1,000 miles before apparently descending "in the almost impassable terrain of the Sierra Madre." A Chihuahua, Mexico, newspaper editor, Guillermo Asunsolo, said, "The light was so brilliant we could see an ant walking on the floor. It was so bright we had to hide our eyes."

At 1:09 A.M. that morning the good citizens of the little town of Pueblito de Allende were awakened by a blinding flash and a tremendous explosion. A shower of fragments sprayed over a 10-square-mile area, one 40-pound piece just missing the local post office building.

Scientists from the Smithsonian Institution scurried to Mexico to recover the fragments, which they identified as "Type 3 carbonaceous chrondites."Translation: metal fragments containing carbon, which is suggestive of organic (living) matter.

Charles Fort examined many of the meteor reports of the nineteenth century and noted that it seemed odd that these things had a habit of appearing repeatedly in the same areas. He also questioned the validity of the theory that these falling rocks and assorted debris were from outer space. Our astronauts have seen very few things in space that could be classified as rocks or meteors. Early fears that such debris might constitute a serious hazard in space have proven to be groundless. Yet there are quite literally thousands of meteor falls annually, and all kinds of junk have been falling from the sky since ancient times. Not just chunks of rock and metal, but also huge blocks of ice, stone pillars, vast quantities of animal and vegetable matter (including real blood and raw meat). Where is all this garbage really coming from?

There are many well-investigated cases in which rocks and pebbles have actually materialized in rooms and fallen to the floor in great quantities. We can't explain these either, but we must seriously consider the possibility that all—or most—of the debris plummeting out of our skies "materializes" in somewhat the same way. Unidentified falling objects pose as many problems as unidentified flying objects. Perhaps the two phenomena are related in some unfathomable way.

There is something above us. This something has always been there, following the same prescribed courses year after year, adhering to the same timetable for at least a century. To claim that this something is from Mars, Ganymede, or Tau Ceti is as absurd as to claim that ornately carved stone pillars falling into fields in France are debris from the asteroid belt.

We have been so preoccupied with trying to understand and cope with our own immediate environment that we have never really made an effort to come to grips with the greater mysteries that lie on the doorstep of our conventional sciences. A thing appears in the sky glowing and dragging a fiery tail. It shows up at a predictable time in a predictable place, follows a predictable course, executes a deft turn, is picked up on radar, photographed, seen by thousands or even millions of people, then it descends, and automobiles stall and great power stations creak to a halt. But the explanation goes that it looked like a meteor, so it must have been one.

What is a meteor anyway?

For our answers we have turned to the same group of experts who were quarreling among themselves over the consistency of the moon's surface until the moment our first successful probe landed.

9
The Physical Non-Evidence

The amusing little mystery of flying saucers slowly evolves into a complicated series of coincidences and paradoxes as we plunge deeper and deeper into the data, excluding nothing, and considering everything as objectively as possible.

Our skies have been filled with "Trojan horses" throughout history, and like the original Trojan horse, they seem to conceal hostile intent. Several hard facts are now apparent: The objects have always chosen to operate in a clandestine manner, furtively choosing the hours of darkness for their enigmatic activities over thinly populated areas, where the possibility of being detected is slight. Perhaps they choose to remain aloof, or perhaps they are involved in long-range preparations for an overt takeover of our planet at some point in the future. This hostility theory is further supported by the fact that the objects choose, most often, to appear in forms which we can readily accept and explain to our own satisfaction—ranging from dirigibles to meteors and conventional-appearing airplanes. We (the ufologists) have really only paid attention to the eccentrics: the objects of unusual configurations. They undoubtedly constitute a minority, and probably a *deceptive* minority, of all the paraphysical objects flitting about in our atmosphere. In other words, flying saucers are not at all what we have hoped they were. They are a part of something else.

I call that something else Operation Trojan Horse.

Those students of UFOs who have made only a superficial study of the historical data have concluded that when ancient peoples encountered flying saucers or "extraterrestrial visitants," they assumed that the phenomena were of religious origin. However, when you really dig into the early literature, it becomes clear that the ultraterrestrials *deliberately conveyed* this impression in much the same way that the mystery inventor tried to create an acceptable frame of reference for the 1896-97 flap.

The phenomenon is constantly reaching down to us, creating frames of reference that we can understand and accept. Then, whenever we see something unusual in the sky, we accept it within that frame of reference and call it a meteor, an airplane, an angel, or a visitor from outer space. The first step to understanding UFOs is to discard all frames of reference and try to view the phenomenon as a whole.

Our earliest religious and occult records fully describe and define Operation Trojan Horse. We have been told throughout history that ultraterrestrials, or superior humanlike nonhumans, have been "assigned" to walk among us. In the Bible, for example, the prophet Zechariah states that he was visited by angels in 520 B.C. and that, "I saw by night, and behold a man riding upon a red horse, and he stood among the myrtle trees that were in the bottom; and behind him there were red horses, speckled and white.

"Then I said, 0 my Lord, what are these? And the angel that talked with me said unto me, I will shew thee what these be.

"And the man that stood among the myrtle trees answered and said, These are they whom the Lord hath sent to walk to and fro through the earth." (Zechariah 1:7-11)

Further on, Zechariah describes how he saw a cylinder-shaped object in the sky, and the "angel" informed him, "*This is the curse that goeth forth over the face of the whole earth.*" (Zechariah V:1-4) The "angel" continued by describing how the objects literally spy upon every human being.

Until 1848, the religious frame of reference was constantly used by the phenomenon. But as man's technology improved and many of our old beliefs were discarded, the phenomenon was obliged to update its manifestations and establish new frames of reference. The phantom armies and angels so frequently reported in the past were replaced by transmogrifications that appeared to match man's own technological achievements. If huge, multi-engined airplanes of the 1934 Scandinavian type had appeared over San Francisco in 1896, they would have created a far greater stir than the clumsy dirigibles which were used in that flap. By 1909, man had learned to build and fly crude machines, so the new transmogrifications of Operation Trojan Horse took the form of biplanes and carefully flew over the areas where the many "soft" objects were busily engaged in their mysterious enterprises.

Still later, when the source of Operation Trojan Horse found it necessary to deploy "eccentrics" over Scandinavia in 1934, airplanes very carefully flew low over the remote, thinly populated villages so the people could see them clearly and have a frame of reference with which they could explain the many strange lights and searchlights in the sky. As with the earlier flaps, the true nature of the phenomenon was carefully hidden from us.

During World War II, and immediately thereafter, the world's skies were cluttered with all kinds of man-made aircraft ranging from helicopters to blimps. While thousands of UFOs were noticed and reported, many thousands of others probably were not. Cigar-shaped objects were assumed to be sub-chasing blimps. Strange "eccentrics" were regarded as secret weapons being tested.

The cessation of hostilities gave the UFO source a new headache. When, for some reason, it became necessary to revisit Scandinavia in 1946, near-hysteria developed. The objects were thought to be Russian rockets. The world was jittery, and the Cold War was just taking shape. If the ghost-rocket transmogrifications were used in other parts of the world, it was possible that they might even have precipitated a new war. A new frame of reference was therefore necessary.

We were now technologically advanced to a point where some of us, at least, were ready to consider and accept the possible existence of "a superior intelligence with an advanced technology." We were a setup for the modern myth of extraterrestrial visitants.

Beginning in 1947, the great "flying saucer" frame of reference was carefully built up by a long series of spectacular incidents and contacts. The whole structure of these events carefully follows the psychological patterns inherent in the earlier flaps. We were seeing no more—and no fewer—anomalous aerial objects in 1947 than had been seen in 1847. We were simply seeing them in a new way. A new game was being played with us.

Small groups of believers quickly sprang up, even though no one bothered to collect and study the hundreds of UFO reports from June-July 1947 to search objectively for the hidden patterns. These believers immediately accepted the extraterrestrial hypothesis, and they spent the next twenty years advocating the idea. Their research followed a singular line: They labored to prove the reliability of witnesses. This meant that if a police officer or pilot observed an unusual object from a great distance, his report was given precedence over the report of a housewife who saw one land in her own backyard. Some of these cults became obsessed with the search for physical evidence. But their criteria for evidence was very strict. Such evidence had to be nonterrestrial. But this was a vicious circle. If a piece of metal fell from a UFO and proved to be ordinary aluminum, it was discarded. If it proved to be made of a puzzling, unidentifiable alloy, it still proved nothing unless the source could also be proven.

A new game emerged: the artifact or hardware game. This game is well known in the Irish fairy lore. The phenomenon has always obliged us by planting false evidence all over the landscape.

The UFO cultists trapped themselves into a hopeless situation almost from the outset. If the UFOs actually were the product of a superior extraterrestrial civilization, then final proof could only come about in one of two ways:

1. A flying saucer would have to make an error and crash or be captured. Then we would have absolute proof that it existed and was from a superior technology. Since 1947, there have been many rumors of such crashes. Author Frank Scully was told by a contactee type that such a crash had occurred in the Southwest in 1948, and that the Air Force had recovered the object, together with some bodies of tiny humanoids. He published this bit of hearsay, and it has become a major ufological myth. The Air Force still receives letters from people asking if it is true that these bodies

are pickled in a bottle somewhere in the AF archives.

2. The ufonauts must, themselves, come forward with the final evidence by landing in a public place, in front of many witnesses, and by entering into direct communication with the heads of state. There have been many reported landings, but, as with the landings of 1897, all of these have taken place in secluded spots with a minimum of witnesses. The apparent purpose of most of these landings seems to have been *to advance belief in the frame of reference*, not to provide absolute proof that the frame of reference is authentic.

After twenty years of this game, it does not seem too likely that such proof will ever be forthcoming. So we must content ourselves with an examination of the actual physical evidence that has been produced at UFO sites all over the world. On the surface, many of these cases seem completely absurd until we search for correlations in other forgotten files. My own criterion is simple enough: If similar events occur in different parts of the world and produce similar details or physical substances, I feel it is highly unlikely that the witnesses in one event could have even heard about the others and could have concocted identical hoaxes. Instead, they were victims of the artifact game.

We can begin with the puzzle of the anomalous anchors. The following story is from the pages of the Houston, Texas, *Daily Post* (April 28, 1897):

> Merkel, Texas, April 26—Some parties returning from church last night noticed a heavy object dragging along with a rope attached. They followed it until in crossing the railroad it caught on a rail. On looking up they saw what they supposed was the airship. It was not near enough to get an idea of the dimensions. A light could be seen protruding from several windows; one bright light in front like the headlight of a locomotive. After some ten minutes, a man was seen descending the rope; he came near enough to be plainly seen. He wore a light-blue sailor suit, was

small in size. He stopped when he discovered parties at the anchor and cut the rope below him and sailed off in a northeast direction. The anchor is now on exhibition at the blacksmith shop of Elliott and Miller and is attracting the attention of hundreds of people.

A small man in a blue sailor suit climbing down a rope from the sky. Rather silly, isn't it? Sillier still, researchers have discovered two identical stories in very obscure historical texts. An ancient Irish manuscript, the *Speculum Regali,* gives us this account from A.D. 956:

There happened in the borough of Cloera, one Sunday while people were at mass, a marvel. In this town there is a church to the memory of St. Kinarus. It befell that a metal anchor was dropped from the sky, with a rope attached to it, and one of the sharp flukes caught in the wooden arch above the church door. The people rushed out of the church and saw in the sky a ship with men on board, floating at the end of the anchor cable, and they saw a man leap overboard and pull himself down the cable to the anchor as if to unhook it. He appeared as if he were swimming in water. The folk rushed up and tried to seize him; but the bishop forbade the people to hold the man for fear it might kill him. The man was freed and hurried up the cable to the ship, where the crew cut the rope and the ship rose and sailed away out of sight. But the anchor is in the church as a testimony to this singular occurrence.

For many years a church in Bristol, England, is said to have had a very unique grille on its doors; a grille made from another anchor that allegedly came from the sky. Around A. D. 1200, during the observance of a feast day, the anchor came plummeting out of the sky trailing a rope. It got caught in a mound of stones, according to the story, and as a mob of churchgoers gathered around to watch, a "sailor" came down the rope, hand over hand, to free it. This crowd succeeded in grabbing him and pushed him back and forth until, according to the Gervase of Tilbury's account in *Otia Imperialia,* another rare manuscript, "He suffocated by the mist of our moist atmosphere and expired." His unseen comrades overhead wisely cut the rope and took off. The anchor remained behind, as in the other stories, and was installed on the church doors.

Researcher Lucius Farish remarked, "Reviewing the similarities of these reports, one is almost tempted to speculate that someone merely updated the ancient accounts. Yet, a citizen of Merkel, Texas, possessing a copy of the *Speculum Regali* [or the *Otia Imperialia]* in 1897 would be fully as fantastic as the reports themselves!"

A farmer fifteen miles north of Sioux City, Iowa, Robert Hibbard, claimed a distressing experience with an anchor-dragging UFO early in April 1897. A dispatch which appeared in the April 5 edition of the Saginaw, Michigan, *Evening News* stated that "Hibbard's reputation for truth has never been bad, and the general opinion is that either he 'had 'em' or dreamed his remarkable experience." The article continues:

> On the night in question, he says he was tramping about his farm in the moonlight.., when suddenly a dark body, lighted on each side, with a row of what looked like incandescent lamps, loomed up some distance to the south of him at a height of perhaps a mile from the ground. He watched it intently until it was directly over his head.
>
> At this point the skipper evidently decided to turn around. In accomplishing this maneuver the machine sank considerably. Hibbard did not notice a drag rope with a grapnel attached which dangled from the rear of the car until suddenly, as the machine rose again from the ground, it hooked itself firmly in his trousers and shot away again to the south. Had it risen to any considerable height, the result, Hibbard thinks, would have been disastrous. Either

his weight was sufficient to keep it near terra firma, however, or the operator did not care to ascend to a higher level.

On the bank of the dry run, where the farmer finally made his escape, grows a small sapling. Hibbard passed near this obstruction in his flight, and as a last resort, grabbed it with both hands. Instantly there was a sound of tearing cloth and the machine went on with a section of Hibbard's unmentionables, while Hibbard himself fell precipitately into the run. He related his experience to several neighbors and despite their grins of incredulity, firmly maintains the truth of the story.

We have only two choices: We can either dismiss all four of these stories as being somehow derivative of one another and pure poppycock; or we can assume that mysterious airships, all dragging anchors, appeared in 956, 1200, and 1897. There are, in fact, a number of other reports in which UFOs were said to be dragging something along the ground. That still doesn't prove that anchors are standard equipment on some of the objects. If they were using anchors, what could the purpose have been? Could some of the early UFOs have been so primitive that the only way they could hover was by being anchored to the ground? Would spaceships from another world require anchors?

Physical Evidence

All kinds of junk have fallen out of the sky throughout recorded history. Ivan T. Sanderson has in his files extensive lists of documented cases going back to Roman times. Ridiculous things such as stone pillars and heavy metal wheels have come crashing out of the blue, and there are countless cases of ice falls—huge blocks of ice, some weighing hundreds of pounds, dropping all over this planet. Charles Fort and others have found reports of ice falls predating the introduction of manmade aircraft, but the popular explanation today, when new incidents occur, is that the ice has fallen from the wings of high-altitude airplanes.

The flying saucers have been spewing all kinds of trash all over the landscape. In nearly every instance, these materials always prove to be ordinary earthly substances like magnesium, aluminum, chromium, and even plain old tin. Each of these incidents gives the skeptics new ammunition.

Here again, I feel that these correlated "negative factors" build into a definite positive factor. In other words, the more negative a piece of evidence seems to be, the more positive it actually is.

We can start with the slag dumped from the sky during the Maury Island, Washington, "hoax" of 1947. Analysis of this material showed it to be composed of calcium, aluminum, silicon, iron, zinc, and other mundane elements. Heaps of this stuff have turned up since in New Hampshire, Michigan, Indiana, Pennsylvania, and many other places following UFO sightings. It has often been found on hilltops and deep in trackless forests, places where it *had* to be dumped from the air. And it was found in Sweden in 1946.

When a wildly gyrating metal disk appeared over the city of Campinas, Brazil, on Tuesday, December 14, 1954, hundreds of witnesses reported that it dribbled a stream of "silvery liquid" into the streets. Government scientists collected some of this stuff, and Dr. Risvaldo Maffei later announced that it was almost pure tin.

The egg-shaped object that police officer Lonnie Zamora said landed outside of Socorro, New Mexico, on April 24, 1964, left behind a metal-like material on some rocks. It proved to be silicon.

Silicon substances have frequently been found at touchdown sites. Sometimes it is mixed with aluminum or other materials to form a purplish liquid. Such liquids have been found in New York State (Cherry Creek, 1965) and dozens of other places.

Witnesses in Texas, Maryland, claim to have watched a shiny disk explode in the air in June 1965. Pieces of it were recovered and were examined at the Goddard Space Flight Center. It proved to be ordinary ferrochromium.

Another exploding UFO, this one at Ubatuba, Brazil, in 1957, left behind particles that were nothing but pure magnesium. And great quantities of tiny strips of aluminum, with traces of magnesium and silicon, are now being found all over the world. Thousands of people in Chiba, Japan, reported seeing a circular flying object eject a flood of these shreds above their city on September 7, 1956. Piles of it have been found in West Virginia, Michigan, and many other places during UFO flaps. It is frequently found laid out in neatly ordered patterns on the ground where witnesses have seen UFOs hovering. I spent a lot of time investigating these cases in 1967. These strips are almost identical to the chaff dispensed by high-flying Air Force planes to jam radar, yet they do not seem to be related to AF operations at all. The UFO chaff is often found under trees or on porches, in places where it could not possibly have fallen from the sky directly. Quantities of it turned up in a burning field outside of Gastonia, North Carolina, in 1966, simultaneously with low-level UFO sightings.

Mysterious hollow metal spheres have also been dropping out of the sky all over the world. Three such spheres were found on the Australian desert in 1963. They were about 14 inches in diameter and had a shiny, polished surface. Australian scientists were baffled by them. On April 30, 1963, Allen Fairhall, the Minister of Supply, appeared before the Australian House of Representatives and told them that all effort to open the spheres had failed. The objects were allegedly turned over to the U.S. Air Force, and that was the end of them.

Other metal spheres have dropped out of the sky near Monterrey, Mexico (February 7, 1967) and Conway, Arkansas (November 1967). The Mexican ball was identified as titanium; the one in Arkansas was stainless steel. Others have been found in Argentina and Africa. They do not seem to be rocket parts, nor would it be possible for a piece of a rocket to go through reentry and land intact as these things have done.

Smaller colored spheres were found scattered over the French countryside in 1966-67, as if it had been raining balls there. Where is all this junk coming from? Why, the answer is simple: from the same place as the stone pillars and the blocks of ice from earlier times.

Innumerable cases of contact and landings have been flushed down the ufological drains because of the deliberate "negative" factors. Sincere witnesses have actually been ruined because the amateur UFO investigators have accused them of being liars or worse.

Consider the case of poor Joe Simonton and his outer-space pancake. It's a classic of the negative factor.

Simonton, a sixty-year-old chicken farmer outside of Eagle River, Wisconsin, said he heard a strange sound outside his farmhouse at 11 A.M. on Tuesday, April 18, 1961. He looked out of the window and was startled to see a silvery metallic machine descending in his yard. As he stepped outside, some kind of hatch slid open in the upper part of the object and three dark-skinned men became visible. He estimated that these men were about 5 feet tall and between twenty-five to thirty years of age. They wore clinging dark-blue uniforms with turtleneck tops and had on apparently knitted headgear, such as is worn under crash helmets. All were clean-shaven, and none of them spoke during the brief episode that followed.

One of them stepped to the hatch, Simonton said, and held out a shiny bucket-like affair which had a handle on either side, indicating that he wanted the farmer to fill it with water. Simonton took it, filled it from his pump, and returned it to the silent man. He noticed that the interior of the craft was black, "like wrought iron," and that one man was busy at some kind of instrument panel, while the other was working at what seemed to be a stove. A pile of pancakes sat nearby. Simonton says he gestured at the pancakes, and the man with the bucket turned, picked up four of them, and handed them to him. He then attached some kind of rope to his belt, and the hatch slid shut. Joe Simonton stood with his mouth open, four warm pancakes in his hands, as the object, which had been humming throughout, began to make a sound like "tires on a wet pavement" and rose slowly into the air, moving off to the south.

At about that same time, an insurance agent named Savino Borgo was driving along Highway 70, about a mile from Simonton's farm, when he saw what he later described as a saucer rising diagonally into the air and flying parallel with the highway.

Eagle River is in a thinly populated section of northern Wisconsin, just a few miles south of the Michigan border and surrounded by forests and small lakes. About a month later, on May 25, there was a widespread power failure throughout the area that also affected local telephone service. On February 24 of that year a B-47 bomber had crashed near Hurley, Wisconsin, about sixty miles northwest of Eagle River. Another B-47 crashed on May 2 *only two miles* from the site of the February accident. The pilot of the second plane was later quoted in the press as saying that, "I felt this weightlessness—I was hanging by my straps," just before his craft went out of control and headed for the ground. There were numerous other incidents and UFO sightings in the area during that period—which was the "lull" from 1959 to 1963.

So once again we have a series of sightings and incidents that corroborate an unusual story. But, unfortunately, we also had those four miserable pancakes. Simonton turned one over to a local judge named Carter who, incidentally, vouched for his honesty and reliability, as did everyone else who knew him. Dr. J. Allen Hynek was given the second one, and a third went to the National Investigation Committee on Aerial Phenomena, which turned it over to a New York researcher, Alex Mebane. Simonton held onto the fourth one. He said he took a nibble out of it, and "it tasted like cardboard."

Were the pancakes made out of exotic Martian mush? Of course not. They were plain old cornmeal, salt, and hydrogenated oil.

Simonton's story got a big play in the national press, and NICAP capitalized on the publicity by issuing statements about their "thorough investigation" which was "under way," etc. But when the press interest died, NICAP dropped the whole thing. The Aerial Phenomena Research Organization investigators stuck with it, however, and when an Eagle River businessman made a joking reference to Simonton having been hypnotized (he later denied this), some leaped on that as the explanation. Cecile Hess, APRO's man in nearby Rhinelander, Wisconsin, didn't buy the hypnotized theory. "If I ever saw a sincere and honest man, it was Simonton," Hess commented.

"If it happened again," Simonton told a UPI reporter in early May, "I don't think I'd tell anybody about it."

Simonton was a bewildered victim of the artifact game. Scores of contactees have been given pieces of junk metal, scraps of paper, and, in many cases, chunks of crystal or tektites (pieces of glass). The contactees display these materials almost proudly as proof of their experiences. One would assume that outright hoaxsters would try to construct better, more impressive, artifacts to support their stories of encounters with the wonderful "space people."

Another fascinating game, which the ufonauts play with a vengeance, is the "repair" gambit. Beginning in 1897, there has been an endless stream of stories and reports, many from police officers, school teachers, and other "reliable witnesses," describing how they encountered a grounded UFO and observed the occupants busily making repairs of some kind. In many instances, the ufonauts deliberately get out of the object and inspect its underside with a flashlight. These instances have been reported in Italy, Australia, Scandinavia, South America, and the United States. The basic details in these stories are so similar that it seems as if the ufonauts are following a carefully rehearsed procedure.

The "superior technology" of Operation Trojan Horse has apparently produced a line of faulty flying machines that constantly break down. Pieces of the damned things are always falling off where they can be grabbed up by eager UFO investigators. If the UFOs were real, it would be logical for a saucer in trouble to seek out a very isolated hilltop to make repairs. Instead, they prefer to land in the fields of occupied farms and on major highways close to big cities.

A fifty-six-year-old electronics engineer from Temple,

Oklahoma, William "Eddie" Laxton, became the center of considerable attention after he reported a bizarre incident in the gray predawn hours of March 23, 1966. At about 5:30 A.M. on that bleak March morning Laxton was driving along a deserted stretch of Highway 70 near the Texas-Oklahoma border, on his way to work at the Sheppard Air Force Base outside of Wichita Falls, Texas, where he teaches electronics, when a huge fish-shaped object suddenly loomed up in front of him. He jammed on his brakes, he said later, and pulled to a stop about 50 yards from where the object was blocking the road at a 45-degree angle. The thing was, he estimated, about 75 feet long and 8 feet deep.

"There were four very brilliant lights on my side," he said. "Bright enough so that a man could read a newspaper by the light a mile away." He also observed that it seemed to be lit up inside and that it "had a plastic bubble in front which was about three feet in diameter, and you could see light through it." It had a tail structure with horizontal stabilizers that measured about 2.5 feet from the leading edge to the trailing edge. Friends and associates have confirmed that Eddie has always been blessed with a phenomenal memory, and they believe him when he says he was able to distinguish a group of earthly numbers painted vertically in black on the side of the fuselage. He remembers them as reading either:

T	or	T
L		L
4		4
7		1
6		6
8		8

Halfway along the fuselage there was a porthole about two feet in diameter. It was divided into four equal sections, and there was a small door below it, measuring about 4.5 feet high and 2.5 feet wide. This door was open and white light was pouring through it.

Directly outside the object a human-looking man was examining the underside of the craft with some kind of flashlight. As Eddie climbed out of his car, this person turned, climbed up a metal ladder, and entered the door. "I'm sure it was aluminum," Laxton noted. "When the door snapped shut, it sounded like when a door closes."

He described the pilot as weighing about 180 pounds and being 5 feet 9 inches tall with a light complexion. He was wearing what looked like a mechanic's cap with the bill turned up.

"I got the impression due to his stooped shoulders he was about thirty to thirty-five years old," Eddie said. "He wore either coveralls or a two-piece suit that looked like green-colored fatigues. I got the idea that he had three stripes above and three below [on his sleeve]. The above stripes were in an arch and the below stripes were in a wide V shape."

A few seconds later "the craft started up… it sounded like a high speed drill. It lifted off the ground about fifty feet high and headed toward the Red River. In about five seconds it was a mile away."

When the machine took off, Laxton reported, "The hair on the back of my hands and neck stood up."

Admittedly excited by what he had seen, Eddie got back into his car and drove about 100 yards when he came upon a huge tank truck parked beside the road. The driver, C. W. Anderson of Snyder, Oklahoma, said that he had seen something following him in his mirror and that he had also watched it fly away toward the Red River. After their story appeared in local papers, other truck drivers came forward with reports of having seen similar objects along Highway 70 earlier in the year.

Eddie Laxton faithfully reported the incident to his employer, the Air Force, and a couple of days later a line of jeeps pulled up in front of his office. "A colonel and other officers wanted to see the spot where the object had been," Laxton said. "I went out with them and showed them the place. They asked me a lot of questions while their men searched the place with all kinds of instruments.

They seemed to know just what they were doing."

In the Air Force files, the object Eddie Laxton saw is officially recorded as "unidentified." As for the man, Eddie claims, "He looked just like you or me. If I met him tomorrow in a bar, I would know him instantly."

Among the great heaps of neglected and ignored UFO data, we find hundreds of "minipeople" accounts. These are very rarely published anywhere because they are so unbelievable. Most of them are identical to the fairy and gnome stories of yesteryear. The minipeople are only a few inches in height. Some dress like spacemen, complete with transparent helmets, while others are described in much the same way as the Irish leprechauns. Witnesses to these events can experience conjunctivitis, akinesia (paralysis), amnesia, and the other effects often noted by witnesses to more conventional UFO events. Many contactees admit that they have seen minipeople cavorting about on their furniture and even riding around in miniature flying saucers.

One of the strangest minipeople stories I have received came from a young woman in Seattle, Washington. In the latter part of August 1965, she awoke around 2 A. M. and discovered she could not move a muscle or make a sound. Her window was open, and suddenly a tiny, football-sized, dull gray object appeared. It floated through the window and hovered over the carpet near her bed. She said she felt no desire to leap up or cry out as three tripod logs lowered from the object, and it settled to the floor. A small ramp descended from it, and five or six tiny people clambered out and seemed to work on some kind of repairs on the object. They wore tight-fitting clothing. When their job was finished, they went up the ramp again, and the object took off and sailed out the window. Then she was finally able to move. She was certain she was wide awake. The case was investigated by J. Russell Jenkins of Seattle.

You can see why very few witnesses to this type of event would be anxious to tell anyone about their experiences. And you can see why almost none of these stories ever appears in print, except in occult-oriented literature. Nevertheless, if we hope to assess the true UFO situation, we must examine all of these stories. We can learn nothing by considering only those episodes that are emotionally and intellectually acceptable to us.

Fewer than two percent of the known UFO sightings are reported to the Air Force at all. Likewise, the various UFO organizations receive only a tiny residue of the data. It is most difficult to judge the situation at all on the basis of such a small sampling. The problem is compounded by the fact that the majority of UFO witnesses and contactees tell no one outside of their own circle of family and friends. I have concentrated, therefore, on the hidden incidents and the little-known, seldom officially reported aspects of the phenomenon.

Individually, the sighting reports are nothing more than anecdotes. Thoroughly investigated, objectively reported cases are very rare. Even so, when you collect together all the available data, as I have tried to do, and view it quantitatively, you naturally expect that this mass of information will reveal some positive factors. Instead, an astounding paradox is presented.

The scope of the phenomenon and the overwhelming quantity of reports negates its validity.

The various UFO organizations and cultist groups, and the few interested scientists, had tried to deal with all this on an anecdotal basis, selecting those anecdotes which seemed to contain the best descriptions and had been reported by the most reliable witnesses. Thus, the actual scope of the phenomenon has escaped them. And the best reports rarely contain details that can provide correlations with other reports. In short, the great bulk of all the anecdotes are worthless and can provide little or no insight into the real problems.

The statistical data that I have extracted, and which I have tried to summarize briefly here, indicate that flying saucers are not stable machines requiring fuel, maintenance, and logistical support. They are, in all probability, transmogrifications of energy and do not exist in the same way that this book exists. They are not permanent constructions of matter.

Operation Trojan Horse has made us believe, first, in angels and phantom armies, later in mystery inventors, ghost airplanes, and ghost rockets, and finally in the splendid Venusians.

Because the scope of the phenomenon far exceeds the limits of the tiny residue of known reports, we can learn almost nothing from studying the observations of a minute group of pilots and police officers.

However, by carefully investigating many flap areas in depth, I have come up with an alternate line of research. I discovered that the witnesses and people living in these areas experienced direct manifestations of a different sort. If we can put the witnesses themselves under our microscope, we may find that a wide variety of psychological and hallucinatory factors are involved. This is something we can investigate thoroughly and systematically.

In 1897, the airships deliberately dropped peeled potatoes, newspapers, and messages at the feet of astonished witnesses to create and support the secret inventor myth. In recent years the same kinds of objects have been dispensing strips of metal and globs of purple goo suggestive of machine oil to support the idea that we are being visited by "a superior intelligence with an advanced technology." Some contactees have produced moon rocks and moon dust as proof of their experiences on other worlds, but these substances have been discouragingly like the rocks in your own backyard. The endless messages from the space people would now fill a library, and while the communicators claim to represent some other world, the contents of those messages are identical to the messages long received by mediums and mystics. I do not believe that the Saratoga was real in 1897. Nor do I believe that the aluminum-spewing spaceships of 1957 were any more real. The engraved message from the *Saratoga* was real; the aluminum shavings are real. But I would hate to have to go into a court of law and prove the reality of extraterrestrial visitants on the basis of such evidence.

Because flying saucers may not actually exist as physical machines, we must study these witnesses and closely examine the experiences which led them to believe that UFOs were real and extraterrestrial. The UFO phenomenon seems to be largely subjective; that is, specific kinds of people become involved and are actually manipulated by the phenomenon in the same way that it manipulates matter. These subjective experiences are far more important to our study than the random, superficial sightings.

Like Canadian scientist Wilbert Smith, Dr. Condon, and so many others, we are obliged to forget about the meaningless sightings and concentrate on the claims and experiences of the contactees.

10
"What Is Your Time Cycle?"

In November 1966, two women were standing in a field outside of Owatonna, Minnesota, watching a familiar sight—what they called little flashers: bright, blinking lights that danced around the sky almost every night. Suddenly one of the objects descended rapidly and hovered at the far end of the field where they stood, swinging back and forth a few feet above the ground. Colored lights flickered around its glowing rim. One of the women let out a little gasp and crumpled to her knees in a trancelike daze. Her friend, Mrs. Ralph Butler, reached for her, but she was immobile, her head dipped down. A strange voice, stilted and metallic, came spasmodically from her lips.

"What...is...your...time...cycle?" The voice asked. Mrs. Butler recovered from her surprise and tried to explain how we measured minutes, hours, and days. "What...constitutes...a...day...and... what...constitutes...a...night?..." The voice continued.

"A day is approximately twelve hours long—and a night is twelve hours long," Mrs. Butler replied. There were a few more innocuous questions, and then the other woman came out of her trance.

"Boy, I'm glad that's over," she remarked simply.

The object shot upward. Believing that they had communicated with a flying saucer through some incredible telepathic means, both women were naturally excited. But later when they tried to discuss the incident with others, they found that they suddenly came down with blinding headaches.

Mrs. Butler wrote to me after reading one of my magazine articles. I immediately called her and spoke to her for almost an hour.

"It's strange," she declared, "but this is the first time I've ever been able to talk about these things without getting a splitting headache."

I asked her all of my weird and seemingly silly questions, and she had all the right answers. She had been having unusual telephone problems and had also been receiving strange voices on her citizen's band (CB) radio.

"Tell me," she asked, "has anyone ever reported receiving visits from peculiar Air Force officers?"

"I've heard a few stories about them," I said cautiously.

"Well, last May [1967] a man came by here," she continued. "He said he was Major Richard French, and he was interested in CB and in UFOs. He was about five feet nine inches tall with a kind of olive complexion and pointed face. His hair was dark and very long—too long for an Air Force officer, we thought. He spoke perfect English. He was well educated."

This man was nattily dressed in a gray suit, white shirt, and black tie. "Everything he was wearing was *brand-new*," she observed. He drove a white Mustang, and her husband copied down the license number and had it checked out later. It proved to be a rented car from Minneapolis.

"He said his stomach was bothering him," she noted. "I told him that what he needed was some Jello. He said if it kept bothering him, he would come back for some."

Early the next morning Major French drove up to the Butler's house again. His stomach was still troubling him, so Mrs. Butler sat him down at her kitchen table and slid a big bowl of Jello in front of him.

"Did you ever hear of anyone trying to drink Jello?" she asked me. "Well, that's what he did. He acted like he had never seen any before. He picked the bowl up and tried to drink it. I had to show him how to eat it with a spoon."

Major French didn't visit any of her friends, and it is something of a mystery why he singled the Butlers out. Later, she said, this same man turned up in Forest City, Iowa, and dropped in on some close friends of the Butlers there.

There proved to be a Richard French in the Air Force in Minnesota, but he did not even remotely answer to the above description.

The Butlers have reportedly experienced all kinds of poltergeist phenomena in their home since the UFO flap began in Owatonna in 1966. Objects have been moving about of their own accord, glass objects have suddenly and visibly shattered without cause, and strange noises have resounded throughout the house.

On another occasion she claimed that while she was standing outside watching some "little flashers," she suddenly felt a cool, comforting hand on her shoulder. She looked around, but there was no one there.

"Sometimes I've seen some kind of activity—men moving around in the trees behind our house at night. But something keeps me from going near them."

No one around Owatonna reported any of the extensive UFO sightings to the Air Force. "We're all disgusted with the government," Mrs. Butler declared. "We know they'd just tell us it was all swamp gas."

There were airship sightings in Owatonna in 1897. And in 1880, the home of a Mr. Dimant was plagued with poltergeist-like activity. Explosions of undetermined origin took place in his house, the doorbell rang frequently when no one was there, and so on. So perhaps this isolated little community of 14,000 is of some special interest to the mysterious ultraterrestrials.

Mrs. Butler's story may sound bizarre, but I have heard the same things too many times in too many different places to dismiss them lightly. In case after case, I have heard about strange men who paid pointless visits and sometimes posed as Air Force officers. The descriptions are always the same—slight of stature, dark olive skins, sharp pointed features. And most of these scattered witnesses specifically noticed that these men were dressed in clothes that seemed *brand-new*. Even the soles of their shoes appear to be unwalked on. If they have occasion to pull out a wallet or notebook, that also is brand-new. (Most men, even

Air Force officers, carry beat-up old wallets.) I have carefully kept many of these small details to myself and have never published them or discussed them. They provide a yardstick by which I can measure the validity of new stories.

The sudden, blinding headaches described by Mrs. Butler are also very common among percipients who have been involved in close sightings or actual contacts.

Finally, there is the curious experience of her friend who was seized by some kind of trance and parroted someone else's words. This, too, has happened far more frequently than one might imagine. But such stories rarely go very far because they are so weird and unbelievable. The phrase "What is your time cycle?" had special meaning to me. I had heard it before, from other percipients.

In December 1967, Tom Monteleone, an aspiring young science fiction writer in Adelphi, Maryland, allegedly had a contact with a grounded UFO and conversed with a man in "shiny coveralls" who identified himself as "Vadig." Because time travel was already a well-established theme in science fiction, Monteleone made up a contactee story about traveling to a distant planet where everyone walked around nude. Asserting that he had been a victim of a time loss, he hit the UFO lecture circuit and appeared on radio talk shows. When he discovered that peddling outer space nudism was a hard way to make a buck, he recanted and spent the next twenty years selling articles about his terrifying brushes with the hardcore UFO buffs, experiences far more chilling than meetings with extraterrestrial nudists.

Aside from Tom's ventures into his inner mind, time is one of the most important aspects of the UFO phenomenon. It plays a strange but significant role. Part of the answer to flying saucers may lie not in the stars but in the clock ticking on your mantelpiece.

Our world exists in three dimensions: height, width, and breadth. We can move in many directions within these dimensions: up, down, sideways, forward, and backward. We measure space in relation to our own size, by inches, feet, yards, miles, light years. If we were 25 feet tall and our planet were the size of Jupiter (many times larger than the earth), we would undoubtedly have adjusted our measurements of space accordingly. Our inch might be equal to an earth foot, our mile might be equal to ten earth miles.

Space does not exist except when we make it exist. To us, the distance between atoms in matter is so minute that it can only be calculated with hypothetical measurements. Yet, if we lived on an atom and our size was relative to its size, the distance to the next atom would seem awesome and beyond reach. The ant lives in a world of giants where even a blade of grass is a gigantic structure and a tree is a whole universe. If ants had measurements, their inch might be the size of the point of a pin, and their mile would be less than a foot.

How dare we try to reduce the universe to our own terms? We can't even see or sense a large part of the world around us. Man is not the final, perfect end product of evolution.

He is the beginning.

There is another man-made measurement called time. Unlike the other three dimensions, time has us trapped. We can move in only one direction through it—forward. This forward motion is governed by physical laws. We cannot leap ahead fifteen years any more than we can slide back to 1848. We are all trapped in this moment of time. This instant.

The only way we can bridge time is to create something that will endure beyond the immediate moment. We construct buildings, pyramids, works of art, and even laws that become material and lasting things. Our moments become seconds, minutes, hours, days, years. Our lives revolve around clocks and calendars. Time becomes very real to us, and it is almost inconceivable that we could live without it.

Yet time doesn't really exist at all.

This moment exists *to us*. The same moment is being shared by other planets and other stars. Or is it?

The light from a distant star may take 30 years to cross space and reach us. We can see a nova (exploding star) 1,000 years after it has actually burst and vanished. With strong telescopes, we can peer into the past. We could see that event 1,000 years after it had happened. Perhaps we could see a planet near that star, see a whole population panic and go mad as their sun started to expand and pour heat and radiation onto them. Perhaps long after our own planet is a dead cinder some dispassionate astronomer in some remote part of the universe will collect the light from this moment and watch us groveling about in this year.

We have learned to measure time by observing the special characteristics of our environment. Our days and nights are measured by the length of time it takes the earth to rotate on its axis. Our years are the number of days it takes to make one complete circuit around the sun. Our lives are scaled by the number of years our delicate organisms can survive. If the earth did not rotate, there would be no days. If it did not circuit the sun, there would be no years. If we were larger or smaller and lived on Ganymede, one of Jupiter's moons, our whole measurement of time would be different.

Assume that a planet exists trapped in a binary (two-star) system. Its orbit is such that all sides of the planet are constantly bathed in light. No day/night cycle exists there. The inhabitants have no way of measuring time—even years—by our standards. They would be living in a timeless void. The Pleiades actually contain more than 200 stars, although only seven are visible to the naked eye, many of them forming binary systems. As close as our astronomers can tell, those stars seem to be dying. In another few million years of our time, the Pleiades will be no more.

From what we know about the Pleiades, the stars there seem to be swirling among great clouds of radiant gases. If they harbor any planetary systems, we wonder what effect those gases might have. An early contactee, Albert K. Bender, wrote a book containing so many far-out details that few ufologists took it seriously. He claimed that UFO entities told him that they lived underground on their home planet because periodically they passed through masses of deadly clouds which destroyed life and created a great blackness.* When Bender's account, *Flying Saucers and the Three Men,* was first published in 1962, it read like the fantasies of a madman. But now many of the things he described have repeatedly occurred all over the world, and the book deserves a careful rereading.

If flying saucers actually exist as extraterrestrial spaceships, then the Pleiades might deserve a place high on the list of possible origins. It is possible that the ancients were so enthralled with the magical number of seven that they placed undue emphasis upon the "Seven Sisters." But it is equally possible that they might have had access to some particular bit of knowledge which has since been lost.

Anthropologists have been amazed to discover that the completely isolated tribes of South America and the aborigines of Australia have much folklore about the Pleiades and even call the cluster the Seven Sisters, just as the ancient Middle Eastern and European cultures did. Much of this independent folklore contends that the Pleiades was the home of the "Sky People." North American Indian tribes have similar legends about the Pleiades, and of all the stars and constellations named and known by the ancient peoples it is interesting to note that even the Bible singles out the Seven Sisters repeatedly. In the Book of Job, 38:31, we find this enigmatic statement: "Canst thou bind the sweet influences of Pleiades, or loose the bands of Orion?"

In modern UFO-contactee lore, beginning in the early 1950s, the constellation of Orion is frequently cited as the home of "evil

---

* The earth, too, has passed through clouds of blackness, according to ancient tradition. Three days of total darkness, during which no light or fire could be seen, are described in the *Book of Mormon,* Third Nephi, Chapter 8. There are many other historical references to this event, not only in the Bible (Exodus 10:22), but in Egyptian. Chinese and Indian texts also. Apparently the phenomenon occurred worldwide. Normal light rays were unable to penetrate the gloom, and human beings found themselves in such a lethargic state they were unable to move. See *Worlds in Collision* by Immanuel Velikovsky, Part 1, Chapter 2, for further references and descriptions of this catastrophe.

spacemen" who are planning to take over the earth. A famous British contactee, Arthur Bryant, claimed that on April 24, 1965, a UFO occupant informed him that "forces from Epsilon are already here in the form of poltergeists." Epsilon Orionis is the central star in the belt of Orion. The Bible and many other ancient works seem to imply that Orion harbors a malevolent force, while the Pleiades is the home of the "good guys."

Stretching Time

Much has been written about the fact that astronauts whizzing through space at 25,000 mph return to earth a fraction of a second younger than the rest of us, because as Einstein discovered, the faster a particle moves through space, the slower it moves through time. Time becomes a hypothetical field. Trapped here on earth, we all move through that field at the same rate. Science-fiction writers have always made a big deal out of this, and there are endless tales of astronauts dashing off to other planets and, upon returning to earth, finding that hundreds of years have actually passed, even though they are only months or years older.

Physicists following Einstein's concepts assert that nothing can exceed the speed of light without becoming infinite mass and being reduced to energy. However, if we want to blow our minds altogether, we can speculate that an energy particle might hit such a high frequency and move so fast that it doesn't move at all. Energies beyond the cosmic rays on our spectrum scale would have such a very high frequency that they would appear to be motionless. A small group of American physicists are now actually trying to build the equipment necessary to test this possibility.

These super-high frequencies would be far outside our time field, yet they could coexist all around us, and we have no way of detecting or defining them. We could only guess at their existence, just as men guessed for hundreds of years about atomic structure before we developed the technology needed to confirm the theories.

To repeat this another way: If an astronaut can move more slowly through the time field by accelerating through three dimensional space, then it might be possible for a super-high-frequency particle moving at super-high speeds to escape or be uninfluenced by our time field altogether.

What I'm trying to do here is reduce the complex Einstein theory to the simplest of terms.

Now then, how can all of this be applied to the UFO phenomenon?

Throughout this book I have tried to explain that UFOs seem to be transmogrifications: seemingly material apparitions that might actually be composed of energies from the high reaches of the electromagnetic spectrum. If this is so, then one additional factor is necessary: order or intelligence.

The UFO phenomenon does seem to be controlled. It does follow intelligent patterns. If the objects themselves are manifestations of higher energies, then something has to manipulate those energies somehow and reduce them to the visible frequencies. Not only do they enter the visible frequencies, but they take forms that seem physical and real to us, and they carry out actions which seem intelligent.

Thus we arrive at the source. The source has to be a form of *intelligent energy* operating at the very highest possible point of the frequency spectrum. If such an energy exists at all, it might permeate the universe and maintain equal control over each component part. Because of its very high frequency, so high that the energy particles are virtually standing still, the source has no need to replenish itself in any way that would be acceptable to our environmental sciences. It could actually create and destroy matter by manipulating the lower energies. It would be timeless, because it exists beyond all time fields. It would be infinite because it is not confined by three-dimensional space.

Within this energy structure there could be other masses of intelligent energy existing on slightly lower frequencies. While these masses would be ultimately under the control of the highest intelligence, they might maintain a certain amount of independence and be able to manipulate the lower energies on their own. But no matter what activities they might engage in, they would be obliged to fit their actions into the plan of the overall intelligence.

A computer relies upon systems that store and direct the course of electrical impulses. A complex system of switches, or transistors that act like switches, form the circuitry, which breaks down information into simple negative and positive pulses. Cyberneticians work with a system of numbers, 0 for negative and 1 for positive. A problem is fed into the computer, and the answer comes back in these numbers; 1010, for example, means 10. These are known as binary numbers.

The human brain functions in much the same way. Billions of tiny switches known as synapses are built into a complex circuitry of nerves. If you handle and smell a rose and prick your finger on one of its thorns, the memory of this event is stored in your brain circuitry by the opening and closing of billions of these synapses. The memory of the odor takes millions, as does the memory of the pain of the thorn and the millions of points of light which were fed from your eyes to your brain and which registered the beauty of the rose. Other circuits form a kind of index so that you can instantly tune into this one particular memory bank and remember the rose clearly.

The brains of small children are filled largely with sensual information. As we grow older, our minds become cluttered with millions of impressions and experiences and with fragments of all that we read, see, and hear. The child's mind, especially before the so-called age of reason when the logic circuits begin to form, is therefore a clear instrument, open and uninfluenced by opinions and conclusions. This is an important point in our UFO mystery.

Our computers and brains are complicated devices developed to cope with the barrage of sensual data from the material world around us. Perhaps if we were in a pure energy state, each particle of energy could serve as a synapse, and information could be stored by a slight alteration in frequency. Thus all of the memory fragments of that rose would be recorded at one frequency, and the whole energy form could tune into that memory at will by adjusting frequencies as we adjust a radio receiver. In other words, no complex circuitry would be required. No body would be necessary. The energy patterns would not need a material form to augment it, circulate food, etc.

If the energy form were infinite, timeless, and permeated the entire universe, it would have total knowledge and total awareness. It would not need eyes and ears and nerve endings for perception. Like Mount Everest, it would be there and would be unaffected by whatever was happening lower on the energy spectrum.

It could surround you completely at this very moment and be totally aware of all the feeble pulses of low energy passing through your brain. If it so desired, it could control those pulses and thus control your thoughts.

Man has always been aware of this intelligent energy or force. He has always worshiped it.

The Modus Operandi of Prophecy

Our first conclusion is that the UFOs originate from beyond our own time frame or time cycle. Our second conclusion is that the source has total foreknowledge of human events and even of individual lives. Because time and space are not absolutes, although they seem to be to us, these two conclusions are compatible.

Visualize a teenaged boy with a microscope. He is studying a tiny microbe with a total life-span of sixty seconds. He takes a fine needle and pokes it into the liquid environment of the microbe—a drop of water on a slide that seems limitless to the minute creature. Suppose that the microbe has some sort of visual or sensory apparatus. The point of the needle would suddenly appear enigmatically before it, a totally foreign object beyond the microbe's experience and frame of reference. The bewildered microbe swims around the object, studies it, then sits down and writes a microbe report on the unexplained object that he saw. When the boy withdraws the needle, the "object" suddenly disappears in front of the microbe because it is no longer part of his environment or his time cycle.

Five minutes later, by the boy's clock, he reinserts the needle into that same drop of water. Now many generations of microbes have passed. A new microbe glimpses this wonder and hurries to the microbe library and uncovers the old report. Strange foreign objects made out of an unknown material and behaving in a most peculiar way had been seen in ancient times, the microbe learns. To the boy, the two events spanned a mere five minutes. To the microbes, many generations had passed. By our time cycle, the two events were almost simultaneous.

Switch things around a bit. Now *we* are the microbes. Could it be possible that all UFO events are interrelated, and although they are widely separated according to our time cycle, they might really be almost simultaneous events to the ufonauts?

I don't mean to imply that some giant is poking needles at us. The microbe's world is a tiny, almost insignificant part of the boy's world, although the microbe had absolutely no knowledge of it. The microbe was not only unaware of the boy's existence, but it could not have possibly comprehended his existence.

It may be that all human events occur simultaneously when viewed by a greater intelligence. The boy peering through the microscope can plainly see a microscopic obstacle looming up in front of the microbe seconds before it even becomes aware of the obstacle. He can thus predict in a limited way the microbe's future. In a single minute of earth time he can watch the birth, growth, reproduction, and death of the microbe. The event is interesting to the boy but not especially important. He can watch a larger predatory microbe swim toward his specimen and consume it. If he wished, he could poke his needle into the drop again and maybe force the predator out of the way, thus saving the microbe's life. He can manipulate the microbe in many ways. But he cannot communicate with it.

If a gigantic superintelligence wants—or needs—to communicate with a much lower form, all kinds of problems are presented. The communication must be conducted in a manner that will be meaningful and understandable to the lower life form.

An acceptable frame of reference must be found and utilized. The superintelligence may wish to convey information of a very complex nature—so complex that it is beyond the comprehension of the lower form. The only way to accomplish this is to pass the information on in very small fragments over many generations, using many modes of communication. All of this might take only a few seconds of the superintelligence's time but would cover thousands of years of the lower form's time cycle.

A long chain of events would be required for such communication. They would have to be arranged in such a manner that they assume singular importance to the generation involved and would be carefully recorded and preserved for succeeding generations. At the end of the chain the assorted fragments would form a whole that would produce the information in tow. Call it a revelation or an awakening if you will.

UFO events seem to occur century after century in the same geographical locations. A majority of these events took place on Wednesdays and Saturdays and were concentrated around the hours of 6 P.M., 8 P.M., and 10 P.M. These facts in themselves are proof that the phenomenon is guided by an intelligence and that the individual events form part of a larger plan. As we progress step by step along this bizarre cosmic trail, that plan becomes slowly more plain. We have misunderstood much of the material passed on to us, and we are just beginning to comprehend the full meaning of the many manifestations of the energies from the higher frequencies.

The UFO phenomenon is frequently reflective; that is, the observed manifestations seem to be deliberately tailored and adjusted to the individual beliefs and mental attitudes of the witnesses. Both the objects and their occupants appear to be able to adopt a multitude of forms, and the contactees are usually given information that conforms to their own beliefs. UFO researchers who concentrate on one particular aspect or theory find themselves inundated with seemingly reliable reports which tend to substantiate that theory. My own extensive experiences with this reflective factor have led me to carry out weird experiments which confirmed that a large part of the reported data is engineered and deliberately false. The witnesses are not the perpetrators of these hoaxes but are merely the victims.

The apparent purposes of all this false data are multifold. Much of it is meant to create confusion and diversion. Some of it has served to support certain beliefs that were erroneous but which would serve as steppingstones to the higher, more complex truth. Whole generations have come and gone, happily believing in the false data, unaware that they were really mere links in the chain. If we understood it all too soon, we might crumble under the weight of the truth. It was first necessary to build man's ego; to make him believe that he had some worth in the cosmic whole. So, lies containing veiled truths were spread among us, and events were staged to make those lies seem valid. Many men—brilliant scholars and philosophers—have clearly seen the truth for centuries. Libraries all over the world are filled with books detailing their findings. But their truths were lost in the waves of organized belief.

This earth is covered with windows into that other unseen world. Perhaps if we had the instruments to detect them, we would find that these windows are the focal points for super-high-frequency waves—the "rays" of ancient lore. These rays might come from Orion or the Pleiades as the ancients claimed, or they might be part of the great force that emanates throughout the universe. The UFOs have given us evidence that such rays exist.

Now, slowly, we are being told why.

11
"You Are Endangering the Balance of the Universe!"

An Air Force plane spiraled clumsily out of the sullen Argentine sky and crashed near Quilino in August 1957, setting the stage for one of the hundreds of "ridiculous" contact stories that have been appearing in newspapers throughout the world for the past twenty years. The Argentine Air Force dispatched three men to the site to guard the wreck until proper equipment could be mustered to haul it back to the base. On the evening of August 20, 1957, two of the men went into the town for supplies, while the third man lounged in their tent.

Suddenly, according to his story, he heard an eerie, high-pitched hum. He stepped outside the tent and was astonished to see a huge luminous metal disk hovering directly overhead. In horror, he reached for his pistol but could not seem to draw it from the holster for some unknown reason, he claimed later.

Standing transfixed, tugging helplessly at his gun, the young man heard a soft-spoken voice coming from the humming object. It addressed him gently in his own language and told him not to be afraid. Then it went on to tell him that the disk was an interplanetary spacecraft and that a base for such craft had been installed in the nearby province of Salta (an area where UFO sightings have been reported constantly for the past fifteen years—"UFO Alley").

"We intend to help you," the voice is supposed to have declared, "for the misuse of atomic energy threatens to destroy you." The voice went on to say that very soon the rest of the world would know about flying saucers.

Then the bushes and trees began to rustle, and the craft ascended straight up and disappeared. The young Argentinean was so upset by this experience that he reported it in full to his commanding officer. The latter took him most seriously and passed the story on to one of Argentina's largest and most respected newspapers, *Diario de Cordoba*, which carried the full account two days later.

Even though the U.S. Air Force and various civilian groups struggle to discount and discredit contactee stories, they continue to turn up everywhere. Many of them contain such ludicrous details that they are easy to dismiss—until you realize that the same ludicrous details are appearing in Italy, Brazil, Sweden, Africa, the Soviet Union, Australia, and nearly every other country on earth.

Consider the improbable tale told by movie actor Stuart Whitman, star of *Those Magnificent Men in Their Flying Machines* and many other big-budget films. According to Mr. Whitman, he was trapped in his twelfth-floor suite in a fashionable New York hotel during the big blackout of November 1965, when he heard "a sound like a whippoorwill" whistling outside his window. He looked out and saw two luminous disk-shaped objects, one blue, the other orange. At least that's what he later told Hollywood columnist Vernon Scott. Then he heard a voice, which sounded as if it were coming from a loudspeaker.

"They said they were fearful of earth," Whitman explained, "because earthlings were messing around with unknown quantities and might disrupt the balance of the universe or their planet...the blackout was just a little demonstration of their power, and they could do a lot more with almost no effort. They said they could stop our whole planet from functioning."

No one else in the crowded streets of darkened New York reported seeing these objects, and no one apparently heard that loudspeaker. But Whitman sticks to his story. Why is anybody's guess. He certainly doesn't need publicity. At least not that kind of publicity.

Senhor Helio Aguiar didn't seem to be looking for publicity, either, when he spun his strange story to Brazilian journalist Joao Martins in 1959. A thirty-two-year-old statistician employed by a bank in Bahia, Brazil, Aguiar not only claimed to have received a message from a UFO, but he took a series of startling pictures to back up his story.

While riding a motorcycle near a place called Piata on April 24, 1959, Senhor Aguiar says he observed a silvery disk with a number of windows visible on the dome on top. The underside of this object bore three markings or symbols, which were actually faintly visible in the originals of his pictures but, unfortunately, do not reproduce well. Aguiar stopped his motorcycle, unlimbered his camera and took three quick shots as the object performed leisurely movements overhead. Then, according to Gordon Creighton's translation of the photographer's original testimony, "He began to feel a pressure in his brain, and a state of progressive confusion overtook him. He felt vaguely as though he were being ordered by somebody to write something down. It was as though he were being hypnotized. As he was winding the film on before proceeding to take a fourth picture, he lost all sense of what was happening."

Like the prophet Daniel, and Joseph Smith of the Mormons, Senhor Aguiar passed out. The next thing he knew, he was slumped over his motorcycle, and the UFO was gone. But clutched in his hand was a piece of paper bearing a message in his own handwriting: "Put an absolute stop to all atomic tests for warlike purposes," the message warned. "The balance of the universe is threatened. We shall remain vigilant and ready to intervene."*

"*The balance of the universe...*" It's a very odd coincidence how this same phrase turns up over and over again in the stories of these "kooks and crackpots."

---

* In the summer of 1963 comedian Red Skelton was loafing alone on a beach in California when, according to what he later told reporter Dick Kleiner (Newspaper Enterprise Association), he lapsed into a semitrance for about an hour. Upon recovering full consciousness, he discovered a terrifying message written in his own hand in the notebook he always carries with him. He doesn't remember writing it or even thinking the words. The message was: "President Kennedy will be killed in November."

Two years before Serihor Agniar's alleged communication from the UFOs, a quiet gentleman in England claimed that he had been taken for a ride. His name is James Cook of Runcorn, Cheshire, and he stated that he saw a strange luminous object in the sky at 2:15 A.M. on September 7, 1957. While he watched in fascination, the object changed colors from blue to white, then blue again, and finally to a dark red. It hurtled out of the sky and settled to the ground only a few feet from him. Then, he claimed, a voice addressed him, inviting him aboard. A ladder descended from the craft, and a voice instructed him, "*Jump* onto the ladder. Do not step onto it. The ground is damp."

He obeyed, leaped onto the bottom rung of the ladder, and climbed into an empty chamber illuminated by a dazzling light from some unseen source. The voice told him to take off his clothes and put on the plastic-like coveralls that were in the chamber. Again, he did as he was told. After he had changed his clothes, he was asked to leave the craft and enter another one that had landed nearby. There, he said, he found twenty people, all of them much taller than he was, and they took him for a ride into outer space. They told him that they were from a planet called Zomdic, which was in another solar system and was unknown to our scientists. Their craft could not operate in damp weather, they allegedly explained to him, apparently because they were surrounded by some kind of electrified field.

They also told him, he said, *that the saucers were used only in the vicinity of the earth and could not operate in outer space.*

"The inhabitants of your planet will upset the balance if they persist in using force instead of harmony," Mr. Cook asserts that he was told. "Warn them of the danger."

"Nobody will listen to me," he says he protested.

"Or anyone else either," one of the giant "spacemen" snapped.

Mr. Cook was deposited several hours later in the very spot where he had first been picked up. He related his story to the authorities and then quietly returned to his garden in the English countryside. Like the majority of all known contactees, he did not write any books or go on any lecture tours. Zomdic was never heard from again, either.

Miss Thelma Roberts of Britain's *Flying Saucer Review* interviewed Mr. Cook, and he showed her a burn on the back of his left hand and told her he had received it when he had left the saucer and had failed to remove his hand from the ladder's railing before his feet touched the wet ground.

Another contactee who has refused to make any fuss over his purported experience with "the people from outer space" is a young Italian engineer named Luciano Galli, who runs a small company on the outskirts of Rome. His story is far more unbelievable than Mr. Cook's, but whether you believe it or not, it contains all of the classic elements that appear in many similar yarns. These elements include terrestrials—people just like you and me—who are in some way connected with the UFO phenomenon. Or maybe they really are our ultraterrestrials in disguise.

Signore Galli left his home after lunch on July 7, 1957, and was headed back to his plant when a black Fiat pulled up and a tall, dark-skinned man with piercing jet-black eyes spoke to him.

"Do you remember me?" the man asked. Galli had seen the man before on the streets of Rome and, for some reason, had felt like speaking to him, but he had disappeared into the crowds.

"I remember you," Galli replied.

"Would you like to come with us?" the man asked.

"Where to?"

"Have confidence." The man smiled. "Nothing will happen to you."

Galli impulsively got into the car. Another man, smaller and with delicate features, was driving. They proceeded to the Croara Ridge outside of Rome where, Galli says, a saucer-shaped machine was waiting for them. A cylinder dropped down from the center of the underside of the craft, and a door opened in it. The tall, dark man led Galli into it, and they rose into the interior, where two bright lights suddenly flashed.

"Don't be afraid," the stranger laughed. "We have just taken your picture."

There was a window-like lens about a yard in diameter in the bottom of the craft, Galli said, and through it he could see the earth fall away as they shot upward. Within minutes they were in space, where they approached a gigantic cigar-shaped object, which Galli estimated to be at least 600 meters (almost 2,000 feet) long. A very bright light surrounded one end of it, and there were a series of ports through which a number of saucers could be seen entering and leaving.

"This is one of our spaceships," the stranger explained. They flew into one of the open ports, and when Galli left the saucer, he found himself in a huge chamber. "There were," he said, "no less than four or five hundred people there... standing and walking around."

He was given a tour of the ship and was shown a large library, lounges, control rooms, and the commander's quarters. Less than four hours later he was back on the ridge outside of Rome. He kept the story to himself and did not really talk about it until a reporter who had heard rumors tracked him down in 1962.

"I don't care what anybody says," Galli declared. "The story is true. You can believe it if you wish."

There were scores of contactee reports during the twelve months of 1957, maybe even hundreds that are now lost to us. One of the most notable of these involved a prominent Brazilian lawyer, Professor Joao de Freitas Guimaraes, a sober middle-aged military advocate in Sao Sebastiao. He said that he went joy riding in a flying saucer on a cool evening in July 1957. For a long time afterward he kept his experience to himself, sharing it with only a few friends such as Sao Paulo judge Dr. Alberto Franco.

On a dull, overcast evening, Guimaraes recalled, he was walking alone along a beach off the coast of Bela Island, Brazil, when he saw a jet of water rise up, and then a pot-bellied machine surfaced and moved toward shore. To his astonishment, two men, both more than 5 feet 10 inches tall, with long, fair hair, wearing tight-fitting green coveralls, clambered out, he said. They approached him directly and silently indicated that they would like him to step aboard. He spoke to them in French, English, Italian, and Portuguese, but they didn't seem to understand any of these languages. Because they didn't seem hostile, and because he was overcome with curiosity, he accepted their unspoken invitation, climbed up a long ladder mounted outside the craft, and with the help of the two men, stepped into the object.

The ladder was retracted and the door eased shut. The professor remained in a small compartment next to a window. He could not say later how many compartments there were in the craft. As the machine lifted into the air, he was surprised to see water splashing against the portholes. "Is it raining?" he asked. He claims that he received a silent reply—he felt it was some kind of telepathy, although he admitted knowing nothing about such matters. Somehow his hosts told him that the water was caused by the rotation of the craft.

For the next forty minutes or so (he said his watch stopped during the flight) the now identified (to him) flying object flitted about in the starlit upper atmosphere. During the trip he noted that he felt pain and cold in his genitals. He tried to ask the men where they were from, but they did not answer. One of them showed him a chart, something like a zodiac, he said, and he had the feeling that they were trying to explain when they would return, and that they wanted him to meet them again. Finally they delivered him back to the spot where they had picked him up, and six months later he told the story to a friend, Dr. Lincoln Feliciano, who contacted a Brazilian journalist. Professor Guimaraes quickly became a celebrity of sorts in Brazil and was, he confessed, amazed by the grave respect his story was accorded.

In John Fuller's account of the bizarre UFO contact of Barney and Betty Hill, *Interrupted Journey*, Barney Hill recalled under hypnosis that he was placed on a table aboard a flying saucer and that he felt something cold being lowered over his genitals. The Hills' watches also stopped during their alleged experience.

The most famous contactee of 1956-57 was a New Jersey

sign painter named Howard Menger. He was "discovered" by Long John Nebel, a New York radio personality who conducted an all-night talk show over station WOR, before moving to NBC. Long John had just begun his career in radio, and he was looking for an angle. He found it in flying saucers and built a huge following with his offbeat interviews with contactees, mystics, and assorted weirdos. Somehow he has managed to remain detached and claims to this day that he doesn't buy most of what his guests tell him. In any case, Menger's initial appearances on Long John's show started a stampede to the little town of High Bridge, New Jersey, Menger's home. According to Howard Menger, the flying saucers were frequently landing on his property, and the ufonauts often dropped in for coffee.

Menger, a gentle, soft-spoken man with a sincere manner, claimed that he had first been contacted by long-haired blond men in automobiles back in his army days in World War II. And in June 1946, a glowing UFO had landed near his parents home in High Bridge, and two men and a beautiful girl had stepped out. The men were dressed in "blue-gray ski-type uniforms," were blond, fair-skinned, and of medium height. The woman, he said, wore a similar outfit of a soft pastel color which almost seemed to glow. She told him she was 500 years old. Basically, she advised him to learn to use his mental powers and to prepare for the important days ahead. She also is supposed to have told him to keep his mouth shut about all of this until 1957.

So he waited. And in 1957, the UFOs began to come to High Bridge. They were seen by many. There were even several witnesses who claimed they had stood by and watched as Howard went out to meet and chat with the "space people."

Menger's book, *From Outer Space to You*, tells an even more bizarre story than George Adamski's. He relates frequent visits with apparent terrestrials who introduced him into the unbelievable underworld of the "silent contactees": ordinary men and women who seemed exceptionally knowledgeable about the UFO situation and who posed as businessmen, real estate dealers, and the like. He was, he said, called out in the middle of the night to take long trips to desolate landing areas. On one occasion he was allegedly instructed to buy a box of sunglasses and leave them in an isolated field at night.

His book is filled with strange stories, most of them completely unpalatable to the UFO researchers who were seeking hardware and solid evidence that the UFOs were from outer space: stories that hinted of occultism, telepathy, extrasensory perception, and, as always, a simplified philosophy based upon the Golden Rule. Although there is some religious commentary in the book, Menger seemed obsessed with health foods and offered diet information that presumably had some relation to what he was learning from the ufonauts. The last sixty-three pages are devoted to a treatise titled, "A New Concept in Nutrition."

Sandwiched in between the landings and contacts, which he tells in a direct and convincing manner, Menger relates things like how a Sergeant Cramer in the village of Bedminister, New Jersey, had pursued a speeding light-green station wagon bearing the license number WR E79. Menger had once owned such a vehicle, and with that license number. He was hauled into court to answer the charges. He had actually been nowhere near Bedminister on the night in question, and Sergeant Cramer's testimony, as quoted by Menger, was most unusual.

Cramer told the judge that he had pursued the station wagon to a red light at an intersection where it simply "disappeared." Because visibility at that particular intersection was good in all directions for some distance, it's a mystery how any car could just disappear there. It's an even bigger mystery how that car could have been one that Menger had junked years before.

"Well, what do we have around here? A phantom car!" the judge allegedly remarked. "I feel like either putting a man in jail for perjury or breaking a sergeant. This is the strangest case I have heard in all my years on the bench!"

The good judge didn't know the half of it!

One of Menger's terrestrial contacts is supposed to have told him, "My friend, this earth is the battlefield of Armageddon, and the battle is for men's minds and souls… there is a very powerful group on this planet, which possesses tremendous knowledge of technology, psychology, and most unfortunate of all, advanced brain therapy…They use people not only from this planet, but people from Mars as well. And also other people of your own planet—people you don't know about. People who live unobserved and undiscovered as yet…"

The Menger book was published by Gray Barker in 1959 and enjoyed a small sale of a few thousand. The UFO hardcore at the time was no more than 30,000, and if a UFO book, particularly a contactee book, sold 3,000 copies it was practically a best seller. Menger didn't stop with the book. He issued a phonograph record which, he claimed, contained music composed by the space people—but it sounded more like Howard Menger plucking clumsily at a badly tuned piano.

Then came the freakish climax, which was almost as fantastic as all that had gone on before.

At one of his early broadcasts with Long John, a crowd had gathered in front of the studio, and in it there was a striking blond girl named MarIa. She and Menger met, and he later divorced his wife so he could marry her. MarIa, Howard confided to friends, was from another planet. MarIa's real name was Constance Weber. "MarIa" was her space name, she explained, and was the pseudonym that appeared on her book, *My Saturnian Lover.* Her Saturnian was Howard, for, you see, the space people informed him that he was originally from the planet Saturn.

In the early 1960s, Long John Nebel landed a television show, and it was natural that he should invite Howard Menger to be one of his first guests. Menger was certain to be controversial, articulate, and enthralling. Or so producer Parris Flammonde thought.

On the night of the show, according to Mr. Flammonde, an unusually quiet and nervous Howard Menger walked into the studio. "I knew that his natural manner could be boyish, even shy," Flammonde commented later, "but on this particular occasion he just seemed *vague."*

Long John sensed this, too, and broke his usual rule of never speaking to a guest before going on the air ("Let's not do the show now," Long John will admonish. "Let's wait until we're on the air."). He said a few kidding words to his old friend, and then the red lights blinked on, and millions of viewers around the Northeast settled back to hear Howard Menger tell about his experiences with the friendly "brothers from outer space."

Instead, Flammonde recalls, "Vaguely, aimlessly, rather embarrassingly, he avoided and vacillated…Howard Menger, Saturnian husband to a Venusian traveler in space, friend of extraterrestrials, annotator of 'authentic music from another planet,' master of teleportation, and saucerological sage *extraordinaire*— recanted! Denied almost everything…His saucers might have been psychic, his space people visions, his and Maria's other planethood, metaphoric.

"As a matter of fact, so did he retreat from his tales of the unreal, the reality of the immediate surroundings seemed to fade momentarily…If he had exuded a sort of translucent indefiniteness when he arrived, he was close to invisible when he left …To this day, the transition of the myth and personality of Howard Menger remains one of the most captivating enigmas of contactology."

Later, in letters to Gray Barker and *Saucer News* editor Jim Moseley, Menger termed his book "fiction-fact" and implied that the Pentagon had given him the films and asked him to participate in an experiment to test the public's reaction to extraterrestrial contact.

He has helped us, therefore, to dismiss his entire story as not only a hoax, but a hoax perpetrated by the U.S. government!

Moseley staged a circuslike Congress of Scientific Ufologists in New York in 1967 and flew Howard and Maria up from their current home in Florida. Howard, Jim reasoned, would be a strong drawing card for the far-out fringe. I met Menger briefly backstage the day he spoke to some 1,500 people gathered at the Congress. Long John introduced him from the stage. Menger was still shy and boyish, and his palms were covered with sweat. Although he had given many lectures and appeared frequently on radio and TV, his nerves were visibly raw that afternoon. "Here," I thought to myself, "is a very scared man."

His brief lecture was a bitter disappointment to the little old ladies who had come to hear a message of hope and faith. His retraction on the Long John show a few years earlier was forgotten, and he made a conscious effort to please the crowd of believers by sticking to a positive pro-extraterrestrial line. He avoided discussing the CIA's alleged experiment and his own misgivings about the reality of UFOs. Instead, he talked about the saucer he was trying to build in his basement, presumably from plans given to him by you-know-who, then he spent several minutes knocking the National Investigation Committees on Aerial Phenomena and its deputy director, Richard Hall, for their attempts to thwart his plans for a UFO convention in Florida, and finally, he got around to his controversial contacts.

"I think the most important thing that happened to me," he said, "was in High Bridge, New Jersey, in the summer of 1956. It was in August. The craft came down from the west. It looked like a huge fireball. I was frightened. Gradually, as it came closer, it slowed down. The pulsations subsided. A metallic appearance was plainly visible. It was no longer a ball of fire, it turned into what looked like a man-made craft, reflecting the sun as it came close to the ground. It was a beautiful sight, very similar to the one on the screen here. [He was showing a UFO movie.] It stopped about a foot and a half from the ground. An opening appeared in the side of the craft. There was a small incline or platform. Two men stepped out, very nicely dressed in shiny space suits, such as what we have today for our astronauts, very similar. Of course, in those days—this was way ahead of the time. One man stepped to the left, and the other stepped to the right, and then another man stepped out, a man I will never forget as long as I live. He was approximately six feet one, maybe six feet two. He had long blond hair over his shoulders—yes, long blond hair. He stepped toward me, and the message he gave, of course, was what most people don't want to hear, a message of love and understanding. He said he had come from outer space, which is what most people really don't believe in. Someday they will.

"I often wonder what would happen to these people who say, 'Well, what proof do you have? If I could see a flying saucer or someone step out of a craft, boy, I would make sure the people knew about it.' Well, I just wonder about that. If you realize what people go through when this happens to them. If you really think you have guts enough to come out and tell people. Of course, nowadays it might be a little easier, but in the early fifties it was very, very rough, especially when you are in business and you are trying to act like a reputable citizen and bring up a family and, you know, things like this in your community."

Yes, it must have been tough. And it must have required more than just a little guts for Howard Menger to first come forward with such a story and then later to publicly recant on television. I have talked with several different people who were around High Bridge in 1956-57. One of them is Ivan T. Sanderson who lives nearby and who knew Howard before, during, and after these episodes. Something strange was definitely happening to Menger and the people around him at that time.

Did Howard Menger get rich from all this? On the contrary. He lost his sign-painting business and his reputation. In the end he had to flee to another state, where he is just barely eking out a living at his old trade.

Howard Menger is not alone. There are many other tormented victims in this incredible drama. One of them was a traveling grain buyer named Reinhold Schmidt. Late on the afternoon of November 5, 1957, Schmidt entered the office of Sheriff Dave Drage in Kearney, Nebraska, and unfolded a tale of contact that was classical in every detail. He said his engine had stalled outside of Kearney, and when he got out of his car to check it, he saw a silver "blimp" in a nearby field. Curious, he walked toward it and was surprised when a kind of staircase opened up and unreeled toward him. A man in conventional terrestrial clothes stepped out to meet him, speaking in perfect German, a language that Schmidt understood.

Repairs were being made, the man explained, and Schmidt was welcome to look around until the work was completed. Schmidt said there were four people aboard, two men and two women, all apparently normal except for one bewildering detail. They did not seem to walk, he noted; rather they seemed to glide across the floor of the craft as if they were on casters. He described glowing tubes of colored liquids inside the craft, but overall, it was as stark and as simple as the interiors described by other contactees.

The four people were not very informative, as usual, but told Schmidt that he would know all about it—and them—eventually. The whole episode sounds very much like the "chance" encounters reported by the 1897 contactees.

After about thirty minutes, Schmidt was asked to leave. The "repairs" were finished. The object took off, and the now-excited grain buyer headed for Kearney. Within twenty-four hours the authorities had him locked up in a nearby mental institution for observation. Air Force officers materialized and branded the poor man as a nut. A search of the alleged landing site revealed puddles of the purple liquid so common at such spots all over the world, and there were indentations in the ground where the object stood. But when the sheriff searched Schmidt's car, he found an open can of oil in the trunk and accused him of having spread it around the site. Schmidt not only denied ownership of the can but pointed out, reasonably, that it would be rather foolish to drive around with an open oil can in the back of any car.

Later, after he was released, Schmidt lectured widely and howled loud and long about the treatment he had received. Ufologists noted that his story improved with age, and new embellishments were added each time he told it. Apparently he claimed other contacts of some sort and revealed that he knew the location of a wonderful quartz mine in California. The space people had told him that this quartz would cure cancer.

He started to raise money to mine the quartz, and eventually some of his investors hauled him into court, where he was indicted as a swindler. Thus, Reinhold Schmidt joined the unhappy ranks of the contactees—a thoroughly discredited man. Yet, his original story made as much sense as any other contactee story, and he seemed to experience many of the same problems reported by the other pawns in this ultraterrestrial game. There were repeated contacts and manipulations that convinced him of the apparent validity of the ufonaut claims and led him down the long road to total disaster.

A massive flap condition existed throughout the world during the week of Schmidt's unfortunate encounter. And there were a number of other contacts, all grouped within thirty-six hours of Schmidt's. Some of these contacts produced details that tended to corroborate the others.

On October 4, 1957, the Soviet Union hurled the first man-made satellite into space. It was not visible to the naked eye. A month later, on November 3, 1957, Sputnik II carried the ill-fated Russian dog, Laika, into orbit. Three days after that, at 6:30 A.M. on the morning of November 6, a twelve-year-old farm boy, Everett Clark of Dante, Tennessee, got up to let out his dog, Frisky, and was nonplussed to see a strange glowing object resting in a field about 300 feet from the house. Thinking that he was dreaming, young Clark shuffled back to bed.

A few minutes later he returned to the door to call his dog, and he saw that the object was still there. Several of the neighborhood dogs, Frisky included, were clustered around it, barking at four people, two men and two women, all normally dressed, who were moving around outside the oblong thing.

One of the men, Clark later told reporters and investigators from the Aerial Phenomena Research Organization (APRO), was trying to grab Frisky, but the dog growled and backed away. He said that these people were talking in a guttural tongue which sounded like the German soldiers he had seen in the movies. The man did catch one of the other dogs, but it snarled and snapped at him, and he let it go. Then the strange quartet turned and seemed to walk right through the walls of the craft, "like walking through glass," Clark said. One of the men had seen the boy watching them and had made a motion for him to approach, but Clark declined.

Dante, Tennessee, lies outside of Knoxville and is a long, long way from Kearney, Nebraska. Schmidt's story of the day before did not appear in the area until after Everett Clark had made his initial report. Reporter Carson Brewer of the Knoxville *News-Sentinel* found an elongated impression in the field where the grass had been pressed down in area 24 feet by 5 feet. APRO's investigators found that Clark was regarded as "a serious and honest boy" by his high school principal, and his grandmother said he had called her immediately after the incident (his parents had already gone to work) and that he was "hysterical."

Later that very night another farmer, John Trasco of Everittstown, New Jersey, reportedly went outside to feed his dog, King, when he saw a brightly glowing egg-shaped object hovering above the ground near his barn. A weird "little man" stepped timidly toward him, he said. He was about 3.5 feet tall, had a putty-colored face with large, bulging froglike eyes, and was dressed in green coveralls.

"We are a peaceful people," Trasco quoted the little man as saying in a high "scary" voice. "We don't want no trouble. We just want your dog."

The taken-aback farmer said he managed to snap, "Get the hell out of here!" The "little man" scurried back to the object, and it shot off into the evening sky.

On Wednesday night, November 6, true to the Wednesday phenomenon pattern, there were the landings in Montville, Ohio; Dante, Tennessee; and Everittstown, New Jersey. Another weird contact took place near Playa del Rey, California, when three cars stalled along a highway called Vista del Mar. The drivers, Richard Kehoe, Ronald Burke, and Joe Thomas, got out to see what was wrong. The answer seemed to lie in the egg-shaped machine sitting on a nearby beach, surrounded by a blue haze.

Two men apparently came from the object and spoke to the trio in difficult-to-understand English. According to Kehoe, the men were about 5 feet 5 inches tall, dressed in black leather trousers and light-colored jerseys. Their skin, he said, appeared to be yellowish green. They asked some very ordinary questions, Kehoe reported, such as, "What time is it? Who were we? Where were we going? And so on." Chalk up still another apparently meaningless contact. After the men flew off in their strange machine, the motorists were able to get their cars started again.

A final contact was reported that morning by a truck driver named Malvan Stevens. He said he was driving near House, Mississippi, about 7:25 A.M. when a large egg-shaped object dropped out of the sky and landed on the highway directly in front of him. Stevens, a forty-eight-year-old resident of Dyersburgh, Mississippi, said that he thought at first that it was some kind of weather balloon. Then he noticed that there seemed to be a propeller on either end and on top of the object. He got out of his truck and was confronted by three people, two men and a woman, all about 4.5 feet tall, with pasty white faces. They were dressed, he said, in gray suits, and they tried to talk to him in a rapid-fire language that he could not understand. One of them tried to shake his hand. After a few minutes of futile attempts at conversation, the beings got back into the object and flew off.

Stevens later told some of his coworkers about the episode, and one of them passed it on to the Meridian, Mississippi, *Star*. Later, when the Aerial Phenomena Research Organization investigated, they found him to be highly regarded as "a reliable family man" and not one to make up tales or play practical jokes.

The big picture for 1957 is awesome in scope. There were apparently reliable contact reports earlier in the year from South America; Professor Guimaraes in Brazil early in July; Signore Galli in Italy, also early in July; the Argentine Air Force guard on August 20; Mr. Cook of England on September 7. And remember, both Cook and the Argentine airman claimed that they had been warned about our upsetting the balance of the universe. Cook had never heard of the Argentine report that preceded his alleged experience by about only three weeks.

The Argentine airman said that "the voice" told him that flying saucers would soon be showing themselves all over the world. That prediction certainly came true in November 1957.

The Contactee Hoax

I have now met and interviewed in depth more than 200 silent contactees who, unlike most of those already named, have never publicly revealed their experiences. They do not write books or go on lecture tours. They show little or no interest in UFO literature. Some of them begin to experience personality deterioration after their initial contact. Others find their previously normal lives disrupted by nightmares and peculiar hallucinations. Poltergeists (noisy, invisible ghosts) invade their homes. Their telephones and television sets run amok. My own educated guess is that there may be 50,000 or more silent contactees in the United States alone. And new ones are being added to the list every month.

Nevertheless, a complex and frightening hoax is involved in all this. But it is not the product of run-of-the-mill practical jokers, liars, and lunatics. Quite frankly, many of these contactees lack the imagination to make up their stories or to construct the complicated "hoaxes" that develop. They are well-meaning, honest people who have undergone an experience that seemed very real to them. In case after case, such people are able to come up with details that correlate and which have received little or no publicity. This would be absolutely impossible if they were simply making up their stories.

No, the real truth lies in another direction. The contactees from 1897 on have been telling us *what they were told by the ufonauts. The ufonauts are the liars, not the contactees.* And they are lying deliberately as part of the bewildering smoke-screen that they have established to cover their real origin, purpose, and motivation.

In recent years we have been informed by seemingly sincere contactees, several of whom have undergone psychiatric and lie detector tests and passed them with flying colors, that the saucers come from unknown plants named Clarion, Maser, Schare, Blaau, Tythan, Korendor, Orion, Fowser, Zomdic, Aenstria, and a dozen other absurd places. There have also been contactees who talk freely about the people of Venus, Mars, Jupiter, Uranus, Saturn, and the moon.

Chances are excellent that the UFOs do not come from any of these places, any more than the great airships of 1897 came from a secret lab in Nebraska. These names are plants, not planets. Whatever the UFOs are up to, they are doing it on a very large scale all over the earth, and it is inevitable that they should come into contact with some of us from time to time, either accidentally or by design. When such contacts do occur, they deliberately hand out ridiculous false information. They exploit our beliefs and hide safely behind the limited credulity of our scientists and governments. It is time that we got wise to this simple psychological trick. They've been pulling it on us for centuries.

Can we really blame the contactees?

Suppose a strange metallic disk covered with flashing colored lights settled in your backyard and a tall man in a one-piece silver space suit got out. Suppose he looked unlike any man you had ever seen before, and when you asked him where he was from, he replied, "I am from Venus." Would you argue with him? Chances are you would accept his word for it. And if you decided to tell the world the news, you would naturally proclaim that the mystery had been solved. The flying saucers were from Venus. You were certain because this very sincere stranger had told you so.

Buried within the context of all the contactees' messages there are clues to an even more complex threat. A direct threat to us. Each contactee has been able to pass on a small fragment of the real truth. The endless descriptions of peaceful far-off worlds and shining cities of glass are only subterfuges. Before I can extend this further, I must present you with some of the other evidence. You must be aware of all the pieces in the puzzle before they can fall into place and make sense. Already you can understand why so many people have been in total confusion for so long. This whole mystery has been designed to keep us confused and skeptical.

Somebody somewhere is having a good laugh at our expense.

12
The Cosmic Jokers

Demonology is not just another crackpot-ology. It is the ancient and scholarly study of the monsters and demons who have seemingly coexisted with man throughout history. Thousands of books have been written on the subject, many of them authored by educated clergymen, scientists, and scholars, and uncounted numbers of well-documented demonic events are readily available to every researcher. The manifestations and occurrences described in this imposing literature are similar, if not entirely identical, to the UFO phenomenon itself. Victims of demonomania (possession) suffer the very same medical and emotional symptoms as the UFO contactees. Demonomania is so common that it has spawned the minor medical and psychiatric study of demonopathy.

Throughout most of history, the manifestations of demonology and demonopathy have been viewed from a religious perspective and explained as the work of the Devil. The bizarre manipulations and ill effects described in the demonological literature are usually regarded as the result of a great unseen conflict between God and the Devil. In UFO lore, the same conflict has been observed, and the believers have explained it as a space war between the "Guardians" (good guys from outer space), who are protecting our planet, and some evil extraterrestrial race. The manifestations are the same, only the frame of reference is different.

The Devil and his demons can, according to the literature, manifest themselves in almost any form and can physically imitate anything from angels to horrifying monsters with glowing eyes. Strange objects and entities materialize and dematerialize in these stories, just as the UFOs and their splendid occupants appear and disappear, walk through walls, and perform other supernatural feats.

Did ancient man misinterpret UFO manifestations by placing them in a religious context? Apparently not. The literature indicates that the phenomenon carefully cultivated the religious frame of reference in early times, just as the modem manifestations have carefully supported the extraterrestrial frame of reference. Operation Trojan Horse is merely the same old game in a new, updated guise. The Devil's emissaries of yesteryear have been replaced by the mysterious "men in black." The quasi-angels of Biblical times have become magnificent spacemen. The demons, devils, and false angels were recognized as liars and plunderers by early man. These same impostors now appear as long-haired Venusians.

All of the major religions, and most of the minor ones, accept the God-Devil conflict, and their scriptures outline some possibly real episodes in which human beings have had some direct experience with this conflict. A large portion of all holy literature consists of material purportedly dictated to men by supernatural beings, and a good part of this seems more allegorical or metaphorical than real. The phenomenon may have passed along information about man's origin and purpose carefully disguised in terms and fictitious episodes that could be understood by the minds of the people during the period when the messages were transmitted. Thus, the story of Adam and Eve might not be the actual truth but merely a great simplification of the truth.

In the *Forgotten Books of Eden,* an apocryphal book allegedly translated from ancient Egyptian in the nineteenth century, we are told that Satan and his hosts were fallen angels who populated the earth before Adam was brought into being, and Satan used lights, fire, and water in his efforts to rid the planet of this troublesome creature. He even disguised himself as an angel from time to time and appeared as a beautiful young woman in his efforts to lead Adam to his doom. UFO-type lights were one of the Devil's devices described in the *Forgotten Books of Eden.* Subtle variations on this same theme can be found in the Bible and in the numerous scriptures of the Oriental cultures. Religious man has always been so enthralled with the main (and probably allegorical) story line that the hidden point has been missed. That point is that *the earth was occupied before man arrived or was created*. The original occupants or forces were paraphysical and possessed the power of transmogrification. Man was the interloper, and the earth's original occupants or owners were not very happy over the intrusion. The inevitable conflict arose between physical man and the paraphysical owners of the planet. Man accepted the interpretation that this conflict raged between his creator and the Devil. The religious viewpoint has always been that the Devil has been attacking man (trying to get rid of him) by foisting disasters, wars, and sundry evils upon him.

There is historical and modern proof that this may be so.

A major, but little-explored, aspect of the UFO phenomenon is therefore theological and philosophical rather than purely scientific. The UFO problem can never be untangled by physicists and scientists unless they are men who have also been schooled in liberal arts, theology, and philosophy. Unfortunately, most scientific disciplines are so demanding that their practitioners have little time or inclination to study complicated subjects outside their own immediate fields of interest.

Satan and his demons are part of the folklore of all races, no matter how isolated they have been from one another. The Indians of North America have many legends and stories about a devil-like entity who appeared as a man and was known as the trickster because he pulled off so many vile stunts. Tribes in Africa, South America, and the remote Pacific islands have similar stories.

Mystery men with strange persuasive powers, sometimes good but more often evil, are described and discussed in many books with no UFO or religious orientation. A dark gentleman in a cloak and hood is supposed to have handed Thomas Jefferson the design for the reverse side of the Great Seal of the United States (you will find this on a dollar bill). Julius Caesar, Napoleon, and many others are supposed to have had enigmatic meetings with these odd personages. These stories turn up in such unexpected places as

Madame Du Barry's memoirs. She claimed repeated encounters with a strange young man who would approach her suddenly on the street and give her startling prophecies about herself. He pointedly told her that the last time she would see him would serve as an omen for a sudden reversal of her fortunes. Sure enough, on April 27, 1774, as she and her ailing lover, King Louis XV, were heading for the palace of Versailles, the youthful mystery man appeared one final time.

"I mechanically directed my eyes toward the iron gate leading to the garden," she wrote. "I felt my face drained of blood as a cry of horror escaped my lips. For, leaning against the gate was that singular being."

The coach was halted, and three men searched the area thoroughly but could find no trace of him. He had vanished into thin air. Soon afterward Madame Du Barry's illustrious career in the royal courts ended, and she went into exile.

Malcolm X, the late leader of a black militant group, reported a classic experience with a paraphysical "man in black" in his autobiography. He was serving a prison sentence at the time, and the entity materialized in his prison cell:

As I lay on my bed, I suddenly became aware of a man sitting beside me in my chair. He had on a dark suit, I remember. I could see him as plainly as I see anyone I look at. He wasn't black, and he wasn't white. He was light-brown-skinned, an Asiatic cast of countenance, and he had oily black hair.

I looked right into his face. I didn't get frightened. I knew I wasn't dreaming. I couldn't move, I didn't speak, and he didn't. I couldn't place him racially—other than I knew he was a non-European. I had no idea whatsoever who he was. He just sat there. Then, as suddenly as he had come, he was gone.

This type of vision is well known to students of psychic phenomena. The immobility or akinesia experienced by Malcolm X is especially common in the "bedroom visitant" cases in which percipients awaken to sense or even see an intruder in their bedroom—an intruder who melts away after passing along a message or a warning. Psychiatrists tend to dismiss this type of phenomenon as hypnopompic; that is, the vision is thought to be a dream that overlaps into the waking state.

Solitary witnesses to UFO landings and contacts frequently complain of akinesia. They find themselves completely paralyzed until the object takes off or disappears. In some cases, the UFO occupant allegedly aimed a tube or weapon of some sort at the percipient, leading ufologists to assume that a technological device was used to induce the paralytic state. Parapsychologists, on the other hand, have long concluded that akinesia is a contributing cause; that the entity materializes by utilizing energy from the percipient himself.

If the UFO phenomenon is largely hallucinatory, and much of the evidence suggests that it is, then the parapsychological assumption may be more valid than the ufological speculation.

Charles Bowen, editor of England's *Flying Saucer Review,* the world's most respected ufological journal, recently observed: "Did these witnesses, widely dispersed on earth, and in time, all have experiences with solid creatures from another world or from another dimension of reality? Or did they suffer hallucinations of a similar kind, where the dream creatures were strikingly similar in many respects?... I pondered over the idea that the frightening, spooky creatures described by some witnesses could be some sort of *psychic projection.* There are noticeable dreamlike qualities about the incidents described in these cases."

The records of demonology are filled with striking parallels. During the outbreak of vampirism in Europe during the Middle Ages, witnesses to vampires were often paralyzed, and the general descriptions of the vampires themselves are identical to the "men in black." The dark skin and angular, Oriental-like faces were commonly reported and were immortalized in the paintings of demons and vampires by artists of the period.

In the UFO reports, innumerable witnesses have described both the little men and the normal-sized ufonauts as sharing these basic characteristics, along with unusually long, claw-like fingers. Malcolm X was not versed in UFO lore, and he assumed that his apparition was a phantom of the Black Muslim religion.

Traditionally, the appearance of one of these evil-looking entities is an ill omen. The witness frequently dies a short time after his vision, or some other terrible tragedy befalls him. Thus, we have the Grim Reaper myth.

Voodoo and black magic are also said to produce such figures. In the early 1950s, Albert K. Bender dabbled in both black magic and ufology, and he created a stir in ufological circles when he claimed that he had been visited by three men with glowing eyes, dressed in black suits. He suffered all of the classic symptoms of demonomania; the fierce headaches, the upset stomach, anorexia (loss of appetite), and lacunar amnesia. He abandoned his UFO studies after these experiences.

I have in my files hundreds of cases, some of which have now been investigated by qualified psychiatrists, in which young men and women obsessed with the UFO phenomenon have suffered frightening visits from these apparitions, been followed by mysterious black Cadillacs which appeared and disappeared suddenly, and have been terrified into giving up their pursuit of the UFOs. Many contactees report similar experiences.

The phenomenon is reflective; the more frightened the victim becomes, the more the manifestations are escalated.

Dabbling with UFOs can be as dangerous as dabbling with black magic. The phenomenon preys upon the neurotic, the gullible, and the immature. Paranoid-schizophrenia, demonomania and even suicide can result—and has resulted—in a number of cases. A mild curiosity about UFOs can turn into a destructive obsession. For this reason, I strongly recommend that parents forbid their children from becoming involved. Schoolteachers and other adults should not encourage teenagers to take an interest in the subject.

Appearances of Angels

There is a balance in nature, and there also seems to be a careful balance in the UFO/psychic phenomenon. People have actually died after exposure to the gamma and ultraviolet rays from UFOs. But other people have had their ailments cured by similar rays. The entities are most often mischievous and sometimes completely hostile to human beings, but there are cases in which people in trouble have been rescued by these characters.

Occult literature is filled with accounts of this type. A man is lost in a blinding blizzard high in the Himalayas, miles from the nearest habitation. Suddenly another man in khaki coveralls appears in the snow and guides him to an abandoned hut and safety, then vanishes. A pilot crashes in the Pacific a mile from a small island. A swimmer appears and hauls the injured man ashore—then vanishes. The island is totally deserted. A child is lost in a swamp, and an unusual man suddenly arrives, takes him by the hand, and leads him out. (There are dozens of these lost-children stories. New ones appear in local newspapers every year. The events are such that routine anonymous Good Samaritans can be ruled out.)

In the Book of Daniel, Chapter 3, King Nebuchadnezzar throws Shadrach, Meshach, and Abednego into a blazing furnace. The trio emerges unhurt after the king observes, "Lo, I see four men loose, walking in the midst of the fire, and they have no hurt; and the form of the fourth is like the Son of God."

Our mystery men have allegedly guided trapped miners out of caved-in shafts.

There are so many of these cases that once again we must ask: Who are all these people? Where do they come from, and where do they go? Could they be the same kinds of entities who were known to the ancients as angels?

Add up all these stories, and it seems as if our planet has always been overrun with angels and devils, vampires, werewolves, ghouls, and ghosts galore; sundry demons killing animals and people and lapping up blood. Good guys and bad guys struggling to hold us together or break us apart.

The Book of the Secrets of Enoch is another apocryphal book attempting to explain, or at least to interpret, the invisible world around us. Earlier we discussed the story of Enoch's trips to other worlds, where he encountered wondrous beings and was given information to take back with him and spread among men. Here is how Enoch is supposed to have vanished at the age of 365 years:

> When Enoch had talked to the people, the Lord sent out darkness onto the earth, and there was darkness, and it covered those men standing with Enoch, and they took Enoch up to the highest heaven, where the Lord is; and he received him and placed him before his face, and the darkness went off from the earth, and light came again.

> And the people saw and understood not how Enoch had been taken, and glorified God, and found a roll in which was traced "the invisible God"; and all went to their homes.

The Bible reduces all of this to a single line (Genesis 5:24): "And Enoch walked with God; and he was not; for God took him."

All of the religious prophets seem to have undergone contactee-type experiences. A man named Hermas, brother to Pius, Bishop of Rome, left behind a controversial book of visions, which details numerous UFO-like events early in the Christian era. Hermas was dictated to write the book by "angels," and in it he describes seeing a great cloud of dust on the desert. As it came closer to him he saw "a great beast, as if it were a whale; and fiery locusts came out of his mouth. The height of the beast was about 100 feet, and he had a head like a large earthen vessel … Now the beast had upon its head four colors; first black, then a red and bloody color, then a golden, and then a white." He also spoke with strange beings dressed in white, with veils over their faces. Some of his "angels" appeared as human beings who could suddenly transform themselves into different persons in front of his eyes. Once, he reports, he was handed a book to read, and as soon as he was finished, it disappeared magically from his grasp.

UFO SYMBOLS

Designs which have appeared on "flying saucers" or which have been attributed to actual writings by the ufonauts. Listed here only by date and place of origin.

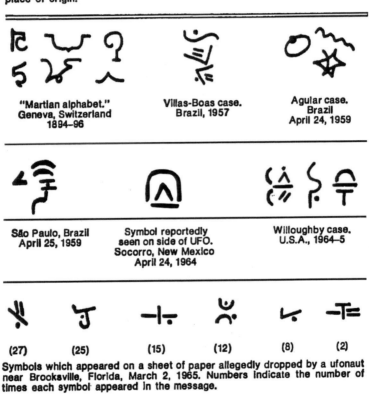

"Martian alphabet."
Geneva, Switzerland
1894–96

Villas-Boas case.
Brazil, 1957

Aguilar case.
Brazil
April 24, 1959

São Paulo, Brazil
April 25, 1959

Symbol reportedly
seen on side of UFO.
Socorro, New Mexico
April 24, 1964

Willoughby case.
U.S.A., 1964–5

(27)   (25)   (15)   (12)   (8)   (2)

Symbols which appeared on a sheet of paper allegedly dropped by a ufonaut near Brooksville, Florida, March 2, 1965. Numbers indicate the number of times each symbol appeared in the message.

Symbols on dials in alleged craft.
Ballard, Washington
February, 1966

Symbol photographed on bottom of UFO
Madrid, Spain
June 1, 1967

The winged angels in gossamer gowns with halos around their heads are the fictional creations of artists. Throughout history, those who have claimed actual experiences with these entities have described them either as radiant beings surrounded by brilliant light, or as very ordinary-looking human beings. They sat down and supped with Lot, just as our modern Venusians reportedly sit down at kitchen tables and drink coffee with backwoods farmers. In the great majority of all these cases, including the numerous UFO stories I have recounted, *these entities appear as very young men in their late teens or early twenties.* We have both male and female entities in our catalogs of the weird, but there seem to be more male "angels" and ufonauts than female. Many witnesses have the distinct impression that these entities are actually sexless (androgynous). The males with their long hair, angular faces, and mincing manners suggest they might be hermaphrodites and homosexuals.

The "inspired" (ghost-written) book *Oahspe*, by Dr. John Newbrough, hammers away at the asexual theme, claiming that the great leaders of early mankind were sexless, as are the great angels. This condition is called *iesu* and is defined as follows in *Oahspe:*

A sexless person; one without the possibility of sexual passion. Some men, as Brahma, attain to *iesu*. Improperly called *iesus*. The Hebraic word *ieue* was made from *iesu*; one who can hear the voice of the Great Spirit. *Ieue* has been improperly confounded with Jehovih. Men who attain *iesu* are said to have attained the state of woman, *i.e.*, to have changed sex.

Leaders such as Alexander the Great were, in fact, suspect as homosexuals or asexuals. One very large religious cult still exists (in the Soviet Union, of all places), which is founded on the belief that asexuals will eventually rule the world. Men in the cult are deliberately castrated. Former Soviet Premier Georgi Malenkov was allegedly a member of this group and his masculinity—or lack of same—has been heatedly debated in several books. Today there is a rampant buffery dedicated to documenting and combating what they assert is a homosexual conspiracy to dominate the world.

Except for those who might be specially constructed for incubus -succubus activities (invisible entities who reportedly fornicate with human females and males), it does appear that our angels and spacemen come from a world without sex—and, very probably, a world without an organized society; a world in which each individual is merely a unit in the whole and is totally controlled by the collective intelligence or energy mass of that whole. In other words, these beings have no free will. They are slaves of a very high order. Often they try to convey this to percipients with their statements, "We are One," "We are in bondage."

Such a world would have no need for money, and contactees are often told that the great civilization in outer space does not use money. Ego would be unknown, and so all of the social problems, conflicts, and ambitions produced by ego would be unknown, too. Even death would hold no terror. To us, death means the end of our enjoyment of material things, of sex, of ego. To them, death means nothing more than the termination of existence. If they are really mere manipulations of energy, as I believe them to be, then they might be reconstructed at some time in the future. Because they lack ego and personality, it would be like taking an automobile apart and using those parts to build another one.

All of the above points have been stressed in the ancient contacts with angels, as well as the modern ufonaut meetings. Sometimes the information is cunningly disguised, but it is always there.

Angelology is a fascinating offshoot of demonology. The appearances of angels have been chronicled down through the ages, and several new angel reports still turn up each year. Once again we find that these reports contain all the basic ingredients of the UFO reports. The same phenomenon is at work, utilizing a different frame of reference or being misinterpreted by devout witnesses.

A writer named Gustav Davidson spent several years of his

life sifting through all the religious, occult, and psychic records to compile his massive *Dictionary of Angels*. The reflective factor, so common in ufology and demonology, seems to have bothered Mr. Davidson, too.

Davidson wrote in the introduction to his book:

> At this stage of the quest I was literally bedeviled by angels. They stalked and leaguered me, by night and day. I could not tell the evil from the good... I moved, indeed, in a twilight zone of tall presences... I remember one occasion—it was winter and getting dark—returning home from a neighboring farm. I had cut across an unfamiliar field. Suddenly a nightmarish shape loomed up in front of me, barring my progress. After a paralyzing moment, I managed to fight my way past the phantom. The next morning I could not be sure whether I had encountered a ghost, an angel, a demon, or God. There were other such moments and other such encounters, when I passed from terror to trance, from intimations of realms unguessed at to the conviction that, beyond the reach of our senses, beyond the arch of all our experience sacred and profound, there was only—to use an expression of Paul's in I Timothy 4—"fable and endless genealogy."

Fable and endless genealogy. That sums up what we face in trying to isolate the UFO phenomenon from the larger and more important "big picture," the overall situation of which the UFOs are merely a small and perhaps even insignificant part.

The Elementals

When I was just a farm boy new to the big city, I met an elderly woman who hired me to type up a book manuscript she had written. It was largely incoherent, and I suspected she was a little bit off her rocker. The book described her interminable conversations with an ancient Roman named Lucretius. She first met him while walking along Riverside Drive one afternoon. He materialized suddenly in front of her, Roman toga and all, and when their conversation ended, he melted away into thin air. He had long flowing hair, aquiline features, and dark, piercing eyes. To the best of my recollection, their discussions revolved around religion and philosophy.

Several times since then I have met other people who claim to have had frequent encounters with similar entities. For some reason, most of these percipients seem to be on the fringes of the art world. They all describe essentially the same type of being. Those who are bright enough quickly realize that their mysterious visitors are capable of assuming any form they wish. One artist told me in great detail of her thirty years of experiences with an androgynous entity who resembled an Indian and who was fond of playing little jokes on her, such as turning up in the form of Abraham Lincoln. She also described his/its volatile temper.

"They're Valkyries, you know," she said. "They have a wonderful sense of humor, but they also get very angry if you contradict them."

Throughout history occultists have called these entities elementals. There are several kinds of elementals in psychic lore. One type is supposedly conjured up by secret magical rites and can assume any kind of form ranging from that of a beautiful woman to hideous, indescribable monsters. Once a witch or warlock has whipped up such a critter, it will mindlessly repeat the same actions century after century in the same place until another occultist comes along and performs the rite necessary to dissolve it. Many hauntings are ascribed to elemental beings. Generation after generation the entity returns to the same spot to walk along a specific course. If a house is built on the spot, it will walk through the house leaving unlocked doors in its wake, parading through bedrooms and pantries, wandering blindly across gardens. There are innumerable documented instances in which knowledgeable occultists have gotten rid of such entities by exercising certain rites and chanting ancient prayers. Sounds ridiculous, but, as with the exorcism rites of the Church, it seems to work.

The leprechauns of Ireland seem to be another form of elemental. They may be akin to the legendary elves of the Black Forest in Germany and the mysterious little "Stick People" of the North American Indians. The Irish have all kinds of stories and lore about the "little people." In 1968, the people in Ballymagroartyscotch were up in arms when road builders threatened to cut down a *skeog*, or fairy tree. According to tradition, some fairies locate themselves in *skeogs*, and woe to anyone who tries to cut them down. Several contractors refused the job of chopping down the tree. One of them, Ray Greene, said, "I heard of a chap with the electricity board, and he cut down a fairy tree, and the next day he fell off an electricity pole and was killed."

The problem was finally solved by diverting the road around the gnarled old tree.

From the days of Moses burning bush to the modern appearances of angels and holy personages, these strange events seem to have concentrated themselves around trees and shrubbery.

A few years ago a *sidhe*, or fairy mound, was found by workmen building an airport in Ireland. They flatly refused to take a shovel or bulldozer to it. Like the *skeog* of Ballymagroartyscotch, the airport *sidhe* became the focal point of a controversy before the builders finally gave in and bypassed it.

At least one man has died on a *sidhe*. His name was Robert Kirk, and he was the minister of the church at Aberfoyle, Ireland, back in the seventeenth century. After a lifetime of scholarly research, he decided that fairies were invisible creatures composed of "congealed air." His body was found on a fairy mound and gave rise to the legend that the little people had carried off his soul.

The brothers Grimm, Jacob and Wilhelm, not only wrote scores of charming fairy stories, but they also studied the occult and wrote books about it. Some of their children's tales were based on the lore they collected. You undoubtedly remember the various stories about how secretive fairies are about their names. In Spence's *The Fairy Tradition in Britain* we are told, "To mention the fairy name either individually or collectively was not permissible. This restriction is associated with the belief that to know the name of a being presupposes a certain measure of power over him."*

In Scotland, the *na fir chlis* were "nimble men" who inhabited the sky. In Ireland and Wales, fairies with reddish skins were called *fir darrig*, and the legendary ancestors of the men who built Stonehenge were known as *fir bolg*, the "men with bags," who lingered in swamps and bogs.

Angels, elementals, and ufonauts all play amusing games with their names, favoring minor variations on ancient languages. The late George Adamski, one of the first UFO contactees to receive publicity in the early 1950s, claimed that he had met an illustrious space person named Fir Kon; a name that was probably derivative from the ancient Gaelic, a language completely unknown to Mr. Adamski.

A forty-six-year-old TV repairman and ham-radio operator named Sidney Padrick was strolling along Manresa Beach near Monterey, California, early on the morning of January 30, 1965, when he reportedly encountered a grounded UFO and was invited aboard by a mysterious voice. He is supposed to have met a 5-foot, 10-inch-tall man with short-cropped auburn hair, very pale skin, a very sharp nose and chin, and unusually long fingers. This ufonaut identified himself by a name which Mr. Padrick later spelled phonetically as Zeeno. Although Padrick had no knowledge of Greek, *xeno* (pronounced *zee-no*) is the word for stranger in that language.

In England, a glass phial filled with silver sand was found at an alleged UFO landing site in April 1965. It was wrapped in a piece of parchment containing Greek lettering which spelled out

---

* In most religions it is regarded as a grave offense to take the accepted name of God in vain, as in the Ten Commandments. Earlier cultures also demanded that the names of the gods be spoken aloud only with the greatest respect. This fear may have been based upon a certain awareness that invoking the name of a god could produce sudden supernatural manifestations.

"*Adelphos Adelpho,*" meaning brother to brother. This was just one of the many curious finds in that Devon field where a gardener named Arthur Bryant reportedly chatted with two ufonauts on April 24, 1965. One of the ufonauts identified himself as Yamski. It was weeks before British ufologists learned that contactee George Adamski had died suddenly in Washington, D. C., on April 23, 1965, only a few hours before the Bryant contact. Mr. Bryant, himself, died of a brain tumor on June 24, 1967—on the anniversary of Kenneth Arnold's "first" flying saucer sighting twenty years earlier. Coincidentally, journalist Frank Edwards, author of two popular UFO books and a longtime researcher, passed away a few hours before Bryant in his home in Indiana. There have been other seemingly coincidental deaths in the UFO field on June 24. Frank Scully, author of *Behind the Flying Saucers,* died on June 24, 1964. Richard Church, a well-known British ufologist and contactee, died on June 24, 1967. And Willy Ley, the pioneer rocket and space authority, suffered a fatal heart attack on June 24, 1969. Perceptive readers will note that many of the events, both modern and historic, outlined in this book occurred on the twenty-fourth of the month.

Another Englishman, Arthur Shuttlewood, the editor of *Warminster Journal,* became involved in UFO investigations when Warminster experienced a spectacular flying saucer flap beginning in December 1964. He was soon introduced into the twilight world of the elementals. First he received a long series of phone calls purportedly from the space people. Later the tall, pale, long-fingered gentlemen in coveralls came knocking on his door to engage him in long chats about cosmic matters. They announced that they were from the *cantel* (their word for planet) of Aenstria. They identified themselves as Caellsan, Selorik, and Traellison. These names were probably plays on old Greek terms. Aenstria could be derived from the ancient Greek story of Aeneas, the son of the Trojan prince Anchises and the Goddess Aphrodite. Aeneas roamed the world for seven years and was the subject of Virgil's history, *Aeneid,* a book Shuttlewood had never even heard of. Caellsan could have had its roots in the story of Caeneus, a Thessalian woman who was supposed to have the power to change her sex. According to legend, she offended Zeus and was punished by being changed into a bird. One of the seven hills of Rome is named Caelian. The name "Selorik" might have come from Selene, the moon goddess of Greek mythology.

The name game is also played at séances, with materializations claiming a variety of names adopted from ancient Egyptian, Greek, and various Indian languages. Apparently the elementals have a language of their own which sounds like double-talk or bad science fiction, and they frequently toss in words and names from that language just to keep things confused.

Thousands of mediums, psychics, and UFO contactees have been receiving mountains of messages from "Ashtar" in recent years. Mr. Ashtar represents himself as a leader in the great intergalactic councils that hold regular meetings on Jupiter, Venus, Saturn, and many planets unknown to us. But Ashtar is not a new arrival. Variations of this name, such as Ashtaroth, Ashar, Asharoth, etc., appear in demonological literature throughout history, both in the Orient and the Occident. Mr. Ashtar has been around a very long time, posing as assorted gods and demons and now, in the modern phase, as another glorious spaceman.

Angels, too, indulge in the name game. Gustav Davidson's *Dictionary of Angels is* filled with names very similar to those that crop up in UFO and occult lore. And, of course, the fairies and leprechauns of northern Europe have played the name game with almost delightful vengeance, particularly during the Middle Ages. There is more truth to Rumpelstiltskin than most people recognize.

Fairies are supposed to possess magical powers—the ability to alter physical matter and to paralyze people through spells. To be bewitched by fairies is to have your mind and body controlled by them.

Accounts of little humanoids with supernatural powers can be found in almost every culture. In *Indian Legends of the Northern Rockies,* Dr. E. E. Clark describes the various Indian legends about little three-foot-tall beings who rendered themselves invisible by rubbing themselves with a certain type of grass. They were supposed to have incredible strength, and in one story an Indian exposed to one of these creatures suffered from a swollen face afterward. As in northern Europe, the "little people" of the Rocky Mountains reputedly kidnapped children from the Indian tribes frequently.

An anthropologist from Berkeley, California, Brian Stross, uncovered some interesting "little men" stories while studying the Tzeltal Indians of Tenejapa in Chiapas, Mexico. The local name for the three-foot-tall hairy humanoids is *ihk'al*. Legend claims that the *ihk'al* fly about with some kind of rocket attached to their back, and they occasionally carry off people. A little farther south, similar beings supposedly live in caves and are able to fly through the air. They are said to kidnap women and force them to bear children.

Far in the interior of Brazil, according to the explorer Lieutenant Colonel P. H. Fawcett, there thrives a dreaded group of "bat people" who live in caves and possess telepathic powers.

Why haven't any of these entities ever been photographed? Sir Arthur Conan Doyle performed a celebrated investigation into one set of photos of fairies taken in England by a couple of children in 1917. Sixty-six years later, in 1983, one of them signed a written confession, explaining how the pictures had been faked.

For some reason, children seem to see the little people more often than adults. Back in 1966, I chatted with a man on Long Island who told me the following story after extracting a promise that I wouldn't use his name. One night that spring, he said, his small daughter ran into the house and told him that there were some little men in silver suits running about the backyard. He tried to shrug her off, but she was insistent. Finally he glanced into the backyard to appease her, and he was amazed to see three tiny figures darting around in the grass. They were less than 2 feet high and were wearing skin-tight metallic suits of some sort. He cautiously opened the door and stepped outside, and the three figures instantly ran to the far end of the yard and vanished.

The historical records certainly indicate that the little people have always existed all over this planet; that they possess the power of flight, the power of invisibility, and, to varying degrees, the power to dominate and control the human mind.

We call them elementals, too. In story after story, the witnesses encountered them near swamps, lakes, and rivers, often carrying out the same actions so often reported by UFO witnesses. Flying lights and spheres are said to accompany some fairies and little people. Witnesses were paralyzed in their presence, just as the unfortunate people who reportedly encountered vampires in central Europe were supposedly frozen in their tracks by some mysterious force or power radiating from the entities. The manifestations have remained the same throughout history. Only our interpretations of those events have changed.

The occult literature asserts that there are several different types of elementals. Fire elementals somehow utilize the energy of flames and materialize in burning houses, fireplaces, furnaces. Then there are water elementals, air elementals, and elementals that feast upon the energy of plants. (Some fascinating experiments with plants have been under way for several years by various independent researchers. Sensitive lie detector devices have been hooked up to potted plants and actually respond when other plants in the room are deliberately injured. The device also reacts to human pain, indicating that all living things might somehow be interrelated by undetermined energy forces.)

The most interesting elemental type is the humanlike being who materializes at séances. Such beings have actually been photographed and examined by medical doctors. The spiritualists have developed their own jargon to describe and explain these unbelievable materializations, but it does seem that these entities are identical to the ufonauts. In these cases, the medium goes into a trance, his or her metabolism declining almost to the point of death. Then a figure slowly begins to appear in the séance room. (In many cases, the room is fully lighted, and the witnesses completely surround the figure, ruling out mundane trickery.)

In the majority of cases, the entity resembles an Indian or an Oriental, with high cheekbones, slanted eyes, and reddish or olive skin. They usually wear robes or Indian garb but have also appeared in the accepted dress of the period. Long hair is a common feature. Both male and female entities have been described. They can speak audibly and carry on conversations with the witnesses. These séance materializations seem to be identical, also, to the Valkyrie types who appear repeatedly before isolated individuals.

Sir William Crookes, the famed physicist, attended no less than forty-five materializations of this kind, photographing and physically examining the entities.

Here is a rather routine description of a materialization event from the late 1800s, as recounted by Archbishop Thomas Colley in a commentary appended to the 1882 edition of *Oahspe*, witnessed by a group of doctors and clergymen: "A spirit form, eight inches taller than Dr. Monck [Reverend Francis Monck, the medium], grew from him by degrees, and building itself up into giant proportions, with muscular limbs developed like statuary of bronze, and of the color, there came into disconnected, independent vigorous life, apart from the medium, an ancient Egyptian ...I now got the spirit to measure hands, placing its palm on mine. The hand was small—like all Easterns', and the wrist was also small, but the arm was massive, muscular, bronzed, and hairy. Its eyes were black and piercing, but not unkindly; its hair lank and jet, and mustaches and beard long and drooping; its features full of life and expression, yet Sphinx-like. Its headdress was very peculiar, a sort of metal skullcap with an emblem in front, overhanging the brow, which trembled and quivered and glistened. I was suffered to feel it, but as I did so, it seemed to melt away like a snowflake under my touch, to grow solid again the moment after."

In a séance room such an entity is automatically regarded to be a spirit—the shade of a long-dead Egyptian. But if the same entity wearing the same metallic skullcap should stride out of the bushes in West Virginia and alarm clandestine lovers in a parked car, he would be considered a spaceman.

Now we can reach another tentative conclusion. In order to materialize and take on definite form, these entities seem to require a source of energy; a fire or a living thing—a plant, a tree, a human medium (or contactee). Our sciences have not reached a point where they can offer us any kind of working hypothesis for this process. But we can speculate that these beings need living energy that they can restructure into a physical form. Perhaps that is why dogs and animals tend to vanish in flap areas. Perhaps the living cells of those animals are somehow used by the ultraterrestrials to create forms which we can see and sense with our limited perceptions. Perhaps human and animal blood is also essential for this process.

The Birth of Spiritualism

In 1823, young Joseph Smith woke up in a farmhouse near Palmyra, New York, to find a faceless "messenger" standing beside his bed. Within a few years, "Spring-heeled Jack" was leaping around the British countryside, his cape fluttering in the still night air. In 1846, the skies went mad with strange lights and peculiar meteorological phenomena. In 1847, the house occupied by the Mitchell Weekman family in the tiny hamlet of Hydesville, New York, *only a few miles from Joseph Smith's former home in Wayne County*, developed a ghost. Somebody kept knocking on the door—but there was never anybody there. An eight-year-old girl in the family screamed that a cold, invisible hand touched her and caressed her body. The Weekman family packed up and moved out—and a family named Fox moved in.

In March 1848, the two Fox children, Kate, twelve, and Margaret, fifteen, not only heard the mysterious rappings and rattlings of the ghost, but they communicated with it.* They developed a simple code for yes and no and for all the letters of the alphabet and carried out conversations with the unseen entity. The

---

*   The date of this breakthrough was March 31, 1848.

story slowly leaked out, and the Fox sisters became famous. What's more, the ghost apparently followed them about, and they were able to hold séances in other towns with the entity communicating with them by rapping on walls or tables.

This single sequence (or was it a communications breakthrough?) was the beginning of modern spiritualism. So here is another freakish coincidence to ponder: Both Mormonism and spiritualism were born in the same county in places only a few miles from each other!

Spiritualism became a rage in the 1850s and 1860s. Mediums blossomed all over the world. Many of them proved to be fraudulent and were merely cashing in on the fad. But others—many others—performed inexplicable feats. Because ghosts and spiritual manifestations seemed to offer proof of religious beliefs, many educated men took an active interest in investigating such phenomena. Leading clergymen, educators, and scientists took up the investigation of these matters as a hobby. Scientific journals of psychic research were founded and published the extensive reports of these above-average "ghost hunters." We have been left a wealth of heavily documented case histories covering most of the nine-teenth century.

Thomas Edison's parents were active spiritualists, and Edison himself privately expressed his belief in the survival of the human spirit after death. He was born in 1847. Sir Arthur Conan Doyle, creator of Sherlock Holmes, spent the last half of his life pursuing and investigating occult matters, as did Sir William Crookes, a physicist who made a number of outstanding contributions to science (he was among the first to study radioactivity, and he invented the Crookes tube, predecessor to X-rays and radio tubes).

I cannot even begin to review all of the occult evidence here, but there are dozens of excellent books available covering the whole spectrum of spiritual events. If you take the time and trouble to examine some of the better literature, you will find precise parallels and correlations with the UFO phenomenon. It appears that the same forces are at work in both situations, the same patterns prevail (particularly the hoax patterns), and the same underlying purposes seem to be present.

In short, we can conclude that spiritualism is just another means of communication between the ultraterrestrials and ourselves. And this form of communication has been in constant use throughout history.

UFOs and Things That Go Bump in the Night

The late Dr. Nandor Fodor, a leading New York psychiatrist, made an extensive study of seemingly genuine trance mediums and even attempted to psychoanalyze their spirit guides, or alter egos. He also performed an outstanding study of the poltergeist phenomenon. In his book, *Haunted People*, written in collaboration with Hereward Carrington, he presented 375 typical poltergeist cases from A.D. 355 to A.D. 1947. A great many of these cases are identical to our modern UFO incidents.

For example, in September 1824, small "symmetric objects of metal" rained out of the sky near Orenburg, Russia. In 1836, globular lights appeared around the home of a Captain Lamber in Szeged, Hungary. Strange sounds were heard in the house, and a "woman in white" appeared and disappeared frequently over a long period. The breaking of glassware and rappings on doors and walls were routine in many of these cases all over the world. "A floating, vaporous body shaped like a football" was seen around a boardinghouse in New York in 1882 and was accompanied by rapping sounds. Dogs frequently reacted with terror during these manifestations. Bedclothes were yanked from beds by unseen hands, and many, many of the victims awoke in the middle of the night to find elusive phantoms standing over their beds.

One of the most celebrated of all poltergeist cases, known generally as the Bell Witch, took place in Robertson County, Tennessee, in the 1820s. The home of John Bell was plagued for years by a mysterious presence that made all kinds of noises, indulged in destructive manifestations, and even talked to the victims and the numerous witnesses. Lights "like a candle or lamp flitting across the yard and through the field" were frequently seen.

General Andrew Jackson (seventh President of the United States, 1829-37) reportedly paid a visit to the Bell homestead. As he neared the place, his horses suddenly halted, apparently unable to pull his wagon farther. The general got down and examined the wheels and the road and could find no reason for the horses' struggle. Suddenly a metallic voice rang out from behind some bushes, "All right, General, let the wagon move," and the horses were able to pull it again. This sounds like our first electromagnetic case—even though no motors or electrical circuits were involved!

Another witness, one William Porter, claimed that he tussled with an invisible entity in the Bell home. He was awakened in his bedroom when someone or something hauled the covers off him. He grappled in the dark and managed to roll the entity up in the quilt. Then he picked the struggling shape up and headed for the smoldering fireplace, intending to throw the cover, "witch" and all, into the fire. "I discovered that it was very weighty," he wrote later, "and smelled awful. I had not got halfway across the room before the luggage got so heavy and became so offensive that I was compelled to drop it on the floor and rush outside for a breath of fresh air. The odor emitted from the roll was the most offensive stench I ever smelled."

A detached, derisive voice frequently spoke to the Bells and the various people who visited them to witness the manifestations. It actually succeeded in breaking up the marriage plans of young Betsy Bell, saying "so many things to Betsy and Joshua [Joshua Gardner, her fiancé] in the presence of their friends of a highly embarrassing nature that the girl in time became quite hysterical and worn out in despair."

This is a common factor in many poltergeist cases. The invisible entities loudly reveal and discuss the intimate secrets of the victims in the presence of outsiders, indicating that they, like the UFO entities, know everything about our life histories. This type of behavior is reported in case after case, extending far back into history. An English poltergeist back in A.D. 1190, for example, "used to talk with people and... it would reveal publicly deeds done from the time of their birth, which least of all they wished others either to hear or know."

(In many modern UFO contact cases, the visible and apparently physical entities nearly always establish at the outset their complete knowledge of the contactee's past, often coming up with information about distant relatives unknown to the contactee which, when checked out, proves to be valid.)

Another common factor in poltergeist cases is the sudden materialization or disappearance of physical objects. Stones have often fallen from the ceilings of rooms in such quantities that they had to be shoveled out every morning. This has even reportedly happened in tents on the desert. Ordinary objects, such as ashtrays, suddenly vanish and are later found in outlandish places. UFO contactees report this same kind of phenomenon shortly after they receive their first visit from the entities.

The controversial contactee Truman Bethurum soberly cited an incident in which the beautiful female captain of a flying saucer, Aura Rhanes, asked him to hold a plastic flashlight on his open palm. She stared at it intently, and it vanished instantaneously, without a trace. This, she told him, was what would happen if we tried to attack "them." We would simply disappear. Demonstrations of this type have been staged since the beginning, as in the case of the prophet Hermas and his magical book which vanished after he had read it.

Bethurum's story is a classic in ufology. He said he was sleeping on a truck on Mormon Mesa, outside Las Vegas, Nevada, on Sunday, July 27, 1952, when he awoke to find himself surrounded by eight or ten men, all under 5 feet in height. They looked like Latins or Italians, he reported, with dark olive skins, jet-black hair trimmed short, and tight-fitting blue-gray jackets and trousers. They spoke to one another in an unknown language but addressed him in perfect English. He was led to a hovering saucer and was introduced to Aura Rhanes. He saw a good deal of Captain Rhanes after that. She even materialized suddenly in his bedroom on a number of occasions, somewhat to the consternation of his wife, who later divorced him. In the UFO name game, "Aura Rhanes" might well have meant the aura reigns.

Truman Bethurum died on May 21, 1969.

Bedroom visitants and poltergeist activity are a common factor in the contactee syndrome. And these poltergeists are not only thieves and mischiefmakers, they are also proven arsonists. In hundreds of cases the haunted houses suffer mysterious fires. As soon as one fire is extinguished in one part of the house, another breaks out elsewhere. Witnesses such as doctors, policemen and firemen have been present and have actually seen the fires suddenly burst out in corners of rooms, curtains, waste baskets, and furniture. There seems to be no earthly explanation for these sudden conflagrations.

When I was visiting Hyderabad in central India, I heard stories of a haunted hut on the outskirts of the city that had been plagued by an arson-bent poltergeist. The local police chief had gone to investigate, and while he was in the hut, his trousers suddenly caught fire. That did it! He ordered the hut vacated and sealed up.

It is traditional that haunted houses eventually burn to the ground. UFO witnesses, researchers, and contactees have this same problem, as I pointed out earlier. Soon after researcher Stephen Yankee acquired a microfilm copy of Morris K. Jessup's Varo Papers (a strange UFO document), his Michigan home went up in flames.

There have also been several cases in which human beings have been found burned to ashes, even though the chairs or beds they were in were only slightly scorched. It takes a very hot flame to reduce human bones to ashes. In recent years, there has been an increasing number of cases in which people have been found totally cremated in their automobiles while the upholstery was only mildly singed.

Water also plays an enigmatic role in the poltergeist phenomenon. Torrents of water from unknown sources have flooded houses, gushing from walls containing no pipes, squirting from ceilings, pouring down staircases, splashing by buckets full out of nowhere to drench witnesses.

Just as the UFO cultists have settled upon the extraterrestrial thesis to explain flying saucers, the occultists have decided that poltergeists are caused by energy radiated from disturbed children or by restless ghosts. The common procedure for investigating poltergeists is to examine the entire history of the house and land. In some cases, it is discovered that someone was murdered there or buried there years—even hundreds of years—before the manifestations began. So the ghost is blamed for the phenomenon. There are, of course, thousands of murders and violent deaths every year, and it might be useful to perform a study of all the scenes of these crimes to determine the percentage of hauntings that occur afterward. I suspect that percentage would be quite small.

Rather, it seems that these events are concentrated in base areas and are merely a side effect of the other things taking place there unnoticed. Small, confined areas all over the world appear to be haunted century after century by mischievous entities who are able to adopt any guise and who maintain such total control over material objects that they can produce any kind of manifestation. Our willingness to accept the restless ghost theories is based upon our ego-inspired need to believe in the immortality of the human soul or spirit. The ultraterrestrials might recognize that need and wickedly take advantage of our beliefs, tailoring their manifestations so that they appear to support our religious convictions.

I have prepared two interesting graphs based upon the independent research of the occultists and the ufologists. One is a chart of the known UFO reports of the nineteenth century. The other is a chart of the recorded poltergeist cases for the same period. We find striking similarities in these patterns. In some cases, the poltergeist wave preceded by a few months or a year or two the UFO activity in the same area. In other cases, the UFO and poltergeist activities occurred simultaneously. Our biggest problem is that the occult phenomena have been more thoroughly investigated, recorded and researched than the UFO phenomena. The occult records are lavish with essential details about the people and the areas involved, while the UFO reports provide little or no details other than descriptions of the objects.

The problems in computing accurate charts from this kind of sampling are obvious, particularly because most of the better poltergeist reports of the period came from Europe, where investigations were better organized and more widely published (this holds true today for UFO coverage). We are forced to estimate that a proportionate amount of poltergeist activity was occurring in the United States in those years. Most of the UFO reports in this particular study were from the United States, and several of them are detailed elsewhere in this book.

Assuming that each discovered historical report represents a larger number of unpublished or undiscovered reports, just as today's published UFO reports represent on the average 250 unreported or unpublished sightings, we can conclude that a flap condition existed in the years 1820, 1834, 1844, 1846, and 1849. We find that there was an outbreak of poltergeists in 1835, 1846, and 1849.

As the nineteenth century progressed, reporting improved, and we are able to make more precise correlations. A UFO flap took place in 1850, and there was also a series of poltergeist cases. A larger poltergeist outbreak occurred in 1867, following flaps in 1863-64. UFO activity became more intense beginning in 1870, and there were notable flaps in 1872, 1877, and 1879. The 1880s produced a major explosion of all kinds of phenomena, including the sudden disappearances of people. Poltergeist cases were in abundance in that decade, particularly in the big flap years of 1883 and 1885.

Morris K. Jessup labeled the years 1877-87 the Incredible Decade after scouring the astronomical journals of the period. Astronomers made some remarkable discoveries during those years. The previously unobserved satellites of Mars popped into view in 1877, new craters appeared on the moon, and all kinds of strange objects flitted around the upper atmosphere. Bonilla photographed unidentified objects while observing the sun during the flap year of 1883 (Chapter 2). The great flap of 1897 was apparently in preparation.

Comparison Chart—UFO Reports and Poltergeist Cases

Dotted lines represent poltergeist reports.
Heavy lines represent UFO reports for the same period.

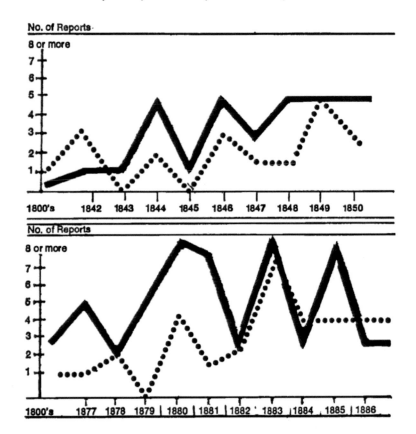

(Jessup's "Incredible Decade")

In 1866, a New Englander named William Denton declared himself to be the first modern contactee. He claim to be in telepathic contact with beings from another planet, and he and his whole family later purportedly visited Venus and Mars. Denton wrote a series of books describing saucer-shaped vehicles in detail, which he thought were made of aluminum. (A commercial process for manufacturing aluminum was not invented until 1886.) He also told his audiences (he lectured widely) that the folks who rode around in aluminum airships looked very much like us. His narratives were, in many respects, identical to those of the modern contactees.

Trance Mediums and Possession

Trance mediums were nothing new in 1850. In the Bible's First Book of Samuel, Chapter 28 describes how Saul consulted a medium ("… a woman that hath-a familiar spirit"). Mediums acted as oracles in ancient times, and people with this peculiar gift appeared in each new generation. Such persons seem to serve as instruments through which the ultraterrestrials can speak to us directly, and they often come up with amazingly accurate prophecies of the future and precise details of events that could seemingly be known only to the dead relatives of the people who consulted them.

Of course, when spiritualism became a national fad, a goodly number of charlatans and hucksters moved in. But most of the genuine mediums exercised their talents carefully and for free. They did not indulge in fancy hocus-pocus and did not need paraphernalia, such as spirit cabinets. They were—and are—people who can apparently summon up unseen entities or alien intelligences and extract information from them.

I am not a spiritualist myself, although I have attended a few séances over the years, usually in the role of a scoffer and disbeliever. As a longtime amateur magician, I have been able to see through the frauds, but I have also been genuinely perplexed by some of the manifestations I have personally witnessed.

Essentially, a trance medium lapses into an unconscious state, and while in this condition, his or her body is taken over by some outside influence. This influence is usually a self-styled "Indian guide" from "the other side." Many mediums have been simple, uneducated people, but when in a trance state they have been able to talk foreign languages fluently. Scientists and clergymen have put countless mediums through severe tests over the years. At one group of séances in the 1920s, sitters, who were all versed in different languages, grilled mediums in everything from ancient Chinese to Swahili, and the controlling entities not only conversed in those languages but corrected the sitters' grammar! The daughter of Judge Edmunds, president of the Senate in the 1850s, gave incredible performances while in a trance, speaking fluently in Greek, Spanish, Polish, Latin, Portuguese, Hungarian, and several Indian languages.

Because the sitters—and the mediums—assume that they are dealing with residents of heaven, they ask mostly spiritual questions. Customarily, the "control" will announce that Mr. Blank is standing next to him and wishes to speak to Mrs. Blank, who is attending the séance. Mrs. Blank excitedly begins to question her dead husband, Mr. Blank. How is life on the other side? Just fine, the control replies, a little bored, everyone lives in vine-covered cottages, and all is sweetness and light. Where did Mr. Blank hide his valuable gold watch before he died? It's wrapped in an old sock and buried under some papers in the bottom drawer of the old rolltop desk, the control answers. Sure enough, when Mrs. Blank gets home, she finds the watch exactly where the medium's alter ego said it would be. Try to convince Mrs. Blank that she didn't talk with her dead husband!

In many cases, the medium even begins to talk in a voice that sounds exactly like the dead Mr. Blank, uses his pet expressions, and even refers to things known only to Mrs. Blank, indulges in their private jokes, and so on. Occasionally, a deceased celebrity will "break through." Recently the late George Bernard Shaw made a tape recording in England that is now circulating in occult circles. Those who knew Shaw claim that it sounds exactly like him, uses his phraseology and vocal mannerisms, and displays his brilliant and distinctive wit.

The trance phenomenon deserves extensive study because so many aspects of it are directly related to the contactee phenomenon. The contactees have been told a hundred different stories of what life is like on other planets. If you review the descriptions of heaven produced at the thousands of possibly genuine séances, you will find the same contradictions. The entities will lie transparently at one point in the séance, and a few moments later will come up with astounding information that could not be based upon simple trickery.

The mediums themselves have always been aware of their controls' mischievous sense of humor. They speak of false shades and malevolent spirits who perform outrageous hoaxes. So the mediums and the professional investigators are always wary. The fact that a control can imitate George Bernard Shaw does not necessarily mean that GBS is doing the speaking from the spirit world.

The fact that a control knows where Mr. Blank hid his gold watch does not necessarily prove that Mr. Blank is standing at his side "on the other plane."

The medium generally remains completely inert while in the trance or "occupied" state but in some instances can become quite animated and make gestures appropriate to whatever is being said. In a very real sense, the medium's mind has been blanked out, and his or her body has been completely taken over by the control. The medium has become a zombie of sorts, possessed by an alien entity, an entity who lacks a physical form of his own.

Contactees often find themselves suddenly miles from home without knowing how they got there. They either have induced amnesia, wiping out all memory of the trip, or they were taken over by some means and made the trip in a blacked-out state. Should they encounter a friend on the way, the friend would probably note that their eyes seemed glassy and their behavior seemed peculiar. But if the friend spoke to them, he might receive a curt reply.

In the language of the silent contactees this process is called being used. A used person can suddenly lose a day or a week out of his life. I have known silent contactees to disappear from their homes for long periods, and when they returned, they had little or no recollection of where they had been. One girl sent me a postcard from the Bahama Islands—which surprised me because I knew she was very poor. When she returned, she told me that she had only one memory of the trip. She said she remembered getting off a jet at an airport—she couldn't recall getting on the jet or making the trip—and there "Indians" met her and took her baggage. She remembered nothing further after that. The next thing she knew she was back home again.

It seems likely the same methods are applied to both mediums and contactees. In the case of the mediums, the mind control serves a useful purpose. It enables the entities to establish direct vocal communication with us and, in many instances, pass along worthwhile information.

This process can also be destructive. A young man from Ithaca, New York, called me some time ago at the urging of William Donovan, president of Aerial Investigation and Research (AIR), to tell me of his close brush with death. One evening in the fall of 1967, he said, he left his home to drive to a meeting. For some reason he couldn't explain, he got out of his car, went back into his house, and carried out several aimless actions such as picking up a book from a table and putting it on the shelf. "Finally, I said to myself, Okay, it's time," he told me. He remembers leaving the house and again heading for his parked car.

The next thing he knew he was in a hospital bed.

He had apparently driven about four miles to a railroad crossing just in time to meet an oncoming train. His car was demolished, but he escaped rather miraculously with only a few minor injuries. If he had not gone back into the house and carried out those meaningless, time-killing chores, he would have avoided the train altogether. It is possible, of course, that the shock of the accident blotted out his memory of that four-mile drive—but he couldn't even remember putting the key in the ignition.

This man had been active in investigating the UFO flap that

took place around the radio telescope installations near Ithaca in 1967-68.

In his book *Passport to Magonia*, Dr. Jacques Vallee, a NASA astronomer and computer expert, touches on all this. "In the Soviet Union, not so long ago, a leading plasma physicist died in strange circumstances," Dr. Vallee states. "He was thrown under a Moscow subway train by a mentally deranged woman. It is noteworthy that she claimed a 'voice from space' had given her orders to kill that particular man—orders she could not resist. Soviet criminologists, I have been reliably informed, are worried by the increase of such cases in recent years. Madmen rushing through the streets because they think the Martians are after them have always been commonplace. But the current wave of mental imbalance that can be specifically tied to the rise and development of the contactee myth is an aspect of the UFO problem that must be considered with special care."

So there seem to be both good and evil forces at work in this type of phenomenon. The good guys latch onto people with particularly receptive minds and turn them into trance mediums. The bad guys use the same methods to tamper with the minds of contactees and even to commit murders indirectly. Because incidents of these types can be traced throughout history, it seems probable that these forces have always been extant on this planet.

When the good guys worked through mediums, they needed some excuse that we would accept. The answer seemed to be "communication with the dead." These communicative efforts led to the foundation of spiritualism, and the entities played the role to the hilt, using their complete knowledge of us and our individual lives to provide us with "proof" of the existence of a spirit world. This is the same precise methodology being employed with the UFOs to build up support for the extraterrestrial thesis. We humans need acceptable explanations for unnatural phenomena, so "they" happily—and often humorously—supply us with all the explanations we can handle. At the same time, they give us tiny fragments of the real truth, hoping no doubt that we will be able to digest them slowly. Ever so slowly.

In earlier times it seems as if they made a complicated attempt to convey the truth to us through mediums and psychics, but we chose to misinterpret these efforts and placed them within the context of our primitive religious beliefs. We are still doing this, and they are going along with it because even misinterpreted communication is better than no communication at all. Religion may not be truth but may merely be a step on the long path of the real truth.

Fragments of the truth have been passed along to us through many different channels of communication. One of these is called automatic writing. The medium holds a pen or pencil loosely, and the controlling entity takes charge, moving the hand to write out the message. Many thousands of people have this gift, and believe it or not, whole books have been written by this process. Hundreds of them have been published over the years and form what is known as inspired literature. One of the most remarkable of these works is a huge volume titled *Oahspe*. It was written by a New York dentist named Dr. John Newbrough in 1880. He was, so the story goes, awakened one morning by a hand on his shoulder and a bodiless voice. He found his room lit up "with pillars of soft light so pleasing to the eyes it was indescribable." His mysterious visitors ordered him to purchase one of the newly invented typewriters and to spend an hour each morning sitting with his fingers on the keys. He didn't know how to type, but he turned out a voluminous manuscript at the rate of about 1,200 words an hour. When it was completed, it was an intricate history of the human race, filled with amazing information about our solar system, such as the Van Allen radiation belt, which has only been recently confirmed by our space program. Much of the historical information in *Oahspe* checks out. A complex language, a mixture of ancient tongues and even Algonquin Indian, is defined and utilized in the text. To research such a book and compile the language would have required many years of study and hard work for a seasoned linguist—which Newbrough was not.

Another popular mode of communication is the Ouija board. This doesn't work for most and produces nothing but mischievous rubbish (probably from the subconscious mind) for others. But some medium types have obtained amazing results with it.

Do the ultraterrestrials *really* care about us? There is much disturbing evidence that they don't. They care only to the extent that we can fulfill our enigmatic use to them.

The Reverend Arthur Ford is one of America's best-known trance mediums. For most of his life he has served as an instrument for an entity who calls himself Fletcher. In 1928, Fletcher announced that Harry Houdini (who had died in 1926) was on hand and had a message which he wanted conveyed to his widow, Beatrice. The message was in a code once used by the Houdinis in a mind-reading act. This code was known only to the couple and had never been published or revealed to anyone. Fletcher, through Ford, was able to give precise details of this secret code, and Mrs. Houdini later confirmed that the message had to come from her husband. This was only one of Ford's many coups. In the fall of 1967, Ford went into a trance on Canadian television and produced a message for Bishop James Pike from his deceased son. Bishop Pike, who was present at this televised séance, avowed that the message seemed authentic and seemed to come from the familiar personality of his son. This well-publicized séance launched a major revival of spiritualism in the United States.

Reverend Ford travels in high circles but has never made any material gain from his peculiar gift. He gives freely of his time—and Fletcher's advice from the other side—at séances all over the country. Mrs. Ruth Montgomery, the well-known author and Washington reporter, tells of the time that Reverend Ford visited her in Washington and lapsed into a trance so she could ask Fletcher for some advice on his behalf. Reverend Ford was then in the process of moving and wanted to know what he should do with some of his things. Fletcher seemed totally disinterested in Ford's problems, Mrs. Montgomery reported, and when she asked if Ford should visit a clinic for a checkup, Fletcher snapped, "He'd better do something. If he doesn't, I can't work through him much longer."

Although Reverend Ford had voluntarily submitted his person to Fletcher's use for nearly half a century, the entity was apparently completely disinterested in his problems and welfare.

This is, alas, rather typical. Even the most helpful entities seem more dedicated to the job of communicating than to any kind of involvement with those to whom (or through whom) they are communicating. The bizarre history of psychic phenomena is filled with Fletchers.

Mrs. Montgomery, incidentally, indulges in automatic writing herself and has received constant messages for the past few years, many of which have been valid prophecies and stern advice meant to govern her future actions.

Psychic Hoaxes

There have been innumerable psychic hoaxes for the past 150 years, and many of these parallel the UFO hoaxes. In 1855, the Fox sisters confessed that their spirit rappings were a hoax. They said they produced the sounds by "snapping their toes." Think about that for a moment. Snapping your toes so that it sounded like a rap on a wall or table would be a most remarkable talent—perhaps even more remarkable than the ability to communicate with the spirit world. I don't believe I would pay ten cents to hear someone talk to a rapping spirit—but I would happily pay five dollars to examine someone who could duplicate the rapping sound by snapping his toes.

Later the two sisters said the confession was false, and they had been bribed to make it.

Mrs. Houdini was genuinely astonished and impressed by Reverend Ford's messages from her husband, and she made numerous public statements to that effect, as well as signing various affidavits. But later, in the 1930s, she chose to deny it all for a time. Then, shortly before her death, she reversed her denials.

In ufology we have to contend with teenagers' hot-air balloons, and in psychic phenomena we have to worry about youngsters firing rocks at houses with slingshots and phony mediums levitating "spirit trumpets" with black thread. But there are many more UFO sightings than there are plastic balloons, and there are more poltergeists dumping rocks in living rooms than there are wild-eyed youngsters with slingshots.

There are also more ultraterrestrial entities than either the occultists or the UFO enthusiasts dream of.

13
A Sure Cure for Alligator Bites

Slag fell out of the sky over Darmstadt, Germany, on June 7, 1846, according to Charles Fort. Slag! Preposterous, of course. Why, slag could no more fall out of the sky in Germany than it could over Puget Sound a century later. Fort detailed more than a dozen other slag-fall cases from the nineteenth century, always carefully listing his sources. I have taken the trouble to check out several items from the works of Fort, and I found that he was painstakingly accurate. His books, all written in the first three decades of this century, recount case after case of strange aerial phenomena that are identical to our modern UFO sightings. So when the late Mr. Fort informed us that 1846 was a most unusual year, we are obliged to take him seriously.

Indeed, 1846 was a most extraordinary year!

It not only rained blood and frogs and slag. There were strange glowing objects circling those garbage-filled skies, and our naughty poltergeists were having a field day, particularly in France. Furniture was floating around a house in La Perriere, France; rocks were being tossed in the home of M. Larible in Paris; dishes were dancing across the tables of Rambouillet, France; and in a field outside of the little town of La Salette a "miracle" was taking place.

Two children, Melanie Calvet, fifteen, and Maximin Guiraud, twelve, convinced skeptical adults that they had seen a religious vision—a great globe of light hovering above the fields. It opened up, they avowed, and a smaller, brighter light moved out. It was some kind of glowing entity who spoke to them in French. The two youngsters, having been schooled in Catholicism, assumed that this entity was Our Lady. She gave them a series of prophecies, accurately predicting the terrible potato famine that struck far-off Ireland in the winter of 1846-47 and the failure of Europe's wheat crops in 1851. In fact, all kinds of droughts and diseases affected crops from 1846 to 1854 throughout Europe, causing great suffering and starvation. She also allegedly stated, "Little children will be seized with trembling and will die in the arms of those who are holding them…" This grim prophecy proved valid, too, when more than 75,000 people, mostly youngsters, died in an epidemic of ague—a malaria-like disease which produced fever and shivering and death.

This was strong stuff in 1846, particularly because the children also reported that the Lady warned, "If my people will not submit, I shall be forced to let the army of my Son fall on them." But, she added, "If sinners repent, the stones and rocks will turn into heaps of wheat, and potatoes will be sown by themselves."

Because it is very unlikely that the two children could have invented these prophecies, we can assume that their story was true, and in fact, it appears to conform to the now-familiar tactics of the ultraterrestrials. Their uncanny talents of precognition (ability to foresee our future) once again served to provide us with "proof" of contact. This tactic is still being used.

The next year, 1847, that spirit moved into the little house in Hydesville, New York, and in 1848 the redoubtable Fox sisters began to communicate with it. Spiritualism began in earnest, and by 1852 there were thousands of adherents in the United States alone. From 1848 to 1851 there was a worldwide UFO flap, and poltergeist cases hit an interesting peak in 1849. Strange, isn't it, that all these things should explode at once? The coming of the UFOs went unnoticed, but the poltergeists and hauntings created a sensation and gave added impetus to the spiritualist movement.

In France, a man named Allen Kardec founded *Revue Spirite* in 1856, and spiritualism became the rage of Paris.

And then, on February 11, 1858, a fourteen-year-old girl wandered into the French hillside and fell to her knees, her eyes filled with a vision of a beautiful woman. The girl's name was Bernadette Soubirous. The hillside was a garbage dump outside the town of Lourdes.

The miracle of Bernadette is so well known that we hardly need comment on it. A local skeptic, one Dr. Dozous, followed the girl on one of her pilgrimages and watched in amazement as she entered a trancelike state, lit a candle, and held her hand in the flame for fifteen minutes without seeming to feel it or harming her skin. Then she scraped away at the ground and a spring suddenly bubbled forth.

Word of Bernadette's visions spread across France, and although she was the only one who could see the Lady, those who accompanied her and watched her in trance experienced unquestioned miracles. Between March 5 and March 25, 1858, a series of miraculous cures took place at the grotto near Lourdes. Paralytics threw aside their crutches after drinking the water from that spring.

The following year, 1859, the UFOs were busy again. And the year after that there was another outbreak of poltergeist cases in France and Switzerland.

Forgetting the worldwide situation for the moment, we can draw some interesting conclusions from these French cases. Two "miracles" occurred in France within twelve years of each other. The incident at La Salette in 1846 was definitely ufological in nature. The events at Lourdes were more subtle and fit more into the "possessed" type of phenomenon. The simultaneous outbreak of poltergeist manifestations in France throughout that period, together with all kinds of aerial and meteorological phenomena (see Fort's *Book of the Damned* for listings of these reports), tends to confirm the thesis that all of these things are interrelated. When and if French investigators burrow into the newspapers and journals of this period, they will undoubtedly uncover many other lost reports that will add to this evidence.

The Curative Powers of UFOs

On September 1, 1965, hundreds of citizens in the Kosice district of Czechoslovakia complained to their commissars about the glowing red and black spheres that were buzzing their towns and villages. A Reuters dispatch from Prague added that this was "the most recent of a series of artifacts of unknown origin which have been seen in the Czechoslovakian skies in recent months…" The Iron Curtain had sprung a leak, and U-2s from another world were pouring through.

Two days later, on September 3, 1965, four metallic blue "plates" swooped out of the sky over the town of Cuzco, in southwest Peru. Hundreds of people, alerted by radio newscasts, went into the streets to stare at the strange formation. The objects entertained them for two hours, performing intricate maneuvers above the town. They made right-angle turns, hovered and skittered about in a manner impossible for any known type of aircraft. When they finally got bored with their audience, they sped away at incredible speed.

Others were seeing lights in the sky that same night and weren't quite so entertained by them as the citizens of Cuzco. Officer Eugene Bertrand of Exeter, New Hampshire, on a routine patrol, came across a trembling woman driver who told him an elliptical red object had just pursued her car from Epping to Exeter. He calmed her but didn't take the incident too seriously. After all, everyone knew that flying saucers were nonexistent, the product of hysteria and hallucination.

A few hours later Officer Bertrand was called upon to investigate the report of an eighteen-year-old, Norman Muscarello, who had also seen something weird in the sky. Muscarello led him to a field near Exeter, and they both saw a large, dark object marked by a straight row of pulsating red lights lift above some nearby trees. It bore down on them and passed within 100 feet of their position. Bertrand started to draw his gun, thought better of it, and radioed for help instead. Another officer arrived shortly afterward, and the three of them watched the object as it silently moved away at treetop level. This was the beginning of the now famous book *Incident at Exeter*, which was carefully and thoroughly investigated by reporter John Fuller.

That same night two other police officers more than 1,000 miles from Exeter were also making an unexpected visit to the twilight zone. It was shortly before midnight, and Chief Deputy Sheriff William McCoy and Deputy Robert Goode were cruising along a highway in Brasoria County, Texas (south of Houston). Goode, who was driving, was complaining to his partner about a sore and swollen finger. Earlier in the evening he helped his son move a pet alligator, and the creature had nipped him on the left index finger. He had bandaged it, but now it was throbbing painfully, and he expressed fear that an infection was setting in. The two men were discussing the need to wake up a doctor at the end of their patrol and have the finger tended when they suddenly noticed a large purple glow in the west, moving horizontally across the nearby oil fields. At first they thought it was just a light from the oil fields. Then it turned and began to move toward them; a great rectangular glob of purple light about 50 feet in height. It was accompanied by a smaller blue light, the men said later. Goode had his window rolled down and was waving his aching digit in the breeze. As the objects rushed toward their car, he said he felt a definite wave of heat on his arm and hand. Whatever the globs were, neither man felt inclined to stop and investigate. Goode jabbed his foot on the accelerator, and when they were some distance away, McCoy looked back and watched the lights rise upward, flare brilliantly, and go out altogether.

The two admittedly frightened men sped back to Damon, Texas, and when their excitement subsided, Deputy Goode noticed that his finger was no longer swelling or bleeding, and the pain was gone. He removed the bandage and discovered that his wound was almost healed! Had he, he wondered, been cured by fright (unlikely, say the doctors) or by the heat from that eerie "something"?

The wire services had a lot of fun with that story—"Alligator Bite Cured by Flying Saucer!" But somebody somewhere took the two men seriously. Low-flying light planes, apparently unmarked, flew back and forth over the area of the sighting for the next two days. Shortly after the incident, two strangers turned up at the sheriff's office looking for Deputy Goode. They tracked the officer down in a local restaurant and immediately proceeded to describe in detail what the UFO looked like—*even before Goode had an opportunity to tell them.* Then they suggested that if he should encounter a similar machine in the future, he should cooperate with its occupants and keep any conversations with them to himself. The identities of these two mystery men have never been determined.

There have been innumerable cases in which witnesses have felt heat radiating from low-flying unidentified flying objects, and there are several heavily documented cases in which people have suffered burns from the objects, but the Texas incident is one of the rare ones in which a wound was apparently healed by such radiation. When this story first appeared, it seemed so absurd that most ufologists neglected it and concentrated on the almost trivial sightings in Exeter. However, we now know that the absurd cases are the most important and that the endless aerial sightings are practically meaningless.

A Major Miracle

Giant winged beings, usually described as headless, are an integral part of the UFO phenomenon. On September 18, 1877 (the year that marked the beginning of Jessup's Incredible Decade) a winged human form was seen cruising casually across the skies of Brooklyn. In 1922, there were two cases in Nebraska of 8-foot-tall winged creatures disembarking from circular flying machines and soaring away under their own power. Headless winged creatures were reported over Scandinavia in 1946, and on November 16, 1963, four teenagers in Kent, England, claimed that they had witnessed the landing of a spherical globe of light while returning home from a dance. A giant, headless figure with bat-like wings waddled from it and terrified them, they said. A decade earlier, a 6- to 7-foot-tall man with wings reportedly appeared in Houston, Texas. UFOs were also seen at the time.

Starting in November 1966 and continuing throughout 1967,

more than 100 people in Point Pleasant, West Virginia, insisted that they, too, had encountered a giant winged creature with blazing red eyes set deep in its shoulders. Most of these sightings took place around the TNT area, a World War II ammunition dump. I have interviewed many of these witnesses and am convinced that they did see something.

Perhaps that something is the basis for many of our legends of angels and demons. And perhaps it was that same something that was flying around Portugal in 1915.

There was a worldwide UFO flap from 1909 to 1914, encompassing Africa, Australia, Oklahoma, and other places. The poltergeist reports hit a peak in 1910 and 1913 and concentrated largely in France and Italy, although there was some activity in Portland, Oregon, during the period.

We are concerned here with the headless winged beings, however. The flap of 1909-14 may have merely been a prelude to World War I and the astounding events which followed, or it may not have been connected with those events in any way. We have no way of knowing. Unfortunately, until more adequate research is done, we have to record much of this evidence as purely circumstantial.

But in 1915, four girls were tending sheep at Cabeco, Portugal, when they allegedly saw a white figure hovering in the air. "It looked like somebody wrapped in a sheet. There were no eyes or hands on it," the young girls reported to their families. (None of the witnesses of that West Virginia winged creature has reported seeing hands or arms on it.) These four children are supposed to have seen this white, headless entity twice again that summer. One of the girls was named Lucia Abobora. She was born on March 22, 1907, and she was to become one of the central figures in the earthshaking drama to follow.

In the summer of 1916, this same Lucia Abobora was playing near a cave with some friends when they saw a light flying just above the nearby trees, moving slowly in their direction. As it drew closer, it became clear that it was a human figure. Later the children described it as "a transparent young man" of about fourteen or fifteen years of age. He settled in front of them near the cave and announced, "Don't be afraid. I am the Angel of Peace. Pray with me." The children knelt beside this "transparent young man" who glowed as brilliantly as crystal and prayed until he dissolved into nothingness.

A few weeks later the angel appeared again before this same group in the same place, and again they prayed together. The initial contact was made. The stage was set.

Europe was in flames and soldiers in the trenches were seeing strange omens in the sky. Blood was spilling needlessly in the most mismanaged war in history. Generals on both sides ordered suicidal attacks that cost thousands of lives without gaining an inch of ground. And men were learning to take to the air, carrying the carnage with them. At first pilots shot at one another with pistols and rifles, but later machine guns were brought into play. Spiritualism flourished as the relatives of the dead and the lost sought communication with their sons and husbands. Thousands of women woke up screaming in the middle of the night, always at the precise time that their men fell on the distant battlefields. This same phenomenon had shored up faith in spiritualism during the Civil War, and it was to be repeated during World War II and the Korean War. It happens still as our young men hurtle headlong into pools of their own blood in Vietnam.

On April 6, 1917, the United States formally entered the Great War. One month later, on May 13, a Sunday, Lucia Abobora, ten, Francisco Marto, nine, and Jacinto Marto, seven, were in the meadows of a place called Cova da Iria outside of Fatima, Portugal, when they saw a flash of light in the clear sky. Thinking that it was lightning, they ran for shelter under an oak tree, and when they reached it, they stopped in amazement, for there, hovering just above a 3-foot-high evergreen nearby, a brilliant globe of light hung suspended. Within this globe there was an entity garbed in a luminous white robe with a face of light that "dazzled and hurt the eyes."

"Don't be afraid. I won't hurt you," the entity said gently in a low, musical voice. The awed children asked her (it was a feminine voice) where she came from.

"I am from heaven," she reportedly replied. "I come to ask you to come here for six months in succession, on the thirteenth day at this same hour. Then I will tell you who I am, and what I want. And afterward I will return here a seventh time."

She asked them to say the Rosary every day and to pray for peace. Then the globe silently rose and floated away. It is noteworthy that only Lucia and Jacinto claimed to hear the voice. Francisco saw the object but heard nothing.

The excited trio rushed home and tried to tell their families about their vision, but the adults refused to take them seriously. Word spread, however, and on June 13, a small crowd of devout pilgrims followed the children to the Cova da Iria and watched from a distance. One of the witnesses, a woman named Maria Carreira, testified that she saw nothing when the children suddenly knelt and began talking to an unseen entity, but she did hear a peculiar sound—like the buzzing of a bee.

Lucia later said that the Lady asked them to learn to read. (A big thing to ask of simple peasants in 1917 Portugal.) On July 13 a much larger crowd gathered as the three children knelt and addressed the entity whom only they could see. Ti Marto, one of the adults, reported that he heard a sound "like a horsefly in an empty waterpot." Hopeful cripples and blind men urged the children to ask for a miracle. Lucia relayed the request and said that the Lady answered, "Continue to come here every month. In October I will tell you who I am and what I wish and will perform a miracle that everyone will have to believe.

"When you shall see a night illuminated by an unknown light," the Lady continued, "know that it is the great sign that God gives you that He is going to punish the world for its crimes... To prevent this I come to ask the consecration of Russia... If they listen to my requests, Russia will be converted and there will be peace."

Naturally, these small and simple children knew nothing of

Russia (the Russian Revolution began on March 8, 1917) and could not have regarded it as any kind of threat.

It was at this July contact that the children were allegedly given a secret which has never been formally revealed. When adults pressed her for details, Lucia would only say that this secret was "good for some, for others bad."

The visions of Fatima were now the sensation of Portugal. In August the children were seized and imprisoned by the Administrator of Ourem, who threatened them and tried to make them confess that it was all a hoax. But the children stuck to their story, even when threatened with death. The three youngsters were still being detained in Ourem when August 13 rolled around, but a crowd of 6,000 gathered at the Cova, and according to their testimony, a flash of light appeared in the sky and then something resembling a small, transparent cloud slowly floated down to rest briefly on top of the evergreen tree. At the same moment, all the faces in the crowd were bathed in a multicolored light.

Lucia, Francisco, and Jacinto were freed and returned to the meadow on August 19. They reportedly saw and spoke with the Lady again on that day. Thirty days later, on September 13, the roads around Fatima were teeming with pilgrims, priests, nuns, poor people, and rich. As is usual in events like this, most of these people came to beg for favors from the Lady; they wanted their ailments healed and their troubles righted. They mobbed the poor youngsters and pleaded for miracles, even though the promised miracle of October was common knowledge, and the children could only repeat that earlier promise.

Among the crowds in the field that day was the Reverend Doctor Manuel Nunes Fromigao, canon of the cathedral at Lisbon and professor at the Seminary of Santarem. He later wrote that he noticed a peculiar dimming of the sun in the cloudless sky as the children went into their trance, but he failed to see the luminous globe reported by other witnesses.

Up until this time the Lady had not identified herself in any manner. She had been seen only by the three children, and her voice had been heard by just Lucia and Jacinto. Determined adults had extracted and embellished a description of the Lady from the youngsters, but they never really saw anything beyond a luminous figure. No hair or features were apparently visible.

An estimated 70,000 people collected at the Cova da Iria on October 13, 1917, in anticipation of the promised miracle. Many of them carried cameras, and primitive hand-cranked movie cameras had been set tip by newsreel men. The weather was sour, with dark, sullen skies and a heavy rain. The meadows and fields were a sea of mud, and the faithful huddled under umbrellas. The three children gathered with their parents in front of the little tree and waited. Shortly after noon, Lucia gasped, and her upraised face flushed as she entered a rapturous trance. The Lady had arrived, even though the crowd saw nothing. The children declared that she held an infant in her arms, and for the first time she identified herself, saying that she was "the Lady of the Rosary." The war was going to end soon, she told them, and all of the soldiers would be returning home. (The war continued for another year.)

Suddenly the crowd screamed, and all the people fell to their knees. Something was coming through the clouds: a huge silver disk which rotated rapidly as it descended toward the mob. Fragile strands of silvery "angel hair" showered from the sky, melting away before any of it could be collected.

The object bobbed up and down, waltzing under the cloud layer, and as it whirled faster, it seemed to change color, going through the whole spectrum. It swooped down and passed low over the terrified people; then it bobbed upward again. These gyrations were continued for a full ten minutes.

Miles from Fatima, others were watching the same object. A well-known poet named Alfonso Lopes Vieira claimed that he saw it from his home at San Pedro de Moel, forty kilometers from Fatima. Eighteen kilometers away in Alburita, Dona Delfina Pereira Lopes, a teacher, and all of her students reportedly witnessed the spectacle. Father Inacio Lourenco described it as looking "like a globe of snow revolving on itself."

Professor Almeida Garrett, a distinguished scientist from Coimbra University, was in the crowd at Fatima and reported: "It was raining hard... suddenly the sun shone through the dense cloud which covered it; everybody looked in its direction... It looked like a disk, of very definite contour; it was not dazzling. I don't think it could be compared to a dull silver disk, as someone said later at Fatima. No. It rather possessed a clear, changing brightness, which one could compare to a pearl... It looked like a polished wheel... This is not poetry; my eyes have seen it... This clear-shaped disk suddenly began turning. It rotated with increasing speed... Suddenly, the crowd began crying with anguish. The 'sun,' revolving all the time, began falling toward the earth, [now] reddish and bloody, threatening to crush everybody under its fiery weight..."

A wave of heat swept over the crowd, drying their rain-soaked clothes instantly. We might speculate that this same wave of heat may have affected the miraculous healings that reportedly took place among some of the sick people in the crowd, just as the heat from that purple glob in Texas seemed to heal Officer Goode's infected finger.

Here we had an event of major importance with 70,000 witnesses, many of them priests, scientists, and journalists. It came at a time when Europe was shuddering with the violence of the First World War and religious faith was being strained by the inanity of sudden death. It would become one of the most thoroughly investigated UFO-type incidents of the period. Innumerable books were written about it, yet none of these books contained photos of the actual object. There were plenty of pictures of the crowds, many of whom were pointing cameras skyward. But what happened to all of the pictures they must have taken? What happened to all of the movie footage? I have tried to locate some of these photographs without success. I can only assume that they were collected by somebody and locked away in some secret archive. Because there was no U.S. Air Force and no CIA to blame this on, who did confiscate those pictures?

In the initial reports of the phenomenon, all the witnesses

agreed that the object was white and seemingly metallic, and that it changed color as the speed of rotation increased. Later, myth and mysticism replaced fact. The disk became "the sun," even though observatories around the world assured the press that the sun remained in its usual place during the miracle. As the years passed, the miracle of "the sun" was gradually played down, and emphasis was shifted to the saintliness of the three children. The silvery angel hair is now described as "rose petals" in most current literature.

Analysis of the Miracle

Fatima was not an accidental contact; it was obviously a carefully planned and deliberately executed demonstration. Dr. Jacques Vallee, Antonio Ribera, and other well-known UFO researchers have written extensively about it, but following the style of contemporary UFO research, they concentrated on the descriptions of the object and the fact that 70,000 witnesses were present, and they studiously ignored the whole pattern of events that preceded the appearance of the object. Those events were far more important than the climactic sighting.

The correlations are very clear. First, Lucia was singled out in 1915 for the cautious initial contacts. She saw something in the sky that summer, and a few weeks later she and her friends were approached by a luminous transparent figure which appeared to be a fifteen-year-old boy. Because the children came from strict Catholic backgrounds, the contact was conducted on a religious level. The boy asked the children to join him in prayer. Fear was replaced by reverence and awe. The experience undoubtedly amplified Lucia's religious beliefs and increased her interest in religious training. A study of her autobiography and the thorough reports written during and after the miracle suggest that she had many of the medium characteristics mentioned earlier and that she willingly prepared her mind for the events of 1917.

In modern contactee reports we find that initial contact is sometimes carried out months or even years before the contactee is finally fully involved in the situation.

(Small children often have a high degree of ESP, but as they grow older and develop reason—and skepticism—and their minds become more disciplined to the material world around them, these powers seem to slip away. A remarkable Italian teacher, Maria Montessori, worked out educational methods that took advantage of this fact, and she founded the school system which bears her name. Four- and five-year-olds in Montessori schools learn to read, write, and work out complicated mathematical problems *by themselves.* The teacher serves more as a consultant and does no lecturing or open teaching. There are now Montessori schools worldwide, and many of her methods have been absorbed into our conventional educational system. It is probable that small children make excellent contactee material because of these factors, and that may explain why so much UFO, ghost, and poltergeist activity seems to surround children.)

The world was in foment in 1917, and the ultraterrestrials may have decided that some form of impressive demonstration was necessary to restore faltering human values. Random appearances of "signs in the sky" could not accomplish this. Nor would a repetition of the miracle of La Salette achieve this.

The world was more sophisticated in 1917 than it had been in 1858. The ultraterrestrials could see our future, and they wanted somehow to guide us and help us try to correct our course. It must have been extremely important to them for them to make such an effort.

They therefore selected three small children in Portugal and launched their careful plan. The events had to be staged so that they would support one another. Valid prophecies had to be made so that the prophecies dealing with the more distant future would be taken seriously. And the whole situation had to fit into the context of the UFO incidents which were still to come.

In May 1917, the first contact was made in the usual UFO manner. A globe of light appeared, and a faceless entity spoke to the children, probably through ESP or the trance state. Little

Francisco could see the entity but could not hear it. Lucia had already been prepared through her earlier encounters so she served as a catalyst. In that first meeting the entity spoke of religious matters in a way that the children could understand and promised to return on the thirteenth of each month for the next six months.

When the children excitedly reported this to adults in their village, some of the more devout were impressed with their obvious sincerity, and the stage was set for the succeeding contacts. Adults who accompanied them to the field in the months that followed heard sounds and saw aerial lights and were convinced by the trance which the children entered into. They spread the word and repeated the Lady's prophecies. During one of the early contacts, she promised a big miracle on October 13. Had this failed to materialize, the whole Fatima thing would have collapsed, but because it did occur precisely as the children said it would months before, we are obliged to take all of their story seriously.

Many of the Lady's statements and prayers, as related by the children, were phrased in perfect Catholic dogma, a fact which impressed the attending priests, because it was very unlikely that the children could have known enough about theology to make such things up. But all these things were probably superficial trappings, quite similar to the endless descriptions of life on other planets given to UFO contactees. The only important things in the statements were the basic prophecies themselves.

Skepticism being what it is, the ultraterrestrials realized that the only way to win attention to these prophecies was to stage a careful demonstration which would be practically irrefutable and that would convince the Church—and the world—that the children had been speaking the truth. Thus the miracle of Fatima came about.

Among the minor prophecies was the prediction that Jacinto and Francisco would soon die. (They were delighted with this in their childlike way because it meant they would be going to heaven.) Lucia entered a convent, became a nun, was renamed Maria of the Sorrows, and was hidden away from the world for many years. The major prophecies of Fatima had been written down, sealed in an envelope, and turned over to the Vatican. They were supposed to be revealed to the world in 1960, but Pope John XXIII "decided it was advisable to preserve the mystery," according to Alfredo Cardinal Ottavianni, head of the Vatican's sacred Congregation for the Doctrine of the Faith, and Pope John took the secret with him to his grave.

Or did he? All kinds of rumors have leaked from the Vatican about that secret. It is said to be a prediction of the end of the world.

Fatima was a modern event, yet it is already clouded with the distortions of belief. The photographs of the object have "disappeared." The key prophecy has been suppressed. Lucia shut herself away from the world. As the years passed, the object was turned into a "dancing sun," the angel hair became "rose petals," and the entire phenomenon was removed from the field of science and entrusted to the religionists.

The carefully planned and deliberately executed demonstration at Fatima was therefore a failure so far as the ultraterrestrials were concerned. Such demonstrations had proved highly effective in Biblical times, but times were changing and new methods were called for. Mankind was getting scientific—so perhaps the phenomenon should be altered to a seemingly scientific framework. A scientific (i.e., seemingly interplanetary) series of demonstrations might capture the imaginations of those who had abandoned religion.

There have been many modern miracles of the Fatima type, but they rarely gain much attention outside of religious circles. The flying saucers get much more publicity than the miracles.

Other Miracles. Other Correlations

Between the years 1937 and 1945, an entity who identified herself as the Queen of the Universe appeared more than 100 times to four young girls in the tiny hamlet of Heede, Germany. The girls, aged twelve through fourteen, were Anna Schulte, Greta and Maria Ganseforth, and Susanna Bruns. These visions began in November 1937 and continued throughout the war, with the Lady urging the world to "pray, pray much, especially for the conversion of sinners." Hitler was probably none too happy about all of this, especially because he openly considered himself to be the Antichrist.

(There are all kinds of stories and rumors that Hitler was a trance medium himself and was in contact with evil entities who advised him and directed many of his genocidal policies.)

Lesser miracles have included weeping statues and pictures that seem to fit into the poltergeist category. A plaster Virgin began crying real tears in Syracuse, Sicily, on August 29, 1953, and continued to "weep" until September 1. Investigators could find no rational cause of the phenomenon. In other cases, pictures and statues have shed human blood.

On Sunday, June 18, 1961, four young girls were playing marbles outside of the little village of Garabandal, Spain, when they suddenly saw an "angel." The girls, Mary Cruz Gonzalez, eleven, Conchita Gonzalez, twelve, Jacinta Gonzalez, twelve, and Mary Loly Mazon, twelve (none of the Gonzalez girls were directly related), said that he appeared to be about nine years old, was dressed in a long, seamless blue robe, had a small face with black eyes, and "fine hands and short fingernails." For some reason, he gave the impression of being very strong. This figure was surrounded by a dazzling glow and faded into thin air without saying a word.

The excited youngsters ran into the village and told everyone that they had seen an angel. Fatima was about to be repeated all over again. Most of the adults scoffed, but those whose faith was extreme listened and spread the word. An angel had visited Garabandal (a village in the heart of the Cantabrian Mountains in northern Spain; elevation about 2,000 feet; it's about 150 miles from Lourdes, France).

Two days later the same four children were walking along a path outside the town when suddenly a brilliant white light exploded in front of them, terrifying them and blinding them briefly. (Brilliant flashes of light from an unknown source are frequently reported by contactees and UFO witnesses. There was an epidemic of such flashes in the spring of 1968. Often people reported that these flashes suddenly occurred directly in front of their moving automobiles. Others said that a flash "like a flashgun going off" burst near them as they stepped outside their homes. These flashes do not seem to be related to the "mystery photographers" who frequently turn up and photograph the homes of witnesses.)

Soon after these initial experiences, the girls began to go into trances (termed a state of ecstasy by the religionists) during which they would see the Lady. Sometimes these trances would last for hours, and the girls would remain fixed in an awkward kneeling position with their heads thrown back and their eyes staring at the vision, totally oblivious of the hundreds of people swarming around them.

One of their first visits with the Lady is of very special interest here. Shortly before 6 P .M. on Sunday, July 2, 1961, the children trooped to their now-sacred spot outside of Garabandal and immediately entered the trancelike state. They were later able to describe in detail what they had seen. These descriptions were dutifully recorded in the religious literature later published by Church-affiliated groups.

The Lady was accompanied by two angels on this occasion. The angels were dressed alike "as if they were twins." *The Lady had long, thin hands, a long angular face "with a fine nose," and lips that were "a bit thin." She seemed to be "rather tall."* Her hair was a deep nut brown, parted in the center. This is, of course, an almost classic description of the "long finger" UFO entities described by many contactees. Even more startling, on the Lady's right the girls said they could see *"a square of red fire framing a triangle with an eye and some writing. The lettering was in an old Oriental script!"*

The angels in all of these cases sound suspiciously like our celebrated "little men." The Lady who has been so glorified by the religionists may merely be a variation of Aura Rhanes.

Conchita and the other children of Garabandal have now experienced more than 1,000 visions, and they have been frequently photographed during their ecstasies. A number of times all four children have awakened simultaneously in their four separate homes and gone dashing into the night to the sacred place as if they were all somehow called by an unseen force. They have been examined by doctors, high government and Church officials, parapsychologists, psychiatrists, by everyone except ufologists (I know of only one ufologist who had ever even heard of this case). The many messages conveyed by the Lady have conformed precisely to Catholic dogma, using phrases and references that are significant to trained theologists but would be meaningless to the children. The message of October 18, 1961, as dictated by the children, read: "We must make many sacrifices, do much penance. We must visit the Blessed Sacrament frequently; but first, we must be good, and unless we do this, a punishment will befall us. The cup is already filling and unless we change, a very great punishment will befall us."

October 18, 1961, fell on a Wednesday.

On Friday, June 18, 1965, Conchita entered a trance and was purportedly given the following statement by the Lady: "As my message of the eighteenth of October has not been complied with, and as it has not been made known to the world, I am telling you that this is the last one. Previously, the cup was filling; now it is brimming over... You are now being given the last warnings."

There is a wealth of evidence and testimony which leaves little doubt that these children of Garabandal were being possessed by some outside influence and were undergoing a supernormal experience.

The messages of Garabandal followed the pattern of all the others received by UFO contactees and religious visionaries alike: stern warnings that the activities of the human race displeased the ultraterrestrials. The religious messages ambiguously threaten worldwide punishment, while the UFO messages are more specific; i.e., stop meddling with atom bombs or "we" will paralyze your whole world.

Can we really afford to ignore these warnings?

The Nation of the Third Eye

There is no reason to think that the four children of Garabandal had ever seen, or even knew about, the eye symbol on the Great Seal of the United States. Nor is it remotely possible that the children, or any of the elders of Garabandal, could have known of the importance that this symbol plays in the silent contactee situation. In fact, very few ufologists are aware of it.

Those mysterious "men in black" who travel around in unlicensed Cadillacs have reportedly been seen wearing lapel pins bearing the symbol. They have also identified themselves directly as being from "the Nation of the Third Eye." So we call the symbol the Third Eye. It would be interesting to find out why some cultures regarded it as evil, while others used it to symbolize the Deity.

Why did the Third Eye appear beside the vision at Garabandal? Was it a symbol of identification? Or was it a warning? The Vatican has been most cautious in the handling of the Garabandal case. The children have promised that a major miracle will take place there sometime in the near future. This miracle is supposed to occur above a grove of pine trees near the sacred place, and it is said that it will somehow leave a permanent mark in the sky. A mark that will endure for the ages.

In the meantime, there have been other miracles around the world. Most of them are greeted by silence from the Vatican. Two occurred within a few days of each other toward the end of March 1968. One was in the Philippines; the other took place half a world away in Cairo, Egypt.

Eight young girls on the island of Cabra in the Philippines began to suffer visions in the early part of the year, and the feminine voice of "the Virgin" promised a miracle. During the last week of March about 3,000 persons poured onto the island and waited. Some, including a university professor, a prominent obstetrician, and an army major, reported seeing a circular object over the island. It whirled and changed through all the colors of the spectrum, they said. Others claimed that a brilliant glowing cross hovered over the island chapel.*

A luminous female figure appeared on the roof of the Church of the Virgin in the Zeitoun District of Cairo in the wee hours of Tuesday morning, April 2, 1968. Thousands of people quickly gathered to view this entity. She has allegedly returned several times since and has been seen by many clergymen of the Coptic Orthodox Church, including Bishop Athanasius of Beni Suef. The Copts have even issued a formal declaration affirming their acceptance of this miracle.

Is the news of these miracles being suppressed? Hardly. *Newsweek* reviewed the Philippine case on April 8, 1968, and the *New York Times* carried a dispatch from Cairo on the events there in its issue of May 5, 1968.

Six young Canadian girls, ranging from seven to thirteen years old, allegedly saw the Virgin Mary on the evening of Monday, July 22, 1968. They reported that a luminous entity appeared before them, hovering in the sky near St. Bruno, Quebec. Four of the girls saw the figure, but only two, Manon Saint-Jean and Line Grise, heard a voice which they described as "soft and slow." It advised them to pray and promised to return again on Monday, October 7. Others in the area reported seeing unusual things in the sky that evening. One boy in neighboring St. Basile is supposed to have called out to his father, "Look, Daddy, there's a man walking in the sky."

Among the many other correlations, you will note that the month of March has often played an important part in these events, just as March and April have always produced many of our principal UFO sightings. These religious manifestations are clearly a variation on the UFO manifestations (or vice versa). The

---

* There were several sightings of glowing, cross-shaped objects over England in the summer and fall of 1967.

same methods of communication are being employed in both phenomena, and the UFO entities bear a marked resemblance to the religious entities.

Our awareness of these correlations presents us with a small dilemma. Are the religious miracles really a manifestation of some extraterrestrial intelligence? Or are the UFOs really some manifestation of God?

The Methods of Miracles

Early in January 1969, a seven-year-old girl named Maria de Carmen Ocampo was walking in a wooded area outside of Uruapan, Mexico, when she reportedly saw a female apparition materialize in front of a large cedar tree. It identified itself as the Virgin of Guadalupe and asked that flowers and candles be placed at the foot of the tree.

After the apparition vanished, an airplane mechanic named Homero Martinez came upon the frightened little girl on his way home.

"She was very nervous," he said. "She told me what had happened and what the vision had said to her. Frankly, I didn't believe her, and I went on my way. A few steps later I heard a rare kind of music—very beautiful—and I turned around and couldn't see anything. I learned later the girl was very sick for a day or two and couldn't talk."

All of the miracles we have discussed here have centered around trees or bushes: a trifling but perhaps significant detail. All have involved children in isolated areas. Information on the Mexican incident is still scanty at this writing, but if the girl really did become sick and voiceless after her encounter, we have another interesting factor to consider. A Wanaque, New Jersey, police officer, Sergeant Benjamin Thompson, was not only temporarily blinded by a UFO in 1966, but he said, "It took away my voice, and I was hoarse for two weeks after that."

Contactees complain that they suffer from nausea, headaches, and general illnesses after their initial meetings with the entities.

But after a series of such meetings their bodies seem to adjust, and they are no longer adversely affected. Normal emotional reactions of nervousness and fear can account for some of these sudden ailments, but not all can be dismissed as mere psychosomatic responses. Some contactee illnesses are suggestive of radiation poisoning, while others seem to be induced by the odors that frequently surround the entities.

Usually the entities connected with these miracles are reluctant to identify themselves. After several contacts they offer vague labels for themselves that can be interpreted in many ways. The Lady at Lourdes finally told Bernadette, "I am the Immaculate Conception," a phrase that had no meaning to the young girl but which greatly excited the theologists. The Lady at Fatima finally declared herself to be the Lady of the Rosary.

By the same token, the UFO entities seem to adopt names such as Xeno (Greek for "stranger") or use variations on ancient Greek and Indian names from mythology. The long-haired Venusians and the long-haired angels are unquestionably part of the same package, coming from the same source but utilizing different frames of reference to approach human beings. It is also highly probable that they do not actually have individual identities but are manifestations of a greater force which is able to manipulate the human mind. This mental (and also emotional) manipulation is the key to our mystery. Possession occurs in both good and evil forms. Possession is part of the overall manifestation. Many contactees display the classic symptoms of possession. Arthur Ford, the medium, was possessed on one level; Dr. Newbrough, author of *Oahspe,* on another; contactees on still another. All are subjects of the same phenomenon—a phenomenon that is not bred in the reaches of outer space but which has always existed with us here in our own immediate environment.

The well-investigated miracles are proof that the human mind can be exposed to induced hallucinations and that information can somehow be inserted into the mind by some unknown mechanism. In most contactee events, the percipient is alone or with a small group when the UFO contact occurs. Such percipients suffer medical effects which indicate that the "contact" was actually hallucinatory, just as the episodes involving children and religious entities have proven to be wholly or partially hallucinatory. The event or vision takes place only in the mind, not in reality. The exterior manifestations are merely part of that mechanism, a byproduct rather than a cause. It is likely that an outsider trespassing on the scene of a UFO contact would see the contactee standing in a rigid trance, just as the witnesses to miracles see only the children in a blind trance state. The contactee's real experience is in his or her mind as some powerful beam of electromagnetic energy is broadcasting to that mind, bypassing the biological sensory channels.

The remembered nonevents are therefore of little or no importance. This process of broadcasting to the mind has always been known as possession or mystical illumination. The modern hippie, under the influence of LSD, often undergoes the same kind of experience and believes that he has tuned in to the cosmic consciousness.

We have made the very human mistake of isolating all of these manifestations into separate categories and studies. The demonologists, angelologists, theologians, and ufologists have all been examining the same phenomenon from slightly different points of view. Aretalogists study the ancient writings describing man's contacts with supernatural or extraterrestrial or ultraterrestrial beings. Spiritualists have been concerned with convincing manifestations indicating that the human soul endures after death and populates some other plane or super-reality beyond human perception. Phenomenologists have endeavored to study larger parts of all this and link them together with abstract philosophical concepts.

For the past twenty years, one group of UFO cultists has been whispering about the approaching "New Age." Now astrologers and hippies are expecting the Age of Aquarius: a new age when the old values and concepts will be tossed aside as mankind somehow merges with the "cosmic consciousness" and our awareness of the supercosmos leads us further along some predestined path.

If the UFOs exist at all, they exist as a minor part of this great explosion. They are the blackboard upon which man's future is being written. To understand the message, we must first develop a pantology which can bring together all of these assorted beliefs and studies to form the whole. All of the assorted literature I have touched upon thus far merely serves as a beginning. We cannot close our minds to some aspects of the fantastic while we happily embrace other equally fantastic parts. The ufologists sneer at the occultists and vice versa. The theologians and religionists frown upon both. Orthodox science laughs at the entire scene.

Open communication with the phenomenon is not something far in our future. It is here. It is happening now.

14
Breakthrough!

Within a year after I had launched my full-time UFO investigating effort in 1966, the phenomenon had zeroed in on me, just as it had done with the British newspaper editor Arthur Shuttlewood and so many others. My telephone ran amok first, with mysterious strangers calling day and night to deliver bizarre messages "from the space people." Then I was catapulted into the dreamlike fantasy world of demonology. I kept rendezvous with black Cadillacs on Long Island, and when I tried to pursue them, they would disappear impossibly on dead-end roads. Throughout 1967, I was called out in the middle of the night to go on silly wild-goose chases and try to affect "rescues" of troubled contactees. Luminous aerial objects seemed to follow me around like faithful dogs. The objects seemed to know where I was going and where I had been. I would check into a motel chosen at random only to find that someone had made a reservation in my name and had even left a string of nonsensical telephone messages for me. I was plagued by impossible coincidences, and some of my closest friends in New York, none of whom was conversant with the phenomenon, began to report strange experiences of their own—poltergeists erupted in their apartments, ugly smells of hydrogen sulfide haunted them. One girl of my acquaintance suffered an inexplicable two-hour mental blackout while she was sitting under a hair dryer alone in her own apartment. More than once I woke up in the middle of the night to find myself unable to move, with a huge dark apparition standing over me.

For a time I questioned my own sanity. I kept profuse notes—a daily journal which now reads like something from the pen of Edgar Allen Poe or H. P. Lovecraft.

Previous to all this I was a typical hard-boiled skeptic. I

sneered at the occult. I had once published a book, *Jadoo*, which denigrated the mystical legends of the Orient. I tried to adopt a very scientific approach to ufology, and this meant that I scoffed at the many contactee reports. But as my experiences mounted and investigations broadened, I rapidly changed my views.

While traveling through some twenty states to check firsthand the innumerable UFO reports, I was astonished to find many silent contactees, and while the physical descriptions they offered were varied, it quickly became obvious that they were all suffering the same physiological and psychological symptoms. Through these silent contactees (people whose stories have never been published) I actually entered into communication with the entities themselves. When a UFO would land on an isolated farm and the ufonaut would visit a contactee, he or she would call me immediately and I would actually converse with the entity by telephone, sometimes for hours. It all sounds ridiculous now, but it happened. My notes, tapes, and other materials testify to the fact.

I developed an elaborate system of checks and balances to preclude hoaxes. Unrelated people in several states became a part of my secret network to that mysterious "other world." I wasted months playing the mischievous games of the elementals, searching for nonexistent UFO bases, trying to find ways to protect witnesses from the "men in black." Poltergeist manifestations seemed to break out wherever I went. It was difficult to judge whether I was unwittingly creating these situations in some manner, or whether they were entirely independent of my mind.

Now, in retrospect, I can see what was actually taking place. The phenomenon was slowly introducing me to aspects I had never even considered before. I was being led step by step from skepticism to belief to—incredibly—disbelief. When my thinking went awry and my concepts were wrong, the phenomenon actually led me back onto the right path. It was all an educational process, and my teachers were very, very patient. Other people who have become involved in this situation have not been so lucky. They settled upon and accepted a single frame of reference and were quickly engulfed in disaster. Several examples will be cited in this chapter.

But let's review some of the game playing first. In May 1967, the entities promised the silent contactees that a big power failure could be expected. On June 4, 1967, the Arab-Israeli six-day war broke out in the Middle East. Early the next morning, June 5, a massive power failure occurred in four states in the northeastern United States. Throughout that month the contactees were warned that an even bigger power failure was due. It would be nationwide in scope and would last for three days, the entities promised, and would be followed by natural catastrophes in July. New York City was scheduled to slide into the ocean on July 2. The contactees did not broadcast these dire predictions, yet the rumors snowballed. By mid-June nearly all of the hardware stores in the flap areas had sold out their supplies of candles and flashlights. Late that May, the UFO entities had also declared that Pope Paul would visit Turkey in the coming months and would be bloodily assassinated and that this would precipitate the blackout and the disasters. Weeks later the Vatican suddenly announced that the Pope was, indeed, planning to visit Turkey in July. Panic prevailed in the secret contactee circles.

I was astonished when I discovered that these same rumors were also sweeping New York's hippie community. People began phoning me late in June to ask me where I was going on July 2. I was not going anywhere. I refused to join the exodus, and Manhattan did not sink into the sea.

Other predictions received that month began to come true right on the nose, however. There were predicted plane crashes; a jet airliner collided with a private plane over Henderson, North Carolina, killing, among others, J. T. McNaughton who had just been appointed U.S. Secretary of the Navy, and the next day, July 20, an identical accident occurred in Brazil, killing some leading Brazilian politicos.

I started to get nervous.

What astonished me most was that these predictions were

coming in from a wide variety of sources. Trance mediums and automatic writers in touch with the spirit world were coming up with the same things as the UFO contactees. Often the prophecies were phrased identically in different sections of the country. Even when they failed to come off, we still could not overlook this peculiar set of correlative factors.

So convincing were these demonstrations that I finally packed up my equipment, rented a car, and drove out to the flap area near Melville, Long Island, to await the assassination and the blackout.

Just before I left Manhattan, I stopped in a local delicatessen and bought three quarts of distilled water. I figured that a three-day power failure would certainly be accompanied by a water shortage. On my way out to Long Island, I stopped in on a silent contactee, and he told me he had received a brief visit from a UFO entity a short time before. This entity had mentioned me, he said, and had given him a message to relay to me. The message didn't make sense to the contactee. It was, "Tell John we'll meet with him and help him drink all that water." (The water was in the trunk of the car, and the contactee had no way of knowing I had it.)

The Pope was not assassinated that weekend, happily, but I saw several UFOs. They seemed to follow me around, as usual. And I was stuck with all that distilled water.

Throughout the fall the predictions continued to come in, and a surprisingly high percentage of them came true. Later in October I had a lengthy long-distance call from a being who was allegedly a UFO entity. He warned me that there would soon be a major disaster on the Ohio River and that many people would drown. He also told me to expect a startling development when President Johnson turned on the lights on the White House Christmas tree in December, implying that a huge blackout would take place as soon as the President pulled the switch. The warning about the Ohio disaster disturbed me enough so that I broke my own silence, and on November 3, I wrote to Mrs. Mary Hyre, a reporter in Point Pleasant, West Virginia, and warned her that we might expect some sort of calamity in the coming weeks. She still has that letter.

Around Thanksgiving I returned to West Virginia for a few days and discovered that a number of people, none of whom knew about my prophecy, had been having horrible dreams of a river disaster. Mrs. Virginia Thomas, who lived in the heart of the TNT area, an abandoned World War II ammunition dump, was one who told me in some detail about her nightmares of people drowning in the river. Mrs. Hyre told me that she had also been having disturbing dreams; dreams of pleading faces and brightly wrapped Christmas packages floating on the dark water of the Ohio.

During my visit I saw more of those puzzling lights in the sky and listened to more eerie tales of monsters and poltergeists. As usual, I stayed in a motel across the river on the outskirts of Gallipolis, Ohio, and every day I drove my rented car across the rickety 700-foot span of the Silver Bridge which joined Point Pleasant with the Ohio side.

There seemed to be an air of foreboding in Point Pleasant that November—something that no one could quite put his finger on. When I caught a plane for Washington, D.C., later I felt decidedly uneasy. I remembered that all of the UFO predictions for July 1967 had come true except the big one. There had been the plane crashes, and an earthquake had taken place in Turkey just before the Pope flew there. Several minor prophecies had also come true. Now, in December, I had a long list to check off. In October, I had been told that "the Hopi and Navajo Indians will make headlines shortly before Christmas." Sure enough, early in December a blizzard struck the Indian reservations in the Southwest, and they did make the headlines as rescue efforts were launched to rush them supplies and medicine

On the morning of December 11, I was awakened by a mysterious caller who informed me that there would be an airplane disaster in Tucson, Arizona. The next day an Air Force jet plowed into a shopping center in Tucson.

On December 15, President Johnson held the usual Christmas tree lighting ceremony at the White House. Because I was expecting a major blackout, I warned a few close friends (who by now must have thought that I was quite balmy) and was joined in my New York apartment by Dan Drasin, the movie-TV producer, and another friend who is a police official. We nervously watched the tree-lighting ceremony on television. The President pushed the switch. The tree lit up, and the assembled crowd oooed and ahhhed. Everything went off as scheduled. The nation's power systems did not blow a fuse.

But thirty seconds after the tree was turned on, an announcer interrupted the news special with a sudden flash.

"A bridge between Gallipolis, Ohio, and West Virginia has just collapsed," he intoned soberly. "It was heavily laden with rush-hour traffic. There are no further details as yet."

I was stunned. There was only one bridge on that section of the river. The Silver Bridge between Point Pleasant, West Virginia, and Ohio.

Christmas packages were floating in the dark waters of the Ohio.

The World Ended Last Night...

A few hours after the collapse of the Silver Bridge, on the other side of the world the Prime Minister of Australia decided to go for a swim on his favorite beach. He vanished. His body was never washed ashore. The elementals had predicted this.

In the Soviet Union, a series of explosions rocked Moscow that weekend. An apartment house blew up. A few blocks away, an automobile belonging to an American newspaperman also exploded into small pieces. There was no one near it at the time. Another prediction come true.

This is the tiger behind the door of prophecy. Some of the predictions are unerringly accurate; so precise that there are no factors of coincidence or lucky guesswork. The ultraterrestrials or elementals are able to convince their friends (who sometimes also become victims) that they have complete foreknowledge of all human events. Then, when these people are totally sold, the ultraterrestrials introduce a joker into the deck. They had me buying distilled water and fleeing to Long Island in the summer of 1967, fully convinced that Pope Paul was going to be assassinated and that a worldwide blackout was going to punish the world for three terrible days.

I was lucky. I didn't cry their warning from the housetops. I didn't surround myself with a wild-eyed cult impressed with the accuracy of the previous predictions.

Others haven't been so lucky.

Dr. Charles A. Laughead, an MD on the staff of Michigan State University in East Lansing, Michigan, started communicating with assorted entities "from outer space" in 1954, largely through trance mediums who served as instruments for Ashtar and his cronies from that great intergalactic council in the sky. A number of minor prophecies were passed along, and as usual, they all came true on the nose. Then Ashtar tossed in his bombshell. The world was going to end on December 21, 1954, he announced convincingly. He spelled out the exact nature of the cataclysm: North America was going to split in two, and the Atlantic coast would sink into the sea. France, England, and Russia were also slated for a watery grave. However, all was not lost. A few chosen people would be rescued by spaceships. Naturally, Dr. Laughead and his friends were among that select group. Having been impressed by the validity of the earlier predictions of the entities, Dr. Laughead took this one most seriously, made sober declarations to the press, and on December 21, 1954, he and a group of his fellow believers clustered together in a garden to await rescue. They had been instructed to wear no metal, and they therefore discarded belt buckles, pens, clasps, cigarette lighters, and shoes with metal eyelets. Then they waited.

And waited.

And waited.

That same year, another doctor named Wilhelm Reich was watching glittering star-like objects maneuver over his home in Rangeley, Maine. The "space people" had a little gift for him, too: a strange theory about cosmic energies called Orgone. Dr. Reich had studied and worked under Freud in Vienna and later held posts at several important educational institutions. He was a brilliant, highly educated man. But somehow he became convinced that Orgone was the vital life force of the universe and that it even powered the UFOs that were flooding the world's skies in 1954. His colleagues and the Food and Drug Administration viewed his theories with some dismay. He was drummed out of the medical ranks, hauled into court, tried, and jailed. He died in prison eight months later, a broken man still convinced that he had unlocked a great cosmic secret.

Two years earlier, in that grand UFO year of 1952, two men were driving through the mountains near Paranã, Brazil, in the state of Sao Paulo, when they encountered five saucer-shaped objects hovering in the air. Later one of these men, Aladino Felix, revisited the spot, and this time a UFO landed and he was invited aboard. He had a pleasant chat with the saucer captain, a being who looked very human and very ordinary, and he went away convinced that the Venusians were paying us a friendly visit.

Then in March 1953, there was a knock at the door of Felix's home, and his wife answered. She reported that there was "a priest" asking for him. Because Felix was an atheist at the time, he was a bit surprised. He was even more surprised when he walked out to meet the man. It was his old friend, the flying saucer pilot, now turned out in a cashmere suit, a white shirt with a stiff collar, and a neat blue tie.

This was the first of a long series of visits during which the two men discussed flying saucers and their mechanics and the state of the universe at large. Mr. Felix kept careful notes of these conversations and later put them into an interesting little book titled *My Contact with Flying Saucers*, under the pseudonym of Dino Kraspedon. It was first published in 1959 and was largely dismissed as just another piece of crackpot literature. However, a careful reading reveals a thorough knowledge of both theology and science, and many of the ideas and phrases found only in most obscure occult and contactee literature appear here. Among other things, the book also discusses an impending cosmic disaster in lucid, almost convincing terms: the same kind of warning that is passed on to every contactee in one way or another.

Dino Kraspedon's real identity remained a mystery for years. The book ended up on shelves next to George Adamski's works. (Like Adamski, Kraspedon claimed that he sometimes met the Venusians in the heart of cities, one such meeting taking place at a railroad station in Sao Paulo.) Then, in 1965, Dino Kraspedon surfaced as a self-styled prophet named Aladino Felix. He warned of a disaster about to take place in Rio de Janeiro. Sure enough, floods and landslides struck a month later, killing 600. In 1966, he warned that a Russian cosmonaut would soon die,* and in the fall of 1967 he appeared on television in Brazil to soberly discuss the forthcoming assassinations in the United States, naming Martin Luther King and Senator Robert Kennedy.

The startling accuracy of his major and minor predictions impressed many people, of course. When he started predicting an outbreak of violence, bombings, and murders in Brazil in 1968, no one was too surprised when a wave of strange terrorist attacks actually began.

Police stations and public buildings in São Paulo were

---

* Many contactees and mediums made similar prophecies. The most startling of these was the report of Gary Wilcox, a farmer in Newark Valley, New York, who said that an egg-shaped object landed in his field on April 24. 1964, and that two little men in silvery suits engaged him in conversation for about two hours. In a sworn statement to Miss Priscilla Baldwin and the sheriff's office, Tioga County, New York, dated April 28, 1964, Mr. Wilcox said, "They also mentioned that Astronauts Glenn and Grissom and the two astronauts from Russia would die within a year..." Virgil Grissom died three years later in the tragic Apollo fire of January 27, 1967. John Glenn is still living. Russian Cosmonaut Vladimir M. Komarov became the first man to die in space on April 24, 1967, exactly three years after Wilcox's encounter. Cosmonaut Yuri Gargarin was killed in a plane crash in 1968. He was the first human being to enter space.

dynamited. There was a wave of bank robberies, and an armored payroll train was heisted. The Brazilian police worked overtime and soon rounded up eighteen members of the gang. A twenty-five-year-old policeman named Jesse Morais proved to be the gang's bomb expert. They had blown up Second Army Headquarters, a major newspaper, and even the American consulate. When the gang members started to sing, it was learned that they planned to assassinate top government officials and eventually take over the entire country of Brazil. Jesse Morais had been promised the job of police chief in the new government.

The leader of this ring was… Aladino Felix!

When he was arrested on August 22, 1968, the flying saucer prophet declared, "I was sent here as an ambassador to the Earth from Venus. My friends from space will come here and free me and avenge my arrest. You can look for tragic consequences to humanity when the flying saucers invade this planet."

Once again the classic, *proven* pattern had occurred. Another human being had been engulfed by the ultraterrestrials and led down the road to ruin. There is no clinical psychiatric explanation for these cases. These men (it has happened to women, too) experienced a succession of convincing events with flying saucers and the UTs. Then they were smothered with promises or ideas that destroyed them.

In the fall of 1967, when Dino Kraspedon was publicly issuing his uncanny predictions in Brazil, another group was battening down the hatches in Denmark, preparing for the end of the world. A man named Knud Weiking began receiving telepathic flashes in May 1967, including a number of impressive prophecies that came true. (Just prior to the capture of the U.S. "spy" ship *Pueblo* off Korea in January 1968, Weiking warned, "Watch Korea.") He was then instructed to build a lead-lined bomb shelter and prepare for a holocaust on December 24, 1967. This seemed like an impossible task because twenty-five tons of lead were needed and the total costs exceeded $30,000. But donations poured in, and voluntary labor materialized. The shelter was built in about three weeks.

On December 22, Weiking and his friends were "told" to leave the shelter and lock it up. A telephone blackout next occurred, lasting throughout the Christmas holidays and cutting off all of the participants from one another.

Meanwhile, mediums, telepaths, sensitives, and UFO contactees throughout the world were all reporting identical messages. There was definitely going to be an unprecedented event on December 24, 1967. Ashtar was talking through Ouija boards to people who had never before heard the name. Another busy entity named Orion was spreading the word. The curious thing about these messages was that they were all phrased in the same manner, no matter what language was being used. They all carried the same warning. People were reporting strange dreams that December, dreams involving symbols of Christmas (such as Christmas cards scattered through a room). There were also reports of dead telephones and glowing entities prowling through bedrooms and homes. Many of these messages, dreams, and prophecies were collected together by a British organization calling itself Universal Links. The stage was set for doomsday. Thousands, perhaps even millions, of people had been warned. At that time I didn't know about Universal Links or many of these predictions. But that Christmas week I received one of those strange phone calls that had become part of my life. At midnight on December 24, I was told, a great light would appear in the sky, and then...

Various contactees began to report in to me from all over the country, all with the same message. Christmas Eve was going to be *it!*

The Danish cult locked themselves up in their bomb shelter that night while I sat by my phone, watching out the window of my apartment on Thirty-third Street in New York City. (I had a good view of the sky.)

After the imaginary crisis had passed, the American wire services finally carried stories about the cowering Danes, ridiculing them, of course. But Mr. Weiking came up with a message that explained it all: "I told you two thousand years ago that a time would be given and even so I would not come. If you had read your Bible a little more carefully, you would have borne in mind the story of the bridegroom who did not come at the time he was expected. Be watchful so that you are not found without oil in your lamps. I have told you I will come with suddenness, and I shall be coming soon!"

It was all a dry run! Actually, it was a rather impressive sequence of events, and it really proved something very important. Many predictions of the December 24 disaster had been documented well in advance of that date. These messages came through in many different countries, from people who had no knowledge of or communication with one another. The UFO contactees received the same identical messages as the trance mediums communing with spirits. A link had been established. It was now clear (to me anyway) that all of these people were tuned into a central source. My earlier speculations seemed true—the UFO entities and the spirit entities were part of the same gigantic system. So more pieces of this tremendous puzzle were falling into place. A long series of events had apparently been staged to warn us of that tiger behind the door. Some of the entities were evil liars. They had ruined the lives of many by producing "proof" which led to false beliefs and irresponsible actions. Kraspedon, Dr. Laughead, and Knud Weiking had been victims in this enormous game.

There were so many others.

One night in the early 1960s (exact date undetermined) a young man named Fred Evans was out driving with his girlfriend when a glowing, saucer-shaped object silently soared out of the night sky and buzzed their car. This marked the beginning of Mr. Evans' research into UFOs and astrology. By 1967, he had installed himself as a prophet and was predicting major black uprisings.

In the spring of 1968, Fred Ahmed Evans moved into Cleveland, Ohio, and opened a storefront with a sign over the door declaring it to be "The New Libya." Then, on the night of July 23, 1968, rioting broke out in Cleveland. Snipers dressed in African clothing killed ten and wounded nineteen before the police brought the situation under control. The leader of the ring of well-equipped, well-organized snipers was Fred Ahmed Evans.

Another UFO prophet had gone wrong.

In California, a man named Allen Noonan claims to have experienced still another variation of this peculiar mind-warping phenomenon. Soon after his discharge from the Army following World War II, Noonan went to work for a company handling outdoor billboards. One day, he says, he was working on a billboard when suddenly he was taken in astral form to a strange place. He found himself in a huge white building filled with light. A group of "elders" were situated around a glowing throne, and a great voice boomed from that throne and asked, "Will you agree to be the Savior of the World?"

Noonan quickly agreed to this role. Then he was told, "You may die in the hands of your fellowmen. Their sin shall remain with you until the Mother Comforter comes to deliver them."

The next thing he knew, he was back in his body working on the signboard. In later experiences, he allegedly visited various planets such as Venus, and he frequently received telepathic messages and instructions from our old friend Ashtar. In this case, he knew it as "the Ashtar Command and the United Planets Organization."

When Noonan was interviewed by Lloyd Mallan for *True* magazine, he revealed, "I believe that I am the Cosmic Master as well as the New Messiah. I believe that a million years ago when this planet was young I was chosen to come to the earth and bring with me a Space Command.

"The Space Command flies in and out of the earth. The earth is hollow and the Higher Command, the Galactic Command, already has bases inside the earth. There are great openings at each pole of the earth, and what we call the northern lights is only the Great Central Sun shining out of these openings. Many people coming from the polar regions have reported seeing flying saucers there which disappeared into the ocean."

The hollow-earth theory is a very old one. In fact, it is one of the oldest and most widely believed UFO explanations around.

A great many books were published about it in the nineteenth century, including a strange little novel called *The Smoky God* which was supposed to be the true experiences of two Scandinavian fishermen who accidentally sailed through the hole at the North Pole and spent a year living among the gentle giants who inhabited the beautiful inside of our planet.

During his interview with Mallan, Mr. Noonan demonstrated his abilities by causing two peculiar UFO-shaped "clouds" to materialize outside his window. Mallan photographed the phenomenon and was hard pressed to explain it. We might point out that many other contactee claimants were able to provide equally convincing demonstrations. Brilliantly glowing UFOs frequently appeared and maneuvered directly over the auditoriums where they were lecturing, waltzing around the skies in front of dozens and even hundreds of fascinated witnesses.

Allen Noonan is not the only Space Age messiah appointed by the Ashtar command. Dozens of humble, ordinary people suddenly turn into UFO evangelists after a flying saucer enters their lives. Dino Kraspedon did a lot of preaching and wrote a "new Bible" before he finally turned terrorist. Lifelong atheists have become religious fanatics almost overnight after their UFO encounters. Such people are now becoming regulars on radio and TV talk shows all across the country.

One night in November 1958, an Arkansas truck driver was unexpectedly introduced into the shadowy half world of the ultraterrestrials. R. D. Smallridge was making a routine trip to deliver a truckload of eggs from Hardy, Arkansas, to Memphis, Tennessee. He stopped for a cup of coffee, as was his habit, at an all-night truck stop near Black Rock, Arkansas. When he left the eatery, he checked his watch with the wall clock. It was exactly 2 A.M. After looking over his tires and truck routinely, he started his engine and headed for the highway again. The next lap of the trip covered 60 miles to Trumann, Arkansas, where he usually stopped for another cup of coffee.

But, according to his story, he never remembers reaching the highway. The next thing he knew he was pulling up in front of the luncheonette in Trumann. When he walked into the restaurant and looked at its clock, he was astounded. It was 2:15 A.M. "I had traveled sixty miles in eight minutes," he declared.

This trip normally required changing highways (from Route 63 to Route 67) and passing over a state weight scale near Jonesboro. He could not remember doing any of this. Somehow he had traveled 450 miles per hour between Black Rock and Trumann!

A wide variety of strange, inexplicable events engulfed Mr. Smallridge after this. Eventually he gave up truck driving and became a minister, traveling about the country and preaching. December 1967 found him in California. Late one night he put aside the book he was reading and strolled over to the clock on the mantel in the home where he was staying. It was exactly 12:05 A.M. Suddenly, he swears, a bright blue light materialized and drifted toward him. Just as it touched him, the room faded away, and he discovered himself standing in another room surrounded by a group of strange humanlike beings. He claims that these people were conversing in an odd language he had never heard before— yet he was able to understand every word and could communicate with them. They told him, among other things, that Martin Luther King and Robert Kennedy would die suddenly in 1968 and that there would be widespread rioting and civil unrest. After about two hours of this, Smallridge was instantly transferred back to the California living room. He was still standing in front of the clock. It was still 12:05 A.M.!

Here, once again, we have a case that can be easily dismissed as too absurd for consideration. But, believe it or not, there is nothing exceptional about Mr. Smallridge's claims. Similar incidents are being reported from all over the world. Because they are so outlandish, they are rarely well publicized.

The strange language mentioned by Smallridge turns up again and again in these stories. It seems to be directly related to the well-known religious phenomenon of speaking in tongues. Sometimes whole congregations enter a trancelike state and begin to babble in this language which is part baby talk, part Greek, part Indian, and part unknown. Many mediums have laboriously copied down whole vocabularies for this unknown tongue. In the 1890s, one Helene Smith in Geneva, Switzerland, a psychic who had UFO-type experiences, produced a veritable dictionary of a "Martian" language. In my first visits with a West Virginia contactee, Woodrow Derenberger, he rattled off the language of UFO entity Indrid Cold, speaking the strange jargon as easily as he spoke English. (It did not seem to be a made-up language or a hoax. It had structure and grammar.) Numerous cases already cited in this book have mentioned how the UFO occupants spoke in a language that the witnesses couldn't understand. But some contactees claim that they were able to understand this language instantly, as if it were a second tongue lying dormant in some recess of their brains. Brazil's Aladino Felix often spoke in what he called "the universal language," described by reporters as "a hodgepodge of Hebrew, Greek, and Latin." This could also describe the language I have heard the other contactees speak. Greek is frequently employed by entities in UFO contacts. A large section of the "inspired" book *Oahspe* is devoted to a complete explanation of a supposedly ancient language known as Panic (language of Pan, a lost continent), complete with vocabulary and written symbols. It appears to be a combination of Hebrew, Greek, Latin, American Indian, and Chinese. To compose such a language as a hoax, Dr. Newbrough, the medium who wrote *Oahspe*, would have had to have been a brilliant linguist, and it would have taken many years for one man to assemble such a complex vocabulary. Buried within the fine print of *Oahspe*, there are many words which I have heard UFO contactees use! Not many people have the patience and scholarship to read *Oahspe*, and I've yet to meet a contactee who had even heard of it!

So here we have another piece of neglected evidence: the actual language of the ufonauts. It is not a secret. It is known and spoken by many.

Time Distortion and Distention

Smallridge's sudden transfer across sixty miles of earthly space might have been caused by a phenomenon known as apporting in occult lore and teleportation in science fiction. There are many documented instances in which objects and human beings have been transported instantaneously over great distances by some unnatural force that defies explanation. This force seems to operate outside the man-made boundaries of time and space. In theory, such events could be caused by converting the energy of atoms into a transmissible beam, projecting that beam to a distant point with the speed of light, and then reconstructing the original atoms. Some scientists think this may eventually be a feasible process for our advancing technology.

But somebody else has been doing it for centuries.

Early in May 1968, Dr. Gerardo Vidal and his wife got into their car, a Peugeot 403, at Chascomüs, Argentina, to drive to the town of Maipu some 150 kilometers to the south. They traveled along National Route 2, following a car carrying two friends who were heading for Maipu to visit relatives. When they reached Maipu, they found the Vidals were not behind them. They turned around and retraced their route, expecting to find the Vidals changing a tire or laboring over the motor. But Dr. and Mrs. Vidal were gone.

Two days later the Rapallini family in Maipu received a phone call from the Argentine consulate in Mexico City—6,400 kilometers away. It was Dr. Vidal, and his incredible story later made headlines in the newspapers in Buenos Aires and Cordoba.

He and his wife had just left the suburbs of Chascomus, he reported later, when a dense fog suddenly appeared in front of them and enveloped their car. The next forty-eight hours were a total blank. They woke up, still in the car, parked on an unfamiliar side road. Both had a pain at the back of their heads but were otherwise unhurt. Dr. Vidal got out of his car and inspected it, finding that it was badly scorched, as if a blowtorch had been applied to its surface. He started driving through the strange scenery, searching for a sign or landmark. When they saw people by the road, they stopped and asked for directions and were dumbfounded to learn that they were in Mexico! Their watches had stopped, but they quickly learned that two days had somehow passed since they first started out from Chascomus.

They drove to the Argentine consulate in Mexico City and told their story to amazed officials. Consul Señor Rafael Lopez Pellegrini advised them to keep quiet while an investigation was held. Their car was shipped off to the United States for examination (no information on whom it was sent to), and later they were given a replacement of the same make.

Dr. and Señora Vidal flew back to Argentina and went into seclusion, hiding from the press. The lid came down on the whole story. But reporters discovered that on the same night they vanished a man had checked into the Maipu Hospital for medical treatment, claiming that he, too, had encountered a strange fog which had left him badly shaken and nauseated.

All these incidents took place in the vicinity of Bahia Blanca, where an Argentine businessman had undergone a similar experience in 1959.

Several of the better UFO books of the 1950s recount other cases in which human beings were suddenly transported through space and time involuntarily. Time lapses and inexplicable periods of total amnesia are a key aspect in the UFO phenomenon, I have now received well over 100 reports in which witnesses have lost from five minutes to several hours immediately after sighting an unidentified flying object. In nearly every case, these people were riding in vehicles at the time. Almost all contactee claimants experience blackouts. Some suffer one or more such blackouts or fainting spells months or even years before they finally seem to undergo direct contact with a grounded UFO. There does not appear to be a verifiable medical cause for this unusual effect, nor does it seem to have a psychological foundation.

In Noonan and Smallridge we have astral projection or classic examples of "instantaneous experience." The body remains apparently in a fixed position (in front of the billboard or the

California clock) while the mind takes a trip of sorts. Based upon what we now know of the phenomenon, it is possible that these two men were actually experiencing the reliving of a hidden memory. In other words, we must consider the possibility that Smallridge had held his two-hour conversation with the entities weeks, months, or even years before he finally remembered it. The memory of this conversation was then suppressed in the same way that the Hills were made to forget their experiences. Then, at a time chosen by the entities, a ray of some sort was directed at Smallridge (the blue light), and his memory was triggered. He was made to remember the earlier conversation as if it had just happened.

There is another type of experience, which I call time compression. Here the witness undergoes a sequence of events that seem to consume a specific period of time. Later he or she discovers that only a few minutes had actually passed, even though the whole sequence seemed to consume hours. Time compression is common among contactees who think they have been taken on visits to other planets.

I do not believe that any of these people are suffering directly from clinical insanity. Rather, the evidence seems to indicate that their minds are manipulated by an exterior influence and that sometimes their intellects are unable to digest the information they are given, and their emotional structure is unable to retain its stability in the face of these experiences. So some of these people crack up under the strain, or at best, they greatly misinterpret these events. Induced confabulation produces memories of experiences that are convincingly real, and a chain reaction of emotional responses creates irrational fanaticism. These people abandon their jobs and devote all of their time and thought to spreading the gospel of the space people. Their family relationships disintegrate because all of their energies are channeled into one direction. They become martyrs to their cause, be it the eminent arrival of the Big Brothers or the Second Coming of Christ; or, as in the case of the run-of-the-mill hard-core UFO enthusiasts, trying to convince the world that flying saucers are real and are extraterrestrial.

What all this really means is that someone or something actually has the power to completely possess and control the human mind. Human beings can be manipulated through this power and used for both good and evil purposes.

We have no way of knowing how many human beings throughout the world may have been processed in this manner, because they would have absolutely no memory of undergoing the experience, and so we have no way of determining who among us has strange and sinister "programs" lying dormant in the dark corners of his mind.

Suppose the plan is to process millions of people and then at some future date trigger all of those minds at one time? Would we suddenly have a world of saints? Or would we have a world of armed maniacs shooting at one another from bell towers?

15
You Can't Tell the Players
Without a Scorecard

Now perhaps we can better understand RAF Air Marshal Sir Victor Goddard's remarks: "The astral world of illusion, which is greatly inhabited by illusion-prone spirits, is well known for its multifarious imaginative activities and exhortations. Seemingly some of its denizens are eager to exemplify principalities and powers. Others pronounce upon morality, spirituality, Deity, etc. All of these astral exponents who invoke human consciousness may be sincere, but many of their theses may be framed to propagate some special phantasm... or simply to astonish and disturb the gullible for the devil of it."

These "illusion-prone spirits" are responsible for nearly all of the UFO appearances and manipulations. The flying saucers do not come from some Buck Rogers-type civilization on some distant planet. They are our next-door neighbors, part of another space-time continuum where life, matter, and energy are radically different from ours. Ancient man knew this and recognized it. The original Biblical texts employed the word *sheol*, which meant invisible world. Somehow, the translators turned this into "hell" and gave it an entirely different meaning.

After spending more than a decade investigating and researching the UFO phenomenon, an engineer named Bryant Reeve published this statement in 1965: "...We began to see that vehicles in outer space were not really the important thing. They were merely an indication of something vastly greater, of earthman's awakening to a tremendous new awareness."

It had taken Mr. Reeve many years to arrive at a conclusion that had apparently been reached in the halls of Washington long before. In January 1953, the Central Intelligence Agency collected together a group of leading scientists to review the flying saucer evidence compiled by Captain Edward Ruppelt and his Air Force Project Blue Book teams. The final report of this blue-ribbon panel was kept in the classified files for thirteen years and was not released to the press until 1966. In that report, these scientists, some of whom later became recipients of the Nobel Prize, declared:

> ...The Panel noted that the cost in technical manpower effort required to follow up and explain every one of the thousand or more reports received through channels each year could not be justified. It was felt that there will always be sightings, for which complete data is lacking, that can only be explained with disproportionate effort and with a long time delay, if at all. The long delay in explaining a sighting tends to eliminate any intelligence value... The result is the mass receipt of low-grade reports which tend to overload channels of communication with material quite irrelevant to hostile objects that might someday appear. The panel agreed generally that this mass of poor-quality reports containing little, if any, scientific data was of no value. Quite the opposite, it was possibly dangerous in having a military service foster public concern in "nocturnal meandering lights." The implication being, since the interested agency was military, that these objects were or might be potential direct threats to national security. Accordingly, the need for deemphasization made itself apparent...

The panel suggested a program for "debunking" UFOs and systematically destroying the mystique that had grown up around the subject. "Such a program," the report stated, "should tend to reduce the current gullibility of the public and consequently their susceptibility to clever hostile propaganda."

As part of a plan for deemphasizing the sightings, the Air Force files were closed to newsmen and researchers for several years, and military personnel were forbidden to discuss UFO material with outsiders. This move inspired the cries of "Censorship!" that are still bandied about in the cultist circles. The phenomenon was much bigger than the U.S. Air Force, and it proved to be impossible to play down or explain all the sightings. Air Force public relations were ineptly handled, and some Air Force officers made incredible tactical blunders, such as telling reporters that airline pilots who saw flying saucers were drunk at the time and trying to explain some sightings as stars that were not even visible in the sighting areas. The UFO enthusiasts were quick to pounce on such careless explanations and used them to reinforce their allegations of official censorship.

Project Blue Book's published record clearly illustrates the official attitude of genuine disinterest. In the 1955 *Project Blue Book Special Report No. 14*, the only accurate summary of AF statistics, 689 sightings were listed as "unknown." Fourteen years later, the Air Force was claiming that a total of 701 sightings were "unidentified," an increase of only 12 over the 1955 total. Air Force statistics were shamelessly juggled year after year, and even the columns of figures were incorrectly added.

On December 17, 1969, Air Force Secretary Robert C. Seamans Jr., announced the termination of Project Blue Book, and Blue Book's files were retired to the archives at Maxwell Air Force Base in Alabama. Thus ended an era of almost unbelievable irresponsibility, on the part of both the Air Force and the UFO enthusiasts who had set themselves up as critics of the Air Force's noninvestigations.

Because the phenomenon is partly reflective, it had played the censorship game in earnest and had worked to manipulate the cultists into believing that some great official conspiracy was under way. Mystery men appeared in flap areas and warned, even threatened, witnesses into silence. Some of these men appeared in Air Force uniforms, and when fragments of these stories reached the cultists, they howled even more about "suppression of the truth."

I have investigated many of these cases myself, and I quickly discovered, to my amazement, that these "Air Force officers" all looked alike. They were slight, olive-skinned men with Oriental eyes and high cheekbones. Some witnesses said they looked like Italians; others thought they were Burmese or Indian. I reported this to the Pentagon and found that other cases had been turning up, and that military intelligence, and even the FBI, were involved in investigating some of them. Early in 1967, I published a newspaper feature on these Air Force impersonators, and it was reprinted around the world.

"Three men in black" have repeatedly driven up to the homes of witnesses in their shiny black Cadillacs to frighten the people into silence. In nearly every case, these men have been described as short, dark-skinned Orientals. For years many of the UFO cultists have believed that these men in black were CIA and Air Force agents, just as they believed that the government was tapping their phones and censoring their mail (much UFO mail seems to go astray). Recently New York's District Attorney Frank Hogan revealed that it takes six men to maintain a full surveillance on a single phone. Phone tapping is a very expensive procedure, and we can seriously question the need or justification for the Air Force or CIA maintaining taps on the phones of teenagers and little old ladies involved in UFO research. But if the phenomenon itself is electromagnetic in nature, it might be able to manipulate our telephone systems just as it seems to manipulate automobile ignition systems.

The real truth is that the UFO cultists have been played for suckers for years, not by the government, but by the phenomenon. Mischievous, even malicious, rumors and nonsense have been passed on to them through the contactees, and they have accepted this rubbish as fact. Other classic UFO stories had their beginnings as clearly labeled fiction in cheap men's magazines. One such story told how a reporter saw officials conducting a hairy spaceman through the White House. A newspaper columnist wryly printed excerpts from it without comment, and it created a sensation among the UFO cultists for years. Irresponsible tabloid newspapers have cashed in on the temporary waves of UFO interest by publishing completely fictitious flying saucer stories as fact. The celebrated tale of a UFO crashing on the island of Spitsbergen in the early 1950s was spawned by such a newspaper and is still being republished as an example of "government suppression." (The Norwegian government denied the story, naturally.)

Situations have been engineered by the phenomenon to make the UFO cultists suspicious of the government and even of one another. The in-fighting between the various groups deserves special study by itself. Many cultists are living in genuine terror. Some no longer trust their own families. Several have suffered nervous breakdowns.

Ironically, the UFO organizations have, themselves, suppressed and censored more UFO reports than the Air Force. When the National Investigation Committees on Aerial Phenomena received a report from one of their members on the sighting by Betty and Barney Hill in 1961, in which they suffered extraordinary effects after they saw human-like figures in the window of a UFO, they hid the full report in their office. The whole story would never have become public knowledge if author John Fuller had not stumbled across the Hills years later during his own independent UFO investigations.

The demonological events discussed in this book have so baffled and confused the UFO organizations that they have dismissed most of them as hoaxes without any kind of investigation. In many cases, they have publicly branded the witnesses liars, publicity nuts, and mercenaries trying to exploit the subject.

There's no doubt that the UFO cultists themselves have thwarted effective research into these matters, and their antics have created the atmosphere of ridicule which surrounds the subject and makes qualified professionals wary of becoming involved.

By early 1967, I had decided that the evidence for extraterrestrial origin was purely circumstantial, and I began to hint in print that perhaps a more complex situation was involved. To my astonishment, my rejection of the outer-space hypothesis focused the wrath and suspicion of the UFO cultists on me. Rumors were circulated nationwide that I was a CIA agent. Later, contactees began to whisper to local UFO investigators that the real John Keel had been kidnapped by a flying saucer and that a cunning android who looked just like me had been substituted in my place. Incredible though it may sound, this was taken very seriously, and later even some of my more rational correspondents admitted that they carefully compared the signatures on my current letters with the pre-rumor letters they had received.

Let's not underestimate the skill of our intelligence organizations. Let's assume that they have been competent enough to collect and assimilate the same kinds of data dealt with in this book. I think we can safely assume that they figured all of this out many years ago and that they are coping with it in their own way as quietly as possible. The huge National Security Agency building outside of Washington, D.C., is filled with James Bond-type electronic gear, and the organization's annual budget exceeds the gigantic budget of our space program. I don't think all that money is going into bureaucratic ratholes. I don't think all those computers and supersophisticated gadgets are sitting there collecting dust. The NSA has orbited ELINT (electronic intelligence) satellites equipped with delicate sensing devices which can instantly detect electromagnetic disturbances on the earth's surface. Other satellites carry infrared detection devices, and still others are designed to eavesdrop on all forms of communication. In 1960, Project Saint was announced; this was a plan to orbit special satellites designed to pursue and investigate unidentified satellites. No further information was ever released on this interesting project.

Even Howard Menger, the contactee, had a few kind words for the CIA (which is merely a subsidiary branch of the National Security Agency) when he said, in 1967, "...Around this great country of ours is a jungle, whether you know it or not, and there are specialized men who know how to deal on the same level with these people on the outside trying to get in and conquer us. These people are trained to deal with these other people on their level.

That's the only way we will ever survive, so don't knock the CIA, please."

It is probable that some small group within the U.S. government first began to suspect the truth about UFOs during World War II. There is curious evidence that Adolf Hitler and his inner circle had some knowledge of the ultraterrestrials and may have even made an effort to communicate with them. Perhaps there were even "men in black" episodes of sabotage and subversion that brought the phenomenon to the attention of the wartime Office of Strategic Services (OSS) and other intelligence groups in the United States and elsewhere. At least we do know that the "Foo Fighters," the World War II name for UFOs, caused considerable concern both in Europe and the Pacific. Subsequent events in the United States in 1945, including the still-unexplained disappearance of six airplanes off the coast of Florida on a single, clear day, probably led to serious and secret investigations.

If the top leaders of the Royal Air Force, such as Sir Victor Goddard, are aware of these incredible facts, then we must certainly admit that the American intelligence community must also have stumbled onto this many years ago. The official anti-UFO position now makes a great deal more sense.

Because our long-haired Venusians are only mischievous impostors, they dare not land on the White House lawn. If a marvelous flying saucer should sweep over crowded Times Square on New Year's Eve and land with its brilliant lights flashing and its antennas rotating, and an awe-inspiring Michael Rennie type should strut down the ramp in a tight, metallic spacesuit, in front of the crowds and TV cameras, it is very probable that he would be whisked off to the Pentagon, never to be heard from again, and a general—or the President—would hold a press conference and soberly reveal that the whole thing was merely a publicity stunt for a new science-fiction movie. It is the nature of the game that such a movie would probably even be in the can, and the wonderful flying saucer would actually be an exact duplicate of the prop used in the film. We have actually been subjected to a long series of hoaxes of this type for the past twenty years, although somewhat less dramatic than this example.

No responsible government could really attempt to explain this bizarre situation to the general public. Our military establishment has therefore been forced to follow a simpler policy, denying the reality of the phenomenon without trying to explain it. If flying saucers are a cosmic hoax, then it follows naturally that many of man's basic beliefs may be based on similar hoaxes. No government is willing to expose these beliefs or become involved in the terrible controversies that would result from such exposure.

The Air Force studies of the early 1950s, and my own recent independent investigations, proved that when the sighting data alone is reviewed quantitatively, it automatically negates itself. The individual sightings are not part of a whole but are part of something else. They form the point of the needle that the ultraterrestrials choose to show us. There are undoubtedly many objects in the sky that we never really notice, but which are a part of all this: strange clouds, weird birds and winged creatures, conventional-looking airplanes. They constitute the real phenomenon. And there are other objects, invisible to human eyes, but discernible, on occasion, to radar and to those people who are more attuned to receiving the signals from those unknown electromagnetic radiations around us.

Sir Victor pointed out that he believed that most UFO sightings were made by people with psychic abilities, and by non-psychics who were standing in the auras of the real percipients and were, therefore, temporarily tuned in. There seems to be some merit to this hypothesis, incredible though it may seem.

However, it would be very dangerous for us to exclude the possibility that a very small residue of sightings may be very real. Most scientists agree that there is a chance that there may be billions of inhabitable planets within our own galaxy, and there is always a chance that living beings from those planets might have visited us in the past, are visiting us now, or are planning to visit us in the future. To regard all UFO sightings as illusions, hallucinations, and paraphysical manifestations would expose us to a potentially volatile situation—an invasion from another world.

There have been many apparently physical sightings and landings which produced markings on the ground and other evidence that the objects were solid machines. But if those events represent the presence of true manufactured spacecraft in our atmosphere, then the overall evidence suggests that they are following a long-range plan—a covert military-style buildup—which will culminate in hostile action.

In psychic phenomena and demonology we find that seemingly solid physical objects are materialized and dematerialized or apported. There are many baffling cases of houses which appeared and disappeared mysteriously. In religious demonic possession, well documented by attending priests and doctors, the victims regurgitated impossible quantities of stones and even sharp steel needles. Apparently these foreign objects materialized in their bodies. Some victims have levitated to the ceiling and had to be forcibly tied to their beds to keep from floating away.

Ufologists have constructed elaborate theories about flying saucer propulsion and antigravity. But we cannot exclude the possibility that these wondrous "machines" are made of the same stuff as our disappearing houses, and they don't fly—they levitate. They are merely temporary intrusions into our reality or space-time continuum, momentary manipulations of electromagnetic energy. When they "lower their frequencies" (as the contactees put it) and enter a solid state, they can leave impressions on the ground. But to enter that state, they need some atoms from our world—parts of an airplane, an auto, or blood and matter from an animal or human being. Or, in some cases, they need to drain off energy from the human percipients or from power lines and automobile engines. This may seem like a fantastic concept, but we have wasted twenty years trying to simplify all this, trying to find a more mundane explanation. The fact is, all of the evidence supports our fantastic concepts more readily than it supports the notion that we are receiving visitors from Mars or Aenstria.

But if we want to be properly cautious and objective, we

find ourselves facing a double-barreled dilemma. On the one hand, all the real facts of the situation, the manifestations and physical effects of the phenomenon, seem to point to a negative, paraphysical explanation. The UFOs do not seem to exist as tangible, manufactured objects. They do not conform to the accepted natural laws of our environment. They seem to be nothing more than transmogrifications tailoring themselves to our abilities to understand. The thousands of contacts with the entities indicate that they are liars and put-on artists. The UFO manifestations seem to be, by and large, merely minor variations of the age-old demonological phenomenon. Officialdom may feel that if we ignore them long enough, they will go away altogether, taking their place with the vampire myths of the Middle Ages.

On the other hand, suppose that some other world, either from another planet or from a region composed of different frequencies and a different kind of physical matter, had designs on this world. Suppose that their time cycle was radically different from ours, and they could launch a plan for take-over that could require thousands of our years to complete? While they were making preparations for this invasion, it would be necessary for them to divert us, just as we planted all kinds of false evidence to convince Adolf Hitler that the invasion of Europe was going to take place far from Normandy. It would then be logical for them to instrument a plan of psychological warfare to keep us confused and even to convince us that flying saucers don't really exist at all. The few thousand people who took a real interest in the UFO reports could be deftly diverted by contacts which assured them that the flying saucers were really being operated by "nice guys," by Big Brothers from outer space who had our best interests at heart.

Contactee Howard Menger reported, "They use people not only from this planet, but people from Mars as well.* And also other people of your own planet—people you don't know about.

---

* The photos returned by our Mariner space probes in 1969 indicate that Mars is uninhabited and uninhabitable.

People who live unobserved and undiscovered as yet..."

What kind of "undiscovered people"? Could he have meant the elementals?

The late General Douglas MacArthur, a man who must have been privy to much secret information, repeatedly made public statements asserting that the next war would be an interplanetary conflict with mankind uniting to combat "evil forces" from some other world.

Having been trained in psychological warfare during my stint as a propaganda writer for the U.S. Army, I have been particularly conscious of this double-barreled threat and particularly concerned over the obvious hoaxes and manipulations apparently designed to foster both belief and disbelief in the reality of the flying saucers. I have tried objectively to weigh all of the factors, pro and con, throughout my investigations and in this book. Frankly, I have gone through periods when I was absolutely convinced that those Trojan horses were, indeed, following a careful plan designed to ultimately conquer the human race *from within.* The physical Trojan horse concept seemed alarmingly valid to me for a long time.

But I am now inclined to accept the conclusion that the phenomenon is mainly concerned with undefined (and undefinable) cosmic patterns and that mankind plays only a small role in those patterns. That "other world" seems to be a part of something larger and more infinite. The human race is also a part of that something, particularly those people who seem to possess psychic abilities and who seem to be tuned in to some signal far beyond our normal perception.

Perhaps the U.S. government was equally concerned with the Trojan horse possibility in the 1940s, and perhaps that explains the peculiar official machinations of the early years. Nobody in Washington has been inclined to confess to me that this is so, but at a press conference in 1954, President Dwight D. Eisenhower told reporters that flying saucers were hallucinatory and existed only in the minds of the observers. In 1966, then-Secretary of

Defense Robert McNamara called them illusions. So it seems probable that, after a period of paranoia in the 1940s and early 1950s, the government settled upon a negative hypothesis based, undoubtedly, on the same kind of material I have outlined here.

If intelligent beings actually do exist on Ganymede or Andromeda, it is even very possible that they, too, have been observing and wondering about the same kinds of unidentified flying objects that haunt our planet. Our astronauts and cosmonauts have frequently sighted mysterious objects deep in space—objects which appeared and disappeared just as enigmatically as the things flitting about the highways and farm fields of earth. The UFO phenomenon may be universal. And it may be unsolvable.

Finally, we come to the problem: How do you investigate something that doesn't exist?

The answer is that you investigate and study the people who have experienced these things. You don't investigate them by checking their reliability. You study the medical and psychological effects of their experiences. This cannot be done by teenagers with telescopes and housewives with tape recorders. It must be done by trained professionals.

We need to know much more about the human mind and how it is linked up to the greater source. We must study the process of confabulation (falsification of memory) which produces the majority of our UFO landing and contact stories and demonological events. These victims *genuinely believe* that they have met splendid space beings, but as Goddard stated, they have really encountered "denizens" who "are eager to exemplify principialities and powers." In my field work I have developed interviewing techniques which separate the confabulations from the real experiences. It can be done. But a large part of the UFO lore is based entirely on confabulations.

The elementals or ultraterrestrials are somehow able to manipulate the electrical circuits of the human mind. They can make us see whatever they want us to see and remember only what they want us to remember. Human minds that have been tuned into those super-high-frequency radiations, described early in this book, are most vulnerable to these manipulations. Discovering and understanding this process should be given top priority.

The symptoms of the contactee syndrome usually appear in early childhood, even though overt contact may not be established until many years later. Many contactees, like Howard Menger, have a long sequence of experiences with the paraphysical entities before their real UFO encounters formally begin. Some contactees begin to receive telepathic messages sporadically years before they have overt contact. Those whose minds misinterpret the information (or the signal) often begin to suffer weird forms of psychic attack. Once they untangle the misinterpretations, the attack ceases, and they become silent contactees and remain in almost constant communication with the source. I do not mean to imply that any of these people are insane. Far from it. But many are *driven* insane when their minds are unable to translate the signal properly. They fall prey to the negative aspects, and their mental confusion attracts induced hallucinations, visits from Oriental gentlemen in dark suits and black Cadillacs, and they can eventually suffer total deterioration of personality. I had to find this out the hard way, only to discover later that Dr. Meade Layne had worked it all out in the early 1950s, but nobody would listen to him.

Dr. Layne tried to express his ideas in occult terminology. He called the ultraterrestrials the Etherians and thought in terms of "ultrasonics" as well as electromagnetic frequencies. In 1955, he published a concise (and time has proven it valid) appraisal of the situation in which he stated: "It is possible that some persons may be less affected by supersonic frequencies than others; this may account for the selection of certain persons by the Etherians. It is also possible that some such persons are now showing signs of amnesia and other physical and mental deterioration."

If Dr. Layne was aware of these factors fifteen years ago, then it is almost criminal that no suitable psychiatric program has been instituted to study and understand this phenomenon. Thousands, perhaps millions, of people all over this planet are being directly affected. My mail is filled with cries for help. I have watched helplessly as witnesses fell into hopeless personality deterioration and went insane or even committed suicide. For some time now I have been working closely with a small group of psychiatrists, but our efforts can be compared only to the proverbial drop in the bucket. The whole UFO subject has been so widely ridiculed and denounced that most qualified men are reluctant to enter into it.

Not all ultraterrestrial contacts are evil and disastrous, of course. But there are many people throughout the world who are deeply involved in all this without realizing it. They have entangled themselves through other frames of reference and, in many cases, have been savagely exploited by the ultraterrestrials in the games being played. These games have been thoroughly documented and defined in the literature of the various frames of reference. The psychology of the elementals or ultraterrestrials is well known and fully described in the fairy lore of northern Europe and the ancient legends of Greece, Rome and India. In fact, we know almost everything there is to know about the entities and their games. Unfortunately, most of this valuable information has been buried in the beliefs of the various frames of reference and clouded by obscure terminology. It will take teams of accomplished and objective scholars to wade through all the literature and distill all the facts. This job should be begun immediately, for the game seems to be headed for some kind of grand climax.

Everything from the Dead Sea Scrolls, the ancient scriptures of the Orient, and the records of early Egypt to the modern messages of the psychics and contactees and the thousands of inspired books indicates that mankind was directly ruled by the phenomenon for many centuries. The god-king system established a universal theocracy which enabled ultraterrestrials posing as gods and superkings to supervise human events. Remnants of this system prevailed until the early 1800s when the United States established a political structure that separated the church from the state. More than fifty major revolutions were staged in Europe in 1848, breaking the back of the god-king system for all time. The phenomenon simply shifted to new frames of reference, notably spiritualism and a new cycle of minor religions based upon the teachings of prophets who were contacted by angels and elementals. Even Abraham Lincoln was a spiritualist and openly admitted that he based some of his decisions upon information and advice he received at séances.

Rapid industrialization and technological development in the Western cultures apparently led to further restructuring of the phenomenon's frames of reference. The inundation of airships in 1896-97 marked the beginning of the modern UFO phase. Although the phenomenon experimented with the "outer space" frame of reference as early as 1866, it did not attempt to advance this concept on a worldwide scale until 1946. By 1950, it had, in a mere four years, firmly established the extraterrestrial visitants idea as a humanly acceptable frame of reference for the flying objects and manipulations.

The study and interpretation of all this belongs in the hands of historians, philosophers, psychiatrists, and theologians. However, physical scientists can also make a contribution by applying standard scientific methods to the wealth of data and preparing statistical studies of the events themselves. My own attempts at this are admittedly very limited, but it is obvious that the phenomenon is controlled by hidden laws and cycles. Psychic and occult events seem to follow the same cycles as the UFO phenomenon. The Wednesday-Saturday phenomenon exists in all the frames of reference. For some reason, the twenty-fourth days of April, June, September, November, and December seem to produce exceptional activity year after year. It is probable that manifestations are dependent upon unknown conditions that have an electromagnetic basis. When specific individuals (people with latent or active psychic abilities) are in specific places (window areas) at specific times (flap periods when the undefined electromagnetic conditions exist), the phenomenon is able to manifest itself in one of its many forms.

These events are staged year after year, century after century, in the same exact areas and often on the same exact calendar dates. Only the witnesses and the frames of reference used are different. The phenomenon can be extremely dangerous, because the objects move through frequency changes that can produce deadly gamma and ultraviolet rays. On Friday, July 4, 1969, Arcesio Bermudez of Anolaima, Colombia, was a witness to a low-level luminous object maneuvering over a farm field. Accompanied by other witnesses, he attempted to signal to it with a flashlight. Representatives of the Aerial Phenomena Research Organization (APRO) investigated this case in depth. The July-August 1969 issue of the *APRO Bulletin* summarized their startling report:

> Within two days of the observation, the principal witness, Mr. Arcesio Bermudez, was taken very ill; his temperature dropped to 95 degrees Fahrenheit, and he had a "cold touch" although he claimed he did not feel cold. Within a few days his condition became far more serious; he had "black vomit" and diarrhea with blood flow. He was taken to Bogota and attended by Dr. Luis Borda at 10 A.M. on July 12 and later by Dr. Cesar Esmeral at 7:30 P.M. At 11:45 P.M., local time, Mr. Bermudez died.

Doctors noted that Mr. Bermudez's symptoms indicated gamma-ray poisoning. Other UFO witnesses have come down with leukemia and died shortly after closely approaching an unidentified flying object. Leukemia can be caused by radiation poisoning.

This is not a subject for teenagers and wild-eyed believers. It demands a cautious, comprehensive, well-financed investigation by independent, objective professionals unhampered by the petty causes of the cultists and the political machinations of the government agencies.

Somebody or something somewhere is trying to tell us about all this. Our skies are filled with Trojan horses and always have been. They are operating on a mysterious timetable, deliberately sowing confusion and nonsense in their wake. The believers and cultists have been crying for us to throw open the gates of the city and wheel the Trojan horse in. But the governments of the world, and the churches, have been trying to nail the gates shut. The Vatican has repeatedly warned that spiritualism is "evil" and the "work of the Devil." When seemingly authentic religious miracles occur today, and there have been many, the theologians and churches approach them with great caution and try to play down their significance. The Bible warns us that during "the last days" this planet will be overrun with wonders in the sky and false prophets and performers of miracles.

There are now many cases in which the voices of deceased persons have seemingly called up their loved ones on the telephone, just as the metallic-voiced space people have been phoning researchers and reporters around the world. To add to our problems, the telephone system, worldwide, is sagging and breaking down, unable to keep up with the increasing load we are placing on it. We face a complete breakdown of all communications within the next few years. Television sets, telephones, ham and citizen's band (CB) radios in flap areas have been going awry on a massive scale during the periods when the UFOs have been most active.

Thousands of people deserted California in April 1969, after hundreds of people had received prophecies in dreams, through Ouija boards, and at séances that the West Coast was about to slip into the Pacific Ocean.

As Sherlock Holmes used to say, the game is afoot. It is happening on every level of our society, manifesting itself in countless ways. The year 1968 was comparable to the year 1848. Great changes are taking place on our college campuses, in our churches, and in the halls of government. The demons of old are marching among us again.

In 1966, 1 was a lifelong atheist raised in the hard school of objective journalism, skeptical but hopeful that I could somehow validate the enthusiasts' speculations about extraterrestrial visitants. The extraterrestrial hypothesis then seemed to me to be the only acceptable explanation. But my experiences over the past few years have changed both me and my outlook, just as similar experiences have changed so many others. I have stood on many a windy hilltop staring in amazement at the multicolored objects cavorting about the night skies. I have dealt with thousands of honest, sincere witnesses by mail, phone, and in person. My skepticism has melted away, and I have turned from science to philosophy in my search for the elusive truth. The late Wilbert Smith, the Canadian scientist who chased UFOs in the 1950s, apparently followed a similar course. "The inevitable conclusion was that it was all real enough," Smith said in 1958, "but that the alien science was definitely alien—and possibly even beyond our comprehension. So another approach was tried—the philosophical—and here the answer was found in all its grandeur…"

All of the various ologies represent the famous blind men trooping to Cathay who encountered an elephant. Each ology has been examining a different part of the elephant and giving it a different interpretation. It is time now for us to gain the total vision necessary for viewing the elephant as it is, not as we would like it to be.

We all seem to be embarked on some new adventure. Our little planet seems to be experiencing the interpenetration of forces or entities from some other space-time continuum. Perhaps they are trying to lead us into a new Dark Age of fear and superstition. Or perhaps they will be guiding us upward to some unexpected destiny. I am not a scientist, theologian, or philosopher. I am only a reporter. My business is asking questions, not answering them. But there are men who do know part of the answers. Among them are our astronauts who have been closer to the infinite than anyone else. One of them, Neil A. Armstrong, the first man to set foot upon the moon, said this when he addressed Congress on September 16, 1969:

"In the next twenty centuries… humanity may begin to understand its most baffling mystery—where are we going? The earth is, in fact, traveling many thousands of miles per hour in the direction of the constellation Hercules—to some unknown destination in the cosmos. Man must understand his universe in order to understand his destiny.

"Mystery, however, is a very necessary ingredient in our lives.

"Mystery creates wonder, and wonder is the basis for man's desire to understand. Who knows what mysteries will be solved in our lifetime, and what new riddles will become the challenge of the new generations?"

Acknowledgments

This book could not have been written without the unselfish, dedicated, and knowledgeable assistance of hundreds of people throughout the world who offered me immeasurable support in my research and provided me with rare documents, reports, forgotten files, and back issues of early journals and publications. The back issues of the Aerial Phenomena Research Organization (APRO) *Bulletin* and the British journal *Flying Saucer Review* were especially valuable, since they had carefully recorded the general history of the UFO phenomenon for the past fifteen years.

I also owe a large debt to those people who have worked for many years without reward, often suffering considerable ridicule and even persecution for their perseverance. There are many who have asked to remain anonymous, such as police officers, sheriffs, and local officials who quietly kept me informed of developments in their areas. And there were also several hundred local newspaper editors, reporters, and stringers who cooperated with me in every possible way and provided me with much valuable background information. In addition to this group, there were thousands of readers of my newspaper features and magazine articles who wrote thoughtful letters offering me testimony of their own sightings and experiences.

Obviously, it is impossible to give full credit to all my sources or to personally acknowledge the help of so many people. Some parts of this book have appeared in slightly different form in *True, Saga, Flying Saucer Review, Flying Saucers, Flying Saucers-UFO Reports, Male, Men,* and in my syndicated newspaper features distributed by the North American Newspaper Alliance (NANA).

Lastly, this book is dedicated to Laocoön. In these past four years I have learned how he must have felt.

Selected Bibliography

This bibliography presents a cross section of the material encompassed in this book. It is by no means complete or comprehensive. Many of the books named in the main text have been deliberately excluded from this list to make room for equally pertinent works.
PP: Privately published and, in some cases, rare.
PB: Paperback editions.

Abbott, Edwin A., *Flatland*. New York, Dover Publications, 1952.

Adamski, George, *Behind the Flying Saucer Mystery*. (PB) New York, Paperback Library, 1967. Originally published in 1961 under the title of *Flying Saucers Farewell*.

Adamski, George, *Inside the Flying Saucers*. (PB) New York, Paperback Library, 1967. Originally published in 1955 under the title of *Inside the Space Ships*.

Angelucci, Orefeo, *The Secret of the Saucers*. Wisconsin, Amherst Press, 1955.

Arnold, Kenneth, with Ray Palmer, *The Corning of the Saucers*. Wisconsin, Amherst Press, 1952.

Bardens, Dennis, *Ghosts and Hauntings*. New York, Taplinger Publishing Co 1965. New York, Ace Books (PB).

Baring-Gould, S., *Historical Oddities and Strange Events*. London, Methuen & Co., 1889.

Barker, Gray, *They Knew Too Much About Flying Saucers*. New Hyde Park, N.Y., University Books, 1956. New York, Tower Books (PB), 1967.

Bayless, Raymond, *The Enigma of the Poltergeist*. West Nyack, N.Y., Parker Publishing Co., 1967. New York, Ace Books (PB).

Bender, Albert K., *Flying Saucers and the Three Men.* Clarksburg, W. Va., Saucerian Books, 1962.

Bernheimer, Richard, *Wild Men in the Middle Ages.* Cambridge, Mass., Harvard University Press, 1955.

Binder, Otto, *Flying Saucers Are Watching Us.* (PB) New York, Belmont Books, 1968.

Binder, Otto, *What We Really Know About Flying Saucers.* (PB) New York, Fawcett World Library, 1967.

Blair, Clay, Jr., *The Strange Case of James Earl Ray.* (PB) New York, Bantam Books, 1969.

Bloecher, Ted, *Report on the UFO Wave of 1947.* (PB) 1967.

Bordon, Richard C., and Vickers, Tirey K., A *Preliminary Study of Unidentified Targets Observed on Air Traffic Control Radars.* Technical Development Report No. 180. Indianapolis, Civil Aeronautics Administration Technical Development and Evaluation Center, 1955.

Bowen, Charles, "Beyond Condon: North American Report on Recent Investigations and Research," in *Flying Saucer Review* (PB) (London, 1969).

Bowen, Charles, "The Humanoids," in *Flying Saucer Review* (PB) (London, 1966). London, Neville Spearman (updated hardcover), 1969.

Bowen, Charles, "UFO Percipients," in *Flying Saucer Review* (PB) (London, 1969).

Brierre de Boismont, Alexandre, *Hallucinations.* Philadelphia (Lindsay & Blakiston, 1855).

Bucke, Richard M., *Cosmic Consciousness.* New York, E. P. Dutton & Co., 1901.

Buckle, Eileen, *The Scoriton Mystery*. London, *Neville Spearman*, 1967.

Cantril, Hadley, *The Invasion from Mars: A Study in the Psychology of Panic*. Princeton, N.J., Princeton University Press, 1940.

Catoe, Lynn E., *UFOs and Related Subjects: An Annotated Bibliography*. Prepared by the Library of Congress Science and Technology Division for the Air Force Office of Scientific Research. Washington, D.C., U.S. Government Printing Office, 1969.

Clarke, Edward Hammond, *Visions: A Study of False Sight*. Boston, Houghton, Osgood & Co., 1878.

Clhbert, Jean-Paul, *The Gypsies*. Paris, B. Arthaud, 1961.

Cleveland, Duchess of, *The True Story of Kaspar Hauser*. London, Macmillan & Co., 1895.

Condon, Edward U., *Colorado University Study of Unidentified Flying Objects*. Prepared for the Air Force Office of Scientific Research.

Condon, Edward U., *Scientific Study of Unidentified Flying Objects*, Daniel S. Gillmor, ed. (PB) New York, Bantam Books, 1969.

Cowan, James, *Fairy Folk Tales of the Maori*. London, Whitcombe & Tombs, 1955.

Crawford, W. J., *The Psychic Structures of the Goligher Circle*. (PP) 1921.

Crowley, Aleister, *The Book of Lies*. Originally published in 1915 and reprinted by Haydn Press, Devon, England, 1962.

Daraul, Arkon, *A History of Secret Societies*. New York, Citadel Press, 1961. New York, Pocket Books (PB), 1969.

Davidson, Gostav, *A Dictionary of Angels*. New York, Crowell Collier and Macmillan, 1967.

Deacon, John, *Dialogicall Discourses of Spirits and Devils*. London, 1601. Various reprints available.

Denton, William, *The Soul of Things*. (PP), Boston, 1875.

Dole, Stephen H., with Isaac Asimov, *Planets for Man*. New York, Random House, 1964.

Downing, Barry H., *The Bible and Flying Saucers*. Philadelphia, J. B. Lippincott, 1968.

Dunne, J. W., *An Experiment With Time*. New York, The Macmillan Company, 1958.

Ewing, Upton Clary, *The Prophet of the Dead Sea Scrolls*. New York, Philosophical Library, 1965.

Farago, Lazlo, *War of Wits: The Anatomy of Espionage and Intelligence*. New York, Funk & Wagnalls, 1954.

Flammarion, Camille, *Urania*. Boston, Estes and Lauriat, 1890.

Flournoy, T., *From India to the Planet Mars*. New York, Harper & Brothers, 1900.

The Flying Saucer Reader, Jay David, ed. (PB) New York, The New American Library, 1967.

Fort, Charles, *The Books of Charles Fort*. New York, Henry Holt & Co., 1941. New York, Ace Books (PB).

Fry, Daniel, *The White Sands Incident*. Louisville, Ky., Best Books, 1966.

Fuller, John G., *Aliens in the Skies: The New UFO Battle of the Scientists*. New York, G. P. Putnam's Sons, 1969.

Fuller, John G., *Incident at Exeter*, New York, G. P. Putnam's Sons, 1966.

Fuller, John G., *The Interrupted Journey*. New York, The Dial Press, 1966.

Gaddis, Vincent H., *Invisible Horizons*. Philadelphia, Chilton Book Company, 1965. New York, Ace Books (PB).

Gaddis, Vincent H., *Mysterious Fires and Lights*. New York, David McKay Co., 1967. New York, Dell Publishing Co. (PB).

Gibbons, Gavin, *They Rode in Space Ships*. London, Neville Spearman, 1957. Retitled *On Board the Flying Saucers*. New York, Paperback Library (PB), 1967.

Hadas, Moses, and Smith, Morton, *Heroes and Gods*. London, Routledge & Kegan Paul, 1965.

Hall, Richard, *The UFO Evidence*. Washington, D.C., National Investigation Committees on Aerial Phenomena, 1964.

Hapgood, Charles H., *Maps of the Ancient Sea Kings*. Philadelphia, Chilton Book Company, 1966.

Harvey, Nathan Albert, *Imaginary Playmates and Other Mental Phenomena of Children*. (PP) Ypsilanti, Michigan, 1918.

Hawkins, Gerald S., *Stonehenge Decoded*. London, Souvenir Press, 1966.

Hayes, L. N., *The Chinese Dragon*. Shanghai, Commercial Press, 1928.

Heard, Gerald, *The Riddle of the Flying Saucers*. London, Carroll & Nicholson, 1950.

Hill, Douglas, and Williams, Pat, *The Supernatural. London*, Aldus Books, 1965. New York, New American Library (PB), 1967.

Hudson, Jan, *Those Sexy Saucer People*. (PB) San Diego, Calif., Greenleaf Classics, 1967.

Huxley, Aldous Leonard, *The Devils of Loudun.* New York, Harper & Row, Publishers, 1952.

Huxley, Aldous Leonard, *The Doors of Perceptions.* London, Chatto & Windus, 1960.

Ireland, William Witherspoon, *The Blot Upon the Brain.* Edinburgh, Bell & Bradfute, 1885.

Jessup, Morris K., *The Case for the UFO.* New York, Citadel Press, 1955.

Jung, Carl G., *Flying Saucers: A Modern Myth of Things Seen in the Sky.* Zurich. Rascher & Cie. AG., 1958. New York, New American Library (PB), 1969.

Keel, John A., *Strange Creatures From Beyond Space and Time.* (PB) New York, Fawcett World Library, 1970.

Keely, John Ernest Worrell, *New Discoveries and Aerial Navigation.* London, Harvey & Co., 1890.

Keyhoe, Donald E., *The Flying Saucer Conspiracy.* New York, Holt, Rinehart & Winston, 1955.

Klass, Philip J., *UFOS — Identified.* New York, Random House, 1968.

Lambert, Helen C., *A General Survey of Psychical Phenomena.* New York, The Knickerbocker Press, 1928.

Lawrence, Lincoln, *Were We Controlled?* New Hyde Park, N.Y., University Books, 1967.

Layne, Meade, *The Coming of the Guardians.* (PP) 1955.

Long, Max Freedom, *The Secret Science Behind Miracles.* Los Angeles, Kosmon Press, 1948.

Lorenzen, Coral and Jim, *Flying Saucers: The Startling Evidence of the*

Invasion From Outer Space. (PB) New York, New American Library, 1966.

Lorenzen, Coral and Jim, *Flying Saucer Occupants.* (PB) New York, The New American Library, 1967.

Lorenzen, Coral and Jim, *UFOs Over the Americas.* (PB) New York, The New American Library, 1968.

Lorenzen, Coral and Jim, *UFO: The Whole Story.* (PB) New York, The New American Library, 1969.

Lorenzen, Coral and Jim, *The Lost Books of the Bible and the Forgotten Books of Eden.* New York, The World Publishing Company, 1926.

Magre, Maurice, *The Return of the Magi: Magicians, Seers and Mystics.* New York, E. P. Dutton & Co., 1952.

McLoughlin, Emmett, *An Inquiry Into the Assassination of Abraham Lincoln.* New York, Lyle Stuart, 1965.

Menger, Howard, *From Outer Space to You.* Clarksburg, W. Va., Saucerian Books, 1959. New York, Pyramid Publications (PB), 1967.

Menzel, Donald H., and Boyd, Mrs. Lyle, *The World of Flying Saucers.* New York, Doubleday k Company, 1965.

Michel, Aime, *The Truth About Flying Saucers.* New York, S. G. Phillips, 1956. New York, Pyramid Publications (PB), 1967.

Michell, John, *The Flying Saucer Vision.* London, Sidgwick & Jackson, 1967.

Miller, R. DeWitt, *You Do Take It With You.* New York, Citadel Press, 1955. Retitled *Stranger Than Life.* New York, Ace Books (PB).

Newbrough, John Ballou, *Oahspe.* (PP),1882. Reprinted in 1960 by the Amherst Press, Wisconsin.

Nicolson, Marjorie Hope, *Voyages to the Moon.* New York, The Macmillan Company, 1948. New York, The Macmillan Company (PB), 1960.

O' Brien, Barbara, *Operators and Things.* New Rochelle, N.Y., Arlington House, 1958. New York, Ace Books (PB).

Oesterreich, T. K., *Possession: Demoniacal and Other.* New Hyde Park, N.Y., University Books, 1966.

Olsen, Thomas M., *The Reference for Outstanding UFO Sighting Reports.* (PP) Riderwood, Md., 1966.

Pascual, F. Sanchez-Ventura y, *The Apparitions of Garabandal.* Detroit, San Miguel Publishing Co., 1966.

Pauwels, Louis, and Bergier, Jacques, *The Morning of the Magicians.* New York, Stein & Day Publishers, 1965.

Project Blue Book Special Report No. 14. Project No. 10075. Air Technical Intelligence Center, Wright-Patterson Air Force Base, Ohio, 1955. Reprinted by the Ramsey-Wallace Corporation, Ramsey, N.J., 1956.

Robertson, Priscilla, *Revolutions of 1848.* Princeton, N.J., Princeton University Press, 1952.

Rulof, Jozef, *My Revelations to the Peoples of the Earth.* (PP) White Plains, N.Y., 1947.

Ruppelt, Edward J., *The Report on Unidentified Flying Objects.* New York, Doubleday & Company, 1956. New York, Ace Books (PB).

Rutledge, Dom Denys, *Cosmic Theology.* London, Routledge & Kegan Paul, 1964.

Sanderson, Ivan T., *Abominable Snowmen: Legend Come to Life.* Philadelphia, Chilton Book Company, 1961.

Sanderson, Ivan T., *Uninvited Visitors.* New York, Cowles Book Co., 1967.

Saunders, David R., and Harkins, R. Roger, *UFOs? Yes!* (PB) New York, The New American Library, 1968.

Schmidt, Reinhold O., *Edge of Tomorrow.* (PP) 1965.

Schonfield, Hugh J., *The Passover Plot.* New York, Bernard Geis Associates, 1966.

Scully, Frank, *Behind the Flying Saucers.* New York, Henry Holt & Co., 1950.

Shklovskii, I. S., and Sagan Carl, *Intelligent Life in the Universe.* San Francisco, Holden-Day, 1966.

Shuttlewood, Arthur, *The Warminster Mystery.*   London, Neville Spearman, 1967.

Sikes, Wirt, *British Goblins.* Boston, James R. Osgood & Co., 1881.

Smith, G. Elliot, *The Evolution of the Dragon.* London, The University Press, Manchester and Longmans Green & Co., 1919.

Smith, Warren, *Strange and Miraculous Cures.* (PB) New York, Ace Books, 1969.

Spence, Lewis, *The Fairy Tradition in Britain.* London, Rider & Co., 1948.

Steiger, Brad, with Joan Whritenour, *Flying Saucers Are Hostile.* (PB) NewYork, Award Books, 1967.

Steiger, Brad, with Joan Whritenour, *The Mind Travellers.* (PB) New York, Award Books, 1968.

Steiger, Brad, with Joan Whritenour, *New UFO Breakthrough.* (PB) New

York, Award Books, 1968.

Steiger, Brad, with Joan Whritenour, *Sex and the Supernatural.* (PB) New York, Award Books, 1968.

Stromberg, Gustaf, *The Soul of the Universe.* New York, David McKay Co., 1948.

Sullivan, Walter, *We Are Not Alone.* New York, McGraw-Hill Book Company, 1964.

Tacker, Lawrence J., *Flying Saucers and the U.S. Air Force.* Princeton, N.J., D. Van Nostrand Co., 1960.

Teilhard De Chardin, P., *The Phenomenon of Man.* London, William Collins Sons & Co., 1959.

Thompson, Josiah, *Six Seconds in Dallas.* New York, Bernard Geis Associates, 1967.

Tompkins, Peter, *The Eunuch and the Virgin.* New York, Bramhall House, 1962.

Trench, Brinsley Le Poer, *The Sky People.* London, Neville Spearman, 1960.

Tuttle, Amber M., *The Work of Invisible Helpers.* New York, Paebar Co., 1945.

Tyrrell, G. N. M., *Apparitions.* (PB) New York, P. F. Collier, 1965.

Urides, Eros ("A Martian"), *The Planet Mars and its Inhabitants.* (PP), 1921. Reprinted in 1956 by James Scott Marshall.

Vallee, Jacques, *Anatomy of a Phenomenon.* Chicago, Henry Regnery Co., 1965. New York, Ace Books (PB, with new additions).

Vallee, Jacques, *Challenge to Science: The UFO Enigma.* Chicago, Henry

Regnery Co., 1966.

Vallee, Jacques, *Passport to Magonia.* Chicago, Henry Regnery Co., 1969.

Velikovsky, Immanuel, *Earth in Upheaval.* New York, Doubleday & Company,1955. New York, Delta Books (PB), 1965.

Velikovsky, Immanuel, *Worlds in Collision.* New York, Doubleday & Company, 1950. New York, Dell Publishing Co. (PB), 1967.

Webster, Nesta H., *World Revolution: The Plot Against Civilization.* Boston Small, Maynard & Co., 1921.

Werner, Alice, *Myths and Legends of the Bantu.* London, George G. Harrap & Co., 1955.

West, Ray B., Jr., *Kingdom of the Saints.* New York, The Viking Press, 1957.

Wilkins, Harold T., *Flying Saucers Uncensored.* New York, Citadel Press, 1955. New York, Pyramid Publications (PB), 1967.

Wilkins, Harold T., *Strange Mysteries of Time and Space.* New York, Citadel Press, 1959.

Wise, David, and Ross, Thomas B., *The Invisible Government.* New York, Random House, 1964.

Young, Mort, *UFO—Top Secret.* (PB) New York, Simon & Schuster, 1967.

Printed by BoD™in Norderstedt, Germany